Ring the Bell

A Memoir
EC STILSON

Literati Publishing
P.O. Box 762
Pocatello, ID 83204

RING THE BELL
Copyright© 2023 Elisa Magagna

The views herein are the author's responsibility and do not necessarily represent the position of Literati Publishing. Names have been changed to protect those written about in this memoir.

Editors: Ruby Stilson and Michael Steven Magagna
Cover Artist: Katie Leoni
Cover Photo Credit: Mike Magagna
Wing Painting on Cover: Art by Rainee
Back Cover Credit (Family Picture): Black Honey Photography

Visit the author at ECStilson.com.

ISBN-13: 9798857379776

Printed in the United States of America.

Dedication

*To all of the people who have encouraged me along the
way, you have brightened even the darkest days,
but especially to Ron and Dottie Barrett,
Adam Burdash, James Chambers, Layton Funk,
Nolan Furniss, Annie Hall, Terry Keating,
Ashley Page-Pete, and Justice Pendray.
Although you left this world too soon,
you will never be forgotten.*

What Others Are Saying

"EC Stilson's cancer memoir is so beautifully written, inspiring, and poignant. The words shine hope into the darkest days."
–Eileen Wharton, Writer of Crime Novels, Women's Fiction, and Children's Books

"EC Stilson's story might not be unique, but her voice is. If anything, it's the universality of her struggle that makes her words worth reading. She brings a light and observant deftness to her prose that belies the severity of her survival. When you read Stilson, you learn that existence is a human condition; it's how we live, how we love, how we laugh, and learn to live within the bedlam we've created that gives us our actual humanity."
–Nick Bruel, Author of the BAD KITTY SERIES

"I have never met EC Stilson in person, but I feel that I know her well enough to feel like she's a close friend. I have read her stories posted on social media for what seems like years and always find them heartfelt, touching, and sometimes funny. And yes, she's made me cry on more than one occasion. She's given me hope that I can overcome my own relatively minor ailments with dignity and a positive outlook."
–William Vaughn, Author of THE SELDITH CHRONICLES

"EC Stilson has been a source of inspiration to me. Her attitude of gratitude is infectious, and her courage to share her walk with others comes through in every one of her stories."
–Mark Gabriel, Managing Director and Owner/Principal Investor of G2 Productions

"EC Stilson shares her profoundly uplifting personal journey from the lowest depths of despair and the insurmountable adversity of cancer to the triumph of unconditional love and an unquenchable thirst for life."
–Joanna Lee Doster, Author of TAILS OF JAXX, a Children's Mystery Series

"Some of Stilson's posts have brought me to tears—and this is coming from a fellow writer. She is so brave in the face of pain and the unknown yet manages to be positive and kind.
–Marya Ashworth, Author of THE ELVEN CHRONICLES

"I am an avid reader of Stilson's work and feel inspired most of all by her sense of balance with regard to honestly reporting about her difficulties, but at the same time finding moments of joy, love, and gratitude within it all."
–Anthony Flacco, Author of THE LAST NIGHTINGALE, a Historical Crime Series

And many, many more, which you can find at the following website: TwoMoreYears.net.

Bonus Content

At the end of this memoir, please find
a special preview of
EC Stilson's upcoming novel, **THE RED FEATHER**,
a fictionalized story of one woman's journey
into the afterlife.

Table of Contents

A New Expiration Date

"She said I have a new brain tumor, and I need radiation immediately," I rebutted, finding it unreal how comfortable I'd become with such conversations.

"Everything shows something else. The head of our department met with the tumor board today," he said, then paused before slightly softening his tone. "They think it's necrosis — induced from radiation."

My heart practically fell out of my body and died on the floor. I never thought I'd discover something worse than cancer. Yet, there I was. "It's been over two and a half years since I had brain radiation. It wouldn't show up this late in the game," I pleaded. Necrosis... my thoughts whirred, frantically grasping for anything to debunk this horrendous possibility. Cancer, I'd come to understand. That felt conquerable. But necrosis? I couldn't believe he'd even mention it. "I... I think you're wrong." The words came out self-conscious and stilted.

"I understand this must be hard for you. God knows you're young, and you've been through more than your fair share." He sighed, and I thought he must have the worst job in the whole damn world, delivering terrible news to nearly everyone. "Necrosis from radiation has been known to surface even after seven years. And it's irreversible."

I gasped. "Will this kill me?"

"Maybe. We don't know for sure if it's necrosis or melanoma again."

No longer satiated by words like "maybe," I wanted facts from this man. "I swear," I whispered, "God is doing this—just to see if I'll stay positive. I feel like a modern-day Job." My head rested in my left hand, fingers massaging my temples, pushing hard into the skin until it hurt and stole my attention from other things. I'd read about Job with one of my Jewish friends. He raved about the ancient story because it poses questions we still ponder today. But I didn't find the topic exciting anymore. "Why do we suffer?" seemed too close to home. Despite that, my friend's words did spark my curiosity, and I researched the etymology of "suffering." Unsurprisingly, I found that the root of "suffer" simply means "to endure."

A considerable breath escaped my gaping mouth, and I returned my attention to the moment: this surreal conversation with a radiation oncologist I'd barely met. He worked as the on-call doctor, and I loathed meeting him this way when I'd responded with uncharacteristic acerbity. I'm sure he didn't enjoy relaying devastating news; who would? I needed to hold my emotions—and anger—at bay until later. But the stinging from the burgeoning mass in my brain kicked up again; it seemed to accompany stress. These excruciating headaches had plagued me for weeks, coming at the absolute worst times and growing in magnitude until not even opioids could mollify the pressure in my skull. "How long do I have to live *this* time?" I blurted. I hadn't meant to sound sarcastic, but I'm sure it seemed that way.

"Elisa, this is terminal. But I have no idea how long you have to live. I've seen other patients in similar situations. Some have lived months. Others have lived several years."

I felt like a wounded animal swimming across some godforsaken lake, watching alligators edge closer.

"This news must be difficult, given how hard you've fought. Are you okay?" he asked. "We have counselors on our team, people you can talk to."

I sighed. "I'll be fine. You guys gave me two years to live almost three years ago; I need to react like I did last time — with humor." Before the conversation ended, I told him that delivering terrible news must be hard. I did feel bad for the guy. But honestly, for just a moment, I felt worse for myself. And later that night, after my four kids went to bed and Mike left to work his graveyard shift, I sobbed in the bathroom.

I'd nearly cried myself hoarse when I did find solace in recent memories. I'd resurrected an old bucket list and begun checking off items with my family.

"Why is this happening?" I finally whispered to God. "I'm so glad I had forewarning, and we've made the most of my time, but I thought you might heal me." I gazed at my reflection in the mirror and wiped the makeup from my puffy eyes. The pressure in my head stung and throbbed at an almost unbearable frequency — the crying had only exacerbated the pain. "God, you must have a plan, but sometimes I don't like it."

As I cinched my eyes shut and willed the pain to abate, I remembered the joys of the past and somehow found hope.

I started panicking during my last set of scans when I'd been in the MRI machine for almost two hours.

Trying to regain my focus, I recalled playing the violin in a band called Rough Stock. We opened for many big-name groups and had fun jamming at private parties and corporate events. Those years felt magical in hindsight, but suddenly, my memory honed in on a specific moment, performing at a farmers' convention. We played intro songs and sat down so the guest speaker could talk. A well-respected farmer got up and began his speech by telling a strange story about a man named Zeke.

"Zeke had an awful year," he said. "All of his crops died. And at one point during the season, he finally asked God, 'Why is this happening to me?' Well, the next year, not only did his crops die, his wife left him, and his kids stopped talking to him too. He again asked God, 'What is going on?'"

The speaker paused for effect, looking around. Many farmers leaned forward. "Well, Zeke got sick the next year, and doctors told him it was terminal. He finally screamed, 'God! Why are you doing this to me?' At that point, the clouds opened, and a booming voice said, 'It's because I hate you, and I just wanna see ya suffer.'"

Everybody in the audience laughed. But I stood there, timidly holding my fiddle offstage. This joke shook me to the core, and I thought, "Oh, my gosh. Does God hate certain people? And if He does, well, I'm no better than anyone else—does that mean He might hate me too?"

Now that I'm older, I do believe God loves everyone. At least, I hope He does. But despite my convictions, this story has always stuck with me.

Anyway, while in the MRI machine this last time, thinking about the farmers' convention and poor, troubled Zeke, I started crying and hyperventilating. No matter how unfounded it seemed, unrealistic thoughts poured through my brain at that moment: Does God hate me? Could it be true?

A tech must've seen me in the camera they use for brain MRIs because her voice shot over the intercom, and she asked if I was okay.

"No." I sobbed. "Can I come out? P–p–please. My atrophied leg is shaking. I'm in so much pain."

"You can come out, but you've almost made it two hours. And if we pause now, we'll have to start all over again."

"No." I took three long breaths. "I... I can do this." I had to calm myself. Mike and my parents waited outside, and they'd been there long enough already.

Looking back, I'm so glad I found the strength to stay. We're all taught that God loves us—to the point that it was the punchline of a farmer's joke:

the idea that God *wouldn't* love someone. But while amid whirring machines on that rock-hard imaging table, I started thinking, "Why do people suffer? Why do we go through such terrible things? Why am *I* going through such hardships with this new brain tumor?" and I suddenly thought about the Hebrew word for God's love.

There are a lot of different words to describe love in Hebrew. This can be romantic or platonic. They even have a word specifically for the kind of love God has for us. The root of *that* kind of love means "loyalty."

I can't tell you how powerful this realization has seemed because loyalty isn't about preventing hardships or stopping pain; it's about sticking by somebody's side even when it's tough and loving them through it all.

As I thought about this, God somehow seemed to be with me, even though I'm flawed and can be an angel with one wing in the fire.

I calmed down and made it through the rest of the scan. And to think, I also learned something along the way. I know that God does love us, but maybe it's not always about intervening in our lives and stunting growth. I just realized God's love is much better than I imagined. He's loyal, and I'm glad He's there, sticking by our sides whenever we need Him the most.

My Bucket List

The origin of my bucket list is anything but glamorous. I could even argue that it's embarrassing since it shows how different I was before doctors removed a tumorous section of my spine and somehow gave me chutzpah and a backbone.

When the man called me at work, I involuntarily flinched. "Why would he be calling me here?" Despite seeing his number on the caller ID, I picked up the phone.

"Burn Unit," I said. I'd been working there for almost a year, so grateful to make a good wage to support my four kids; I finally only needed one job instead of two.

His voice came out husky and soulless. "The world would be so much better off without you in it."

I should've hung up. It would've taken less than a second to slam the handset on the receiver, yet, as if suffering from paralysis, I remained frozen.

"You're a burden on your parents," he said. "You know you make them worry." The kids and I would see them nearly every weekend, and they did seem stressed when we would come over.

"The kids wouldn't have to travel between two houses... if you weren't alive," he seethed. "That would be a lot better for them." He paused for effect. "And Mike—"

17

I finally gained the courage to speak. "Mike and the kids love me."

"Sure they love you." His words felt slippery and evil, velvety and sweet. "But didn't Mike always want a biological baby?"

I finally hung up and saw a counselor immediately after. I picked her because she was named after a state, Georgia, and I've always liked people named after states.

"I don't mean to be," I told her one day, "but I'm sad."

"You've let his words burrow into you and fester. You know you aren't a burden on anyone."

I broke down, crying. Trying to stay strong for my kids wasn't easy, being the only adult in a houseful of children. If something went wrong, it was my fault. Yes, Mike had begun coming over more often, but I did feel like an island most of the time.

She wheeled over to her desk and pulled out a piece of paper. "What are things you enjoy doing? Things you could do almost any day at the drop of a hat?" And over the next twenty minutes, she helped me create a "fun list."

"Why are we doing this?" I asked.

"To distract you when you're sad. But this list isn't enough. You also need long-term goals. You need a bucket list."

I raised my brows, surprised.

"I won't call you actively suicidal—because you don't have a plan—but I do think you're verging on situational depression because of this narcissistic, maybe even sociopathic, man."

"A bucket list?" I scoffed. "I'm in my early 30s. Why would I make a bucket list?"

"So, you have something to look forward to."

Almost a year passed after my sessions with Georgia, and my life changed. Mike and I got married, moved with the kids to another state, and began settling into life in Idaho. "What's this?" my youngest daughter, Indiana, asked. I'd just gotten home from work and set my briefcase by the front door. "Ma... ma." she sang. "What *is* this?" Her chubby five-year-old hand traced the paper I'd taped to the inside of a kitchen cupboard. I couldn't help grinning at that kid as she perched whimsically on a wooden chair we'd bought from a yard sale.

Trey came over, curious. "Yeah, Mom. What is that?" He read some of the words, "Jam with a stranger in Italy."

I smiled, lifted Indy off the chair, and gave them snacks at the table.

"That's my fun list and my bucket list. If I ever get stressed or have a hard time, I do something on the fun side. Look, you're on the list."

I pulled the paper down, and both of them looked at it with wonder.

"Go get a coffee," I read. "Write a blog post. Call Grandma Dee or Maureen. Visit Noni and Papa. Go for a walk with Trey and Indy. Go shopping with Ruby and Sky."

Ring the Bell

Indy's feet kicked happily under the table. "Mama, can we go for a walk right now?"

The memory shifted as I found myself years removed from those moments. Indy walked past me, no longer five but a preteen now.

"I'm going to hang out with Brooklyn."

"Okay." I nodded. "Be back in time for dinner."

I sat on the same wooden chair Indy had perched on many years before and studied my bucket list.

The left side of the list had saved my life. It's amazing how a quick, distracting activity can completely change the momentary climate of our lives. I shook my head, finding it odd I'd once let some man's terrible words have power over me. At certain times, I thought that maybe the world would be better off without me. Yet, now, seeing how much my friends and family needed me, how devasted they were by my terminal diagnosis... I never knew I'd be willing to fight so hard. It's because I finally realized how much I did matter. After all, flaws and everything, the people in my life loved me—even sometimes despite reason.

My eyes moved from the simple list on the left to the more complex items on the right: my bucket list.

Strangely, Mike and I began checking items off long before I had cancer, almost like we knew my life would be cut short.

I laughed, thinking about playing my violin in the New York Subway, visiting Jamaica, skinny dipping, or traveling to Canada for a weekend trip.

But, as always with life, there seemed to be so much more I wanted to do.

And despite doctors' warnings that I should stay home and rest—they panicked over every sniffle—I began concocting a plan. I would finish my bucket list well before doctors claimed I'd die.

I looked at the biggest items: jam with a stranger in Italy and go skydiving again. Envisioning my doctors' reactions to this made me chuckle.

Whether oncologists liked it, I knew what I wanted to do. They might have given me an expiration date, but that didn't mean I had to die before I finished living.

A Nice Barista

"This is taking *forever*," the woman fumed, even though it had been less than three minutes. "You're making me late for work." She'd already complained about rolling her window down all the way and yelled since they were out of a specific syrup.

The teenage barista frantically took another order at the drive-through, started a simultaneous fourth coffee, and handed the cranky lady her drink.

"You know," the woman hissed, "I'm having a terrible day because of you. You've made me late. I'll pay for the person behind me so at least someone can have a nice day."

The barista could have cried. She'd had a tough day too: Everyone had called out sick because of COVID, she'd been treated terribly by two customers already, and she worried about her mother—whose cancer seemed to be worsening.

But the barista didn't share any of this with the insensitive woman. Instead, she nodded and tried not to cry. "Okay." She forced a smile. "I hope you'll have a... nice day."

The woman must've slightly registered her childish behavior because she paused. "You must think I'm a terrible person. It's just that I still need to get my coffee today. That always makes me irritable."

Ring the Bell

Yes... That was it. She'd yelled at a child because she hadn't had her coffee yet. *That* made everything better.

Following this tirade, she drove off. And even though she had paid for the person behind her, she had also momentarily derailed the little barista's day.

When my daughter, Sky, told me what happened to her at work, I got so upset. With everything we're going through, we try to be extra kind to other people because you never know what trials they're facing. I can't imagine treating someone so terribly over coffee. Plus, it makes me sad that someone treated *my* 17-year-old kid this way. She's doing her best and dealing with more than any teenager should.

Sky ran away the year before, and after returning home, time and new experiences somehow bound us together even closer than ever before.

We would've floundered without her after Mike broke his right foot a couple of months ago and was temporarily unable to drive. I would bring him to work at 4:30 a.m., and she would bring him home. It felt depleting, but Sky made all the difference for us, and I still don't know what I would've done without her.

Life can feel crippling when hardships litter the way. Maybe that's why this tart customer's actions upset me so much. I bet she'd be appalled to hear about our struggles and how pubescent she seemed, throwing a tantrum over a raspberry mocha with two espresso shots.

Ring the Bell

I started writing a column for the Island Park News right before my diagnosis. This was slated to be a personal column about my life in Idaho, but I had no idea it would turn into stories about my battle with cancer. I sent in my weekly articles through hospitalizations, surgeries, treatments, and more, sometimes writing them on napkins or hospital bills before typing them into the computer. Looking back, writing each week buoyed me through some terrible times. One day, I excitedly typed, "I got through brain radiation by pretending to be a violin. I imagined that God was fixing me and giving me a tune-up." I could hardly wait for this to be published for my "Island Park pen pals" because it feels like a message in a bottle, going out into the vast world.

Unfortunately, tragedy struck, and the soundpost in my violin broke. This wooden dowel holds up the entire top plate of the violin. It's tiny and seemingly insignificant, but without it, a violin will sound hollow and weak.

I take everything so symbolically that this felt like a bad sign from God. After all, that violin is part of me. It's gone nearly everywhere I've traveled for 25 years. I busked as a homeless street musician with it in Hawaii. That fiddle has been with me all across the world. Canada and Mexico—all over America from California (Berkeley to Venice Beach) to the New York subway, Hawaii, Colorado, North Dakota, Missouri, Kansas, Florida... And now, to hear it sound so frail. And right after doctors delivered terrible news. More testing. Before even having results, they've thrown out scary ideas like "surgery," "palliative care," and "end-of-life planning."

"Mom," I said after she brought me in for labs, "we have two hours before the spinal tap. I need to get my violin fixed; would it be okay to drop it off since we're in Utah?"

The place where my parents bought my violin in Salt Lake, Scoggins and Scoggins, closed years ago, but I found a local luthier named Carrie Scoggins online. She quickly responded to an email saying "yes" she could fix my violin, and without knowing more, my mom and I drove to her home between appointments.

Carrie explained that she owned Scoggins and Scoggins with her first husband before he died. "We bought this violin from you 25 years ago!" I spouted. "It's been with me everywhere—even as a homeless street musician." I went to hand her my precious instrument, but as I extended my arm, I remembered the bandage conspicuously wrapped around my left elbow where nurses had drawn my blood. Carrie must've seen it too. And although I didn't need to explain myself, I decided to anyway. "I... I go to the Huntsman Cancer Center for treatments," I told Carrie, wondering if she'd spied my bandage.

"Sorry to hear you're going through that," she said.

We remained quiet for a moment, and then my mom and I became instantly mesmerized as Carrie took my violin, flipped it upside down, removed the endpin, and did all sorts of magic to the inside of my instrument.

"You know... I read the Island Park News," she said, still working wonders. "Up in Idaho—near Yellowstone, there's a woman who writes a column. She has cancer too. You might like to read some of her stuff."

My mom and I gaped at each other. "That's... " I paused. "Carrie, that's me. I'm EC Stilson. I write for the Island Park News... about my journey with cancer."

She set my violin on the table in front of her. "Really?" She gasped. "Wait... Really?"

"Yes." I could hardly hold my enthusiasm in check. "Page nine. Every week." I wanted to jump around and dance. Because someone actually read my articles!

"I've been reading your column for years—and so has my husband."

"I... I can't believe this. You have made my year!" I turned to my mom and giggled because she seemed stunned. "To think, the woman I bought my violin from 25 years ago... is reading my column all the way in a different state."

Carrie shook her head in wonder and then began doing more fantastical things to my fiddle. "What you needed to be fixed, your 'soundpost,' in Italian means 'soul.' It helps the violin vibrate and produce sound."

Her words hit me, filling my entire being like I'd just gotten my own figurative soundpost back. I could hardly take it in, the enormity of the situation.

Ring the Bell

My violin wasn't broken before, not really. But without that soundpost, it would be a husk without a soul to give it life. It just needed a little tweaking from a master craftsman.

"Wow," my mom said as the words took root.

Carrie fixed my violin in moments and made it sound even more perfect than before. "I take everything so literally," I admitted, "I thought maybe this was a sign from God. Not to be dramatic," I whispered, "but I thought God was about to kill me."

She laughed. "Yeah. Not to be dramatic — at all." Then she grinned, and the moment seemed electric and exciting. "This was an easy fix."

I held my violin out, so amazed just staring at the beauty of it. This master luthier had somehow swept into my life, fixed the soul of my violin, and given me my courage back.

As my mom and I returned to the hospital for my spinal tap, I couldn't help feeling a sense of peace.

"I think God is trying to tell you that He's looking out for you — and everything will be okay."

"I think so too," I said. Then I thought about the master luthier who'd fixed my violin. She brought new life to my fiddle and gave me hope that if I place my faith in God, He'll take care of me and even make my soul shine.

Fiddling in New York

My bucket list contains some strange things, but each of them has the capability of making a great memory for myself—and, hopefully, the people around me. I thought about one of the items: play my violin on the subway and in New York.

A few years ago, Mike surprised me and bought airplane tickets to New York. I could hardly wait to get there and play.

But the subway wasn't what I'd imagined, and things didn't go as expected. Many people wore earbuds or looked at social media on their phones. I might as well have played alone in a dark alley for all I accomplished. I played a Vivaldi piece I'd once performed with an orchestra. And when I finished, pure energy pulsed from my fingers. Yet almost everyone got off at the next stop, still glued to their phones as if I didn't even exist.

"Oh, Elisa," Mike said. "That sounded so great. Don't feel bad."

Sweet Mike. He's the most fantastic guy, and after I put my violin away, I hugged him.

"You're still okay bringing that to Staten Island?" he asked, and I nodded.

"Who knows what adventure might happen there." Even though the subway thing hadn't gone like I'd dreamed, I could hardly wait to see what the future would hold.

Ring the Bell

Mike and I drank smooth, black coffee on Staten Island when suddenly, a guitar melody drifted from nearby.

We followed the notes and ended up in the large room where droves of people waited for the return ferry to New York. Almost every person watched a guitarist playing anything from Jamaican rifts to a mix of Latino and rock harmonies.

I wished more than anything that I could jam with him. So, I went and gave him a tip. But as I turned to walk away, he saw my violin case and stopped playing. "Are you pretty good?" he asked.

"I've played since I was five."

"You wanna jam?"

"Oh, my gosh! Are you kidding? Yes, I want to jam!"

I took out my fiddle, and we played—right there in front of the ever-growing crowd.

After several measures, he leaned over to me and said, "You are good. Let me turn down my guitar so people can hear you."

Music is life-changing—it's math that we can hear. He played a third, so I played a fifth. Then I knew he'd drop back again, so I countered with a root note. After a few minutes, my mind stopped making predictions, and the music poured straight from my soul. Toward the end of the third song, I felt so connected with the melodies it sounded as if this man and I had played together for years. That's the thing about music, it brings out your soul, all barriers removed, and that's when we can connect, even with strangers.

Ring the Bell

"Oh, shoot," I said at the end of the last song. "Our ferry is almost here. I've gotta go."

"But what's your name? When will you be back? Who are you? We need to jam again—we could get a contract!"

As I frantically packed up my fiddle, I felt like Cinderella leaving the ball. "I don't live around here."

"I play at Staten Island every Sunday. I'm Mohammed—you have to come back... Where are you from, anyway?"

"Idaho."

"Idaho? Huh." His grin widened. Then as I slid my bow into my case, Mike got the guy's number.

Before going, I gave Mohammed a huge hug. "This moment—what you did for me... Letting me jam with you in front of all these people… I'll never forget it. You made my entire year.

He lit up with happiness. "Keep in touch!"

As Mike and I boarded the ferry, I asked him if that whole thing surprised him as much as it floored me. I'd traveled there to play my violin on the subway, yet playing in Staten Island had been far more memorable. Thank God life doesn't always turn out how we hope; it often plays out much better.

"Typical day." Mike shrugged. "Come to a city you've never been in. Meet some guy. Get propositioned to play music with him on Staten Island every Sunday. No, Elisa, I'm done being surprised. Life with you has always been an adventure."

Ring the Bell

I gazed up at my wonderful man. "You're such a good guy to stick by me through all my crazy antics. Not everyone can be as supportive as you are. I love you so much, Mike."

He winked at me, and I snuggled into him as we sat on the ferry.

They found another tumor in one of my legs. It doesn't even matter which leg at this point because it's just another bump in the road.

The kids asked me last night how many tumors I have.

"One in each vertebrae, one in my hip, shin, leg... neck, brain." I tried to act bravely. "It's not a big deal anymore. Who's counting?"

"Wow. I guess that's one way to find something good," my son said.

"I'm just done focusing on the bad. It's like studying for a test and still failing. I'm just gonna stop focusing on my score."

"I'm so sorry this illness has been hard on you," a friend said when I told her about the new tumor later that afternoon.

I hate that. Wouldn't it be hard on anyone? I don't want people treating this like leprosy or something, but simply calling stage 4 melanoma an "illness" is like calling a fart a unicorn. Talk about the ultimate minimization. This *illness*... Blah.

I said goodbye and hung up right before calling Ruby, my 19-year-old who is seriously — no bias — one of the most extraordinary people you could ever meet. At the time, she was almost a tattoo artist (working on finishing her apprenticeship) and recently got herself a motorcycle instead of a man. That kid knows what she wants, and she gets 'er done regardless of obstacles.

"Ruby," I said. "This isn't a pity party, but I should probably give you the latest update."

"Okay?" she said in this adorable way that only she can.

"There's a new tumor in my leg and a lump in my boob."

I heard her inhale sharply. "Oh, Mom. I'm so sorry."

"It's no big deal. I'm just becoming a nonprofit tumor factory. They say, 'Do what you're good at'—and I took their words to heart."

"Mom," she laughed, "I love you so much." And somehow, her response made everything bearable.

I called Mike later. "If they cut off my leg and my boob, will you still be proud I'm your wife? Will you still love me?"

"Depends on which boob." Mike smirked.

"What?" I nearly bellowed.

"You're ridiculous—and dramatic. Of course, I will always love you. You'd still be you."

"Yeah. But I'd look a lot different in my fancy dresses." Then we made some inappropriate jokes.

"Hey, did you hear Chrissy has stage 3 kidney cancer?" I asked him after we'd stopped laughing about me being "half the person I used to be."

I sighed. "She said she feels dumb complaining to me—after everything we've been through."

"Why? No two situations are the same."

Ring the Bell

"That's exactly what I said. She shouldn't minimize what she's going through. Our situations are both hard—I can't imagine what she's enduring. I'm glad we have each other's backs and can find the good together."

So, that day seemed good because I still had two legs, two boobs, a sense of humor, and doctors competent enough to find new tumors.

They slated me to start treatments again soon after being on steroids for what felt like a lifetime. I counted down the days so we could fight this thing again. The best we could do was try—while still focusing on the good. So, that's what I did. I decided to get busy seeing the good side of life so I couldn't focus on anything else. "'Tis only a scratch."

It Came Back Around

Her words made my blood burn with anger. "I don't want a Black man narrating my book."

"Excuse me?" I balked. She suddenly seemed like some Neanderthal. It was 2013. Who thought something like that?

At the time, I co-owned a publishing company. Other editors, writers, investors, and I had worked to publish over a hundred authors in just over a year. But the joy had been short-lived, and authors—like this woman—had begun irritating me.

As a first-time author, she'd submitted a list of demands. Her book had yet to sell well, and now she wanted book signings in key New York locations and reviews in publications that would cost thousands of dollars each. We couldn't do all of that, but I'd tried something else and had luck; a famous man had agreed to narrate *and promote* her audiobook. But when we finished the project, and we'd slated it for release, the author didn't want a Black man connected with her book. I had never heard something so idiotic, something so wholly infantile.

"I'm terminating your contract," I immediately told the woman. "You wanted your book to sell, so we found a well-known narrator who kindly agreed to narrate your book, and you're upset because of what he looks like? I'll email the details to you, but we will no longer fund this project."

Ring the Bell

She screamed, and I hung up. Within the next hour, my editors talked about the situation and agreed; we would not support an author like that.

I truly appreciated my editorial team. They knew how hard we'd worked to establish the publishing company, but they also understood that we'd reached a critical point. I'd just filed for divorce, and because of my ex's financial involvement, none of us knew if we'd be able to keep the company going through a split like that and while I adjusted to being a single mom to four young kids.

So, long story short, the company, my dream, dissolved. I think it somehow ended well for everyone. I taught authors how to self-publish; they even got to keep the rights to their covers and promotional materials.

But as for the famous narrator, he wouldn't be making anything off the project he'd worked so hard on. Just the idea of that irked me because he'd been so exceedingly kind throughout the ordeal.

"How much would you charge for something like this if you weren't getting a percentage of the profits?" I asked, and he gave me a number. It was a small fortune to me, but I'd made up my mind.

He had no idea where the money came from or what I'd just gone through. But, as a single mom, I worked extra hours, and through two different jobs and over six months, I paid the man what he should have made.

"Why are you doing this?" one of the previous editors asked. "The company went under. I don't think you need to front the cost."

Ring the Bell

"It's the *right* thing to do. He worked hard. He deserves to get paid." I'd begged him to narrate the book. How could I not pay him after he'd gone out of his way to help me?

I remember making the final payment. It felt so good. That day I'd looked up the author—the racist one. She'd self-published her book, which hadn't sold well. And to think, she'd almost had it narrated by someone who could've made it a bestseller.

I thought about all of this today because we've had some pretty astronomical medical bills. I spent a chunk of yesterday afternoon fighting debilitating pain and our insurance company. Anyway, I opened my email, discovering that someone had given us a bit of money, precisely what we needed to get by. It was the narrator whom I'd worked so hard to pay off as a single mom. I read his name about three times, totally stupefied. I hadn't heard from him for over seven years, yet there it was, a random email and a gift.

Tears streamed down my face. I can't believe he's following my story or that he came to help me in my time of need.

"It's like watching an innocent little animal get cancer. I feel so bad, and I don't know what to do. Or what to say. I feel helpless. No one wants to see a bunny—or a baby otter—with cancer. You're like… Thumper," my friend said, flummoxing me.

First off, I am a certified badass. Was she seriously comparing me to a bunny? Secondly,

Ring the Bell

Thumper is a boy. And last, I want to be a fearsome predator—not a cute, pansy-ish woodland creature. I thought about all of this as I looked at a painting in my bedroom. It's of bunnies battling a storm. There's just something romantic and inspiring about their tenacity. Maybe it's because I want that tenacity. I want to persevere like those fearless creatures. Even when failure is guaranteed, I want to embody that moxie.

At least the "woodland creature" conversation reminded me of my aspirations; that's one thing.

So, as I woke up today and looked at the painting on my wall, I had to smirk.

Bring on the storm. Even if I *am* like a bunny, I will face this head-on with a determination that'd make Captain Ahab envious. Take that, Thumper.

As if trapped in an hourglass, the sands of time cascade around me, and I'm stuck up to my waist. Sand continues dumping, getting caught in my hair and occasionally my mouth and eyes, but it's not falling as quickly now. "You'll live longer than we initially thought," a doctor recently told me. And although I'm exceedingly grateful, I can't help thinking of the initial two-year diagnosis in 2020 and that death still circles like a vulture in the sky.

If my time is quickly approaching, what do I have to show for the recent past? What have I even accomplished since my diagnosis? I've decided the key is to *keep* living, even while dying.

Ring the Bell

I scanned through pictures, and memories poured over me, just like the sand in that hourglass. I remembered fiddling for cancer patients; losing my hair; being selected as the angel family; enduring debilitating surgeries, infusions, and radiation; fighting liver failure and sepsis; and losing several friends who died too soon (suicide, overdose, cancer, and car accidents). And then I found pictures of Mike and the kids. I reminisced over when family and friends came to visit. I couldn't help grinning about road trips and time fishing, card games and movie nights.

Then it hit me: how much I've bonded with those who matter most. This has brought us closer. And although I'm still scared, and we are living scan to scan, I am proud that *we* have made it through so far. Even that is a breadcrumb from God.

A Beacon in the Darkness

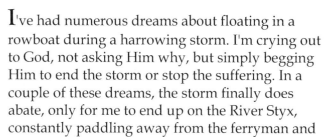

I've had numerous dreams about floating in a rowboat during a harrowing storm. I'm crying out to God, not asking Him why, but simply begging Him to end the storm or stop the suffering. In a couple of these dreams, the storm finally does abate, only for me to end up on the River Styx, constantly paddling away from the ferryman and smacking away bony hands that try climbing into my boat from the river. Of course, I don't have a coin for passage; I'll be "damned," trying to make my own way even up until the end.

I thought about all of this as I studied my bucket list again. Unfortunately, many of the activities on it would be too difficult now that I often need a wheelchair. Although I'm a natural faller, I can't imagine skydiving again—I don't know how I'd land. And backpacking across Europe? That's unfathomable. But the most impossible wish on my list, which I hope to check off more than anything, is to "ring the bell." Many people don't know what this means, but it's like conquering the world to a cancer patient because it means you've finished treatments. Sometimes I'll be sitting during infusions only to hear the bell. That means someone has either made it out of this journey alive or they've decided it's time to quit. I always hope they're healthy and can move on with their lives. I want that more than anything for them. I want that… for me too.

39

Ring the Bell

My dreams have shifted from seeking adventure to just wanting to live so I can see my children grow up, find their dream careers, get married, and have children. I'm not shooting for the moon, not really.

I told Mike all of this, and with tears in his eyes, he said he had a surprise. "I've been looking at your bucket list. You know how we keep saying we'll see your family in Seattle? Well, I found cheap tickets. We're going to see them. We're doing it, Elisa."

I hugged Mike because he's the most incredible person in the world. And before I knew it, we'd gone to Seattle and sat looking at a massive lighthouse with two of my favorite cousins: Lori and Gabby Brush.

"It's saved many ships during storms," I heard an old man say as he passed us on the walkway.

I scoffed and stared at the unimpressive building again. It didn't look newsworthy, but that's what, I decided, made it so special. A layman could deem it an old, irrelevant building. Instead, it tells a story of life, just like ringing the bell.

I have seen the strangest beacons at such fortuitous times, especially recently, and they've carried me through the storms.

The next day, before we flew out from Seattle, Mike decided to surprise me. "We're driving somewhere before we leave."

Mike guided me slowly, and I carefully traversed a small portion of lush forest before reaching a different lighthouse from days before.

A piece of driftwood became the perfect seat because it faced the wind, and as the salty sea air turned my earrings into tiny windchimes, I felt liberated next to that lighthouse.

"Mike," I said, "something's bothering me."

"What's that?" he asked.

"I've gotten a few strange messages from people lately. They say I'm proof that God doesn't exist. Because why would God do something like this to me." My voice faltered. "I'm not religious, but I do love God with all my heart. Why would my journey bring people further away from God? Even if I do die, death is a part of life. When will people stop getting mad at God for something that was part of the deal anyway? I have peace that there's a plan. When I'm supposed to die, it'll be my time."

Mike thought hard and stared out at the ocean. He doesn't believe in God per se, but he's awfully supportive of people believing what makes sense to them. "Elisa, if they stopped believing after hearing your story, it isn't about you. They're placing their doubt on you. That's a burden you don't need to carry."

I closed my eyes and faced the wind again. I pretended that lighthouse was shining right into me, guiding me in the storm. In my imagination, the light went through me, leading me to be the person I'm meant to be without regrets, burdens, or even sadness over cancer and doubt.

I heard some people approaching because they started screaming excitedly. Mike and I followed their gazes to see a pod of orcas jumping and dancing in the waves right before us. "Orcas." I squealed. "They're *real* orcas. This is the best. Day. Ever."

Ring the Bell

I hugged Mike so hard, and he looked down at me instead of the magnificent fish in the ocean. "You're so darling," he said.

"The orcas are my beacon for today." I no longer worried that I might never ring the bell or get better. I stopped thinking about people who supposedly lost faith because of my journey. I didn't even worry about the 18 pills I had to take every single day because, at that moment, everything seemed incredibly doable. Whether I'm magically healed someday or end up on the Styx sooner than later, I'll keep looking for beacons because God's lighthouse is leading me home.

"We'll go dancing and clubbing," one lady said. "We'll drink all night long."

"And we can run together each morning. And maybe even get in a little rock climbing."

I could tell that the two ladies were just a little older than me, yet they could do so much more. I finally arrived at the front of the line. Mike had gone to the bathroom, and I decided to help out so we wouldn't miss our flight. It seemed great in theory, but my back and legs ached so much that my knees began shaking. "I requested a wheelchair," I told the woman behind the ticket counter. "There's no way I can walk through the airport anymore." Why did I feel the need to justify myself to this woman?

As she printed out boarding passes, I thought about the two ladies in front of me and how they could run, dance, and rock climb. Tears began filling my eyes because I missed all of that so much. I wish that the last time I'd done everything, I would've appreciated it with due credit. But now, all of it is just a memory.

"Do you see that man sitting in a wheelchair over there?" the lady asked after a while.

I spotted a man who resembled Mr. Potter from IT'S A WONDERFUL LIFE. He sat grumpily next to the other wheelchairs.

"Just go sit in a wheelchair by him, and someone will be with both of you shortly." After I gave her my luggage, she paged someone and motioned for me to go.

"Mr. Potter" looked like his namesake for a reason. I tried being social, but his drab countenance could've killed even a chipper angel's spirit. "Why do you need a wheelchair?" he asked accusatorially. "And why do you walk all hunched over?"

"I've been walking much better. It gets worse when I'm tired. Dragging my luggage was rough."

"Maybe you shouldn't pack so goddamn much," he said.

"I have cancer," I finally retorted. "Why are *you* in a wheelchair."

"I have cancer too. It's almost eaten all of me now." I spied scabs on his arms and legs, something I've come to see a lot at the cancer center. I've even had some myself after itching from treatments or medications.

"I used to be able to do so many things. I looked years younger." After saying the words, he glanced around almost hungrily at the healthy people scurrying around us. "Bet someone else deserves this more than I do."

We stayed quiet for a couple of minutes. "Has anyone helped you?" a woman asked. She spoke so slowly, as if we were mentally handicapped.

"A woman at the ticket counter paged someone, but that was quite a while ago," I said so fast that I'd hoped she'd realize we were mentally capable. "Can you call someone just in case?"

So, she did. And when she walked away, Mr. Potter couldn't say enough bad about her. "You know people are just nice because they know something is wrong with us? That's the only reason. We make them feel better about themselves."

My mouth dropped. "Sir, I find your outlook on life... not to be my favorite. I've *always* expected the best from people. Now I get to see it almost every day. People find out I have cancer, and they rise to the occasion. I've seen the kind of generosity written about in books."

"Oh. So, you're a Pollyanna."

"Maybe I am. But I'd rather be that than a Mr. Potter."

I couldn't believe I'd said it. And unfortunately, the man—who was quite a bit older than me—got the reference. "You need a wheelchair. What can you find to be *glad* about that?"

"Because it reminds me... " I paused. "Even though there's a lot I can't do, being in a wheelchair reminds me of the things I can be grateful for."

"Such as?"

Ring the Bell

"Well, now I'm doing a lot of things on my bucket list. And... my kids aren't cranky teenagers. They're somehow grateful for everything."

Mike walked up. "You got the passes and checked the luggage?"

I nodded.

"I can't believe you did all of that." He glanced down at his feet briefly. His right foot was still healing after surgery. "Sorry I took so long to find you after I went to the bathroom."

My phone lit to life after I tapped it. "I must not have reception in here. Thank God that you found me." Mike had arrived at the right time, like he always seems to.

The fact was that this man, Mr. Potter, had shaken my resolve. He'd said so many things that worried me. Sometimes sickness is hard, and I feel myself teetering on a knife's edge. I could be just like this man if I didn't fight to be positive. The battle to remain happy and appreciative despite hardships is sometimes more complex than fighting cancer.

Several workers came up together at that point. Just before the cranky man got whisked away, he turned to me. "Did I really remind you of Mr. Potter?"

"Yes," I said. And as he disappeared into the crowd, I thought of how important it is to focus on what I can do instead of what I can't. I felt suddenly grateful for Mr. Potter. He inadvertently gave me the wake-up call I needed.

"Making friends?" Mike asked.

"Not this time," I said, surprising even myself.

Live to the Fullest

Two attendants wheeled me through the massive airport as Mike walked behind us with our carry-ons and my violin. "I'm training John," the shorter man said. "You don't mind if he tags along?"

"The more, the merrier." I grinned. It's taken some time, but I've overcome my embarrassment of needing a wheelchair for long stints.

So, Mike and I talked with the men: John and Matt. We joked and laughed about life, and soon the young men told us about their hopes and dreams.

"This isn't your dream job?" I asked Matt.

"I want to stage houses."

"But—let me guess—it doesn't make any money. Right?"

He nodded.

"Okay," I said. "I had a similar problem. I wanted to be a writer; I even wrote nine books, but I only made enough each month to eat off the dollar menu at McDonald's. So, I found something close to writing where I *could* make money. I had to work hard for it, but now I'm an editor. Sure, I'm not writing young-adult fiction like I hoped, but I'm surprisingly happy with my career."

"How can I possibly make money staging houses? I don't have any experience."

I thought for a minute. "You could become... a realtor. Stage homes and then make money selling them. Get contacts and, down the road, start your own staging business for fellow realtors who've grown to love you."

"This is so weird," he confessed. I joined a realtor class, and it's about to expire. Then my mom, who has no idea, just gave me silly realtor socks as a joke."

"And *now* we're talking about it. It's a Godwink for sure."

John, the other man who'd just started this job, said he got it to pay his way through college. "I want to become a pilot."

"That's awesome," Mike said, and we found ourselves so impressed with the two that we bought them coffee.

"Listen," I finally said, "I have stage 4 cancer. I thought I'd raise my kids and see the world when they got older. I always wanted to visit Italy. I wanted to see Canada and Mexico again. But look at me. My oldest is an adult, and my 17-year-old is close behind. Now that I'm closer to 40—the age when I'd hoped to travel—I'm too sick to do everything I wanted. Time goes too fast, and if you don't work to accomplish your dreams and do what you want, you might look back and realize life passed you by. Tomorrow is uncertain at best."

We resumed our journey then, our ragtag band moving steadily through the airport. I couldn't help watching as different people occasionally looked at me kindly, sadly, curiously, callously... I even caught an elderly woman grimacing as if nothing looked "wrong" with me.

Ring the Bell

We finally arrived at our terminal, and Mike and I turned to the men. "You can do anything if you just work hard to get there," Mike said.

"I'm so energized." Matt grinned. "You guys totally changed my whole perspective."

"It was nice to meet you," Mike said.

"You too," they both replied.

They left soon after, and another representative, seeing the wheelchair, asked me to approach the customer service desk. "Which flight?" she asked.

"7350," Mike said.

"I saw you in the wheelchair," the representative said. "Can you walk?"

I nodded.

"We'll have you board first, so you'll have enough time to make it onto the plane."

"Thank you," I gushed. This meant so much because it's embarrassing when business people seem impatient for me to find my place. They don't always have much empathy when they're in a hurry.

Mike wheeled me from the customer service area, and we waited to board. That's when I noticed a few younger people studying me with pity. I'm not sure why their prying eyes hurt, but they did.

"Mike, can we go over there, where there aren't many people?"

He peered down, concerned. "What's going on?" he asked when we reached the vacant corner.

"I think," I bit my lip, trying to keep it from trembling, "God made me all wrong." Mike seemed so shocked that I immediately regretted my words. God doesn't make mistakes—that's Religion 101.

Plus, I probably got melanoma from fake baking at tanning salons or getting burned when I was homeless in Hawaii as a teenager.

Hawaii... Now, there were some memories of living to the fullest. Fiddling all night, then blending in with tourists, and sleeping on the beach all day had risks. If you slept too hard, you'd wake up lobster-red when the shade moved. Nope. Melanoma wasn't God's fault; it was mine.

"I shouldn't have said that," I added. "But it's true that I do feel like there's something wrong with me. Maybe we all feel like that sometimes. Perhaps I've just felt that way more than many people. It doesn't help that people have told me I'm a one-upper (so contrary, I go against everyone) or that I'm an acquired taste. But I don't want to be someone who has to grow on you like a fungus.

"You're perfect," Mike said, bringing me from my thoughts and making tears brim my eyes.

"You are." I gazed up at my dream man. "It *is* mentally exhausting having cancer, though, wondering about death and so many of life's deep questions."

"Like why this is happening? Why you're sick?"

I nodded. "And then there's the whole concept of 'me,' the fact that any of us even have consciousness. I mean, who am I really? A collection of my own perception and what other people think about me? What impression am I leaving behind? And then it instantly feels as if everything that's wrong with me is manifesting in my body so everybody can see it on the outside too.

Ring the Bell

Maybe I was always a mess, but now everyone knows."

"You are not a mess, Elisa. Even now, you're handling this better than anyone I know would." Mike leaned down and kissed me on the forehead before letting his right thumb grace my cheek.

"I'm not feeling bad for myself," I said. "Really."

"I know, sweetheart." He pressed his forehead against mine and stared into my eyes. "I think you're just grieving. You're young. You shouldn't be facing all of this. Thinking about leaving all of us so soon." His voice caught on the last couple of words.

"Neither should you," I whispered.

It's hard being unable to do some things by myself. I can't reach up high or climb on counters when I need the largest dish. I can't even sleep through the whole night anymore because my body pulses with pain. But what's worse is knowing this has negatively affected my family.

"You know what's crazy, Mike? People ask me when I'll be able to walk 'normal' again."

"You seem to be standing straighter every day."

I smiled. He's trying so damn hard to make things better. But the fact is, I'll probably never walk the same again. I'm just glad he somehow loves me through it all and sees the best in me even when I don't see it in myself. "I've also had friends ask when the swelling in my face will go away." It's called moon face—something that happens when you take steroids. Doctors made me take them after immunotherapy caused an infection so bad that I almost died... again. My face will thin out in days or months. I. Don't. Know. But honestly, that's the

least of my concerns right now. And that's what
Mike told me before we boarded the plane.

The last few minutes before boarding, the airline
staff must've moved my seat from an emergency
row to the front of the plane. "But I want to sit by
you," I whispered. They'd moved *my* seat but not
Mike's.

"It'll be okay," he said. "Maybe this will give you
a chance to rest in a nice seat."

I didn't necessarily want to close my eyes, but
Mike seemed tired. "Mike, you sit in the front. I'll sit
in the back."

"Are you kidding?" He laughed. "This is so you
won't have to walk far." After reassuring me that
he'd be okay sleeping in the emergency row, I sat
and watched as passengers boarded the plane.
Rows behind me, Mike closed his eyes almost
immediately, and I couldn't help gazing fondly at
that man. He's always doing so much for everyone;
I wished I could do something nice for him.

An overwhelming peace fell on me, and my
worries faded as I stared out the window,
wondering who might sit next to me. Toward the
end of the boarding process, a tall stranger took the
seat, and I decided to strike up a conversation.
Everything happens for a reason, right? Maybe I
had something to learn from this man.

When I told him about my battle with cancer, he
didn't judge or show an overt amount of sympathy;
he just treated me like an average person. And then,

we talked about everything: religion, philosophy, and family.

"They changed my seat at the last minute," he said.

"Mine too," I replied. And then, as we talked more, I discovered he was from the same small town as me. And he only lives a few miles from us. Our kids are the same ages—and even attend school together.

Despite just meeting, I said this was a Godwink, and we exchanged information after deciding to get together with our families sometime. When almost the whole plane deboarded, Mike led me down the aisle, and I told him about the exchange. The words came out quickly, with such excitement that I stood a little taller. It wasn't because I felt better physically but because someone had treated me normally. This stranger gave me the courage to move on from a sobering moment. I'm still alive. I'm able to move around. And I can live life to the fullest—to my own capabilities. "It's time for me to *stop* measuring myself against everyone else's view of me. And measure myself against what I am capable of, what I want, and what I *can* do about it," I said.

Mike eyed me like I'd taken advantage of the plane's wine list.

"I just realized that regardless of how people treat me, finding inner joy is always worth it." The root of joy is synonymous with perseverance. It's something you must fight for. "Joy is something you choose," I said to Mike. "So that's what I'm going to do. Today, I choose joy." I couldn't help wondering over my handsome man, whose eyes shone bright like they always do first thing in the morning. "What-did-*you*-do? Who-did-you-sit-next-to? How-was-your-flight?" I blurted so quickly that Mike blinked and shook his head.

"I slept," he responded, and both of us laughed.

The Power of Gratitude

I've relived certain moments from my life dozens of times. Do you have experiences that you go to sleep thinking about because they were so fantastic or memories so nightmarish they wake you from the deepest sleep?

Sometimes I fall asleep remembering what it was like when my mom held me in a rocking chair. I would nestle in so close, and she'd snuggle me in one of those fuzzy blankets. I just remember the love.

Other times I think about watching fish in a huge tank we owned. My black and white cat—Bootsie—would curl up on my stomach. He loved watching the fish just as much as I did. And if I turned away for too long, sometimes he'd go fishin'. I could hear the TV and music from another part of the house. All four of my closest family members were there, happy and healthy.

I love looking back on those moments, but some parts of my life are less kind.

She was four years older than me, and I remember she hated raisins. The girl told me we could do strange things at night, under the covers. I wanted it to stop, but she said we'd already gone too far. I'd just started school the first time it happened. "I'll tell your mom," she said one time. "Then she'll know how dirty you are." I offered to give her my allowance, favorite toys... my decorations. I didn't want my mom to know how gross I'd become.

When I finally got brave enough to talk about it, an adult told me, "It doesn't count as molestation."

"Why?" I balked.

"She was a girl. And she was just a child too."

"But she was a teenager the last time it happened—and four years older than me."

The woman shook her head, solidifying the fact that some adults will never see reason. "She was a girl" seemed like saying a declawed lion isn't dangerous.

Other memories haunt my dreams too, like an exorcism that zealots performed on me at church, years later when my son died, or the moment that led to the dissolution of my first marriage.

Luckily, as I've aged, more recent memories have replaced the old ones.

When I met Mike, everything bloomed. Every day of falling in love with him, the world unfolded with new adventures. We got married at Antelope Island—a state park—because it had become a place of magic for me and the kids when I was a single mom. We all loved going there and watching the wild animals.

As my dad walked me down that outdoor aisle, I could hardly wait to stand next to Mike, gaze into his eyes, and tell him I'll love him forever—my Mike. My handsome bachelor gave me and my four kids the world. He took those vows about "sickness and health" so seriously. Who knew I'd get terminally ill a few short years into our marriage and that he'd take care of the kids whenever I drove to the out-of-state cancer center or got hospitalized?

So, when I think of the key memories that make up my life, I realize what a strange mishmash they are. Each one has molded me and taught me something.

The moments I've re-experienced through imaginings or dreams are intriguing because they have collectively made up a human life.

Sometimes I find it fascinating that I'm here at all, breathing... thinking. It really does make you wonder: Where did we all come from? Did God always exist? If not, who in the hell made God? And what key experiences make up His existence too?

Months ago, I started feeling something new: hope. I even entertained the thought that someday I might be in remission, ringing the bell so loud the whole country would hear it as I beat the odds. But today, I'm crushed. It takes courage to hope, and now, after falling into momentary despair, I've realized maybe I'm only a brave fool.

Previously, I never understood how people could say, "The cancer didn't kill them; it was the treatment." Now, I get it. So far, immunotherapy has caused me to have liver failure, colitis that led to sepsis, and now serious struggles with my endocrine system.

This is so hard on my body—and exhausting—that I'm sleeping all night and then an additional four hours a day. Limping to a finish line that I may never cross.

I contemplated all of this when Mike found a package on the front porch. "It's for you," he said, bounding into the room like a golden Lab.

Despite my worries and pain, I grinned at my darling husband. It's hard to be glum around Mike.

"But... " I read the sender's name, Sheri Neeley. "She has cancer too. She's so sick, Mike. The fact that she sent *me* something — when she's having such a hard time... People astound me."

I set the package on my bed and wondered over numerous pick-me-up gifts and fun winter hats. The irony hit me after I donned a beanie and looked in the mirror. Sheri is undergoing chemo and just lost her hair. Yet, she still found the courage and fortitude to think of someone else. I so hope Sheri will beat this.

Anyway, I'm taking medications to bolster my endocrine system and wearing a hat from my new friend. If my body can withstand treatments long enough for the immunotherapy to kill the cancer, I'll have a chance. My organs just need to survive this.

I know God has a plan; maybe part of this is just learning to be at peace regardless of the outcome.

Indy got incredibly sick, and to see her like that was devastating. She's one of the happiest people on earth. Someone in her middle school could be insulting, and she'd hope for the best: "They'd never mean it *that* way," or "We should give them another chance."

But on Sunday, I knew something was wrong when Trey teased her, and she mumbled, "What a jerk."

Two hours later, Indy had a full-blown fever, a sore throat, and even hallucinations. The doctor dubbed it strep and gave us antibiotics. But the next night, Indy still struggled, so I slept by her on the couch despite how much it made my body ache and how sick I felt from treatments.

After a while, I fell asleep and had a wonderful dream about a beautiful valley. It felt so different, lying in the grass—and I realized it was simply the absence of pain.

Indy woke up. "Mama, I'm cold." She shivered.

"I've got you. You're okay." I covered her with an extra blanket.

"Mama." She quaked moments later.

"What, sweetheart?" I held her close.

"It's just that you're so sick. Now, you're staying up and not getting rest because of me."

"Don't worry about me. I'm okay," I said, amazed by that kind of altruism at such a young age. "I wouldn't want to be anywhere else," I said, even shunning the beautiful valley from my dream. Mike and the kids are my Heaven. "You're my baby. I want to be with my kids, always. Especially when you need me."

She rolled over, and her big eyes filled with concern for me even though *she* still fought a fever. "You know how you said you feel like you always have the flu?"

Ring the Bell

I nodded.

"I just realized how terrible that must be. It must be so bad." Then these massive tears rolled down her cheeks. And she hugged me like she might never let go. "Mama, I'm sorry you're sick."

I hugged her. "It's okay. It really is. It's not as bad... as it sounds. Indy, I'm just so sorry that *you* are sick." And as I thought about how terrible cancer can be—and I felt those darling arms around my neck—I remembered the reason I'm fighting so hard. It's for my family.

Indy finally started feeling better hours later. I'm so glad she's on the mend, painting her nails crazy colors and harassing her cat again.

Later, when I woke up from a nap, the kids had already been home from school for an hour. I instantly wished I could give them more: hike, climb, play, and not need to rest all the time.

Instead, the best I can offer now is to appreciate everything—even if I'm living in a new normal. Things will never be the same for me ever again, but at least I'm still here.

I'm waiting in a massive line. It doesn't matter why I'm there; it just matters how I feel in the moment. I'm standing on a steep incline, and soon I shift uncomfortably. As a teenager, I always carried a deck of cards and a hacky sack in my tattered purse. So, I start kicking the hacky sack around, knowing it will make strangers my friends. Others in line introduce themselves and form a circle where we can all play.

I soon discover the power of words. Having an epiphany that asking the right questions is like getting a key to someone's door. You can hear many amazing things—and learn so much—if you dare to ask the deep stuff. It's a shortcut to the soul.

"I've never told anyone that," a woman says, serving the hacky sack to the man beside her. "I feel so relieved that I'm not alone."

"I think we've all felt like that at one time or another," a gypsy-looking girl says in the wispy voice of a fairy.

But the hill makes things difficult—even for budding friendships. We persist for a bit, but after a while, the sun beats down unapologetically, and we all grow tired.

I decide to try resting. Nobody cares because even my new buddies are doing the same thing. I fluff my ragged purse on the ground and use it as a pillow, but the hill isn't ideal. The gravel bites into my hip and shoulder, and the deck of cards only adds to my lumpy purse. I roll, but I can't get comfortable on that hill no matter how hard I try.

After an eternity, a man yells, and I see that employees are finally letting people into the event. We all press forward like a herd of cattle. Everyone looks relieved. And I'd never been so happy to be on flat ground in all my life.

As I struggled to rest today, I couldn't help remembering when I tried sleeping on a gravel hill. That's what cancer has become for me. I'm in the same reality as everyone else—we're all searching for purpose—but I'm on a hill now, fighting hard to be on flat ground again. Nothing is ever quite comfortable. And this realization has me reeling.

Life is that way right now. There's no changing it. I'm fighting to live—and I'm just not ready to get out of this metaphorical line yet.

Cancer isn't easy. Hell, *life* isn't easy, even when you level the playing field. Thank God for things like my hacky sack or enjoying the utter magic of hearing strangers' stories.

Proving Patty Wrong

I clutched the sides of the restaurant's copper sink and stared at the river of mascara on my cheeks. I'd worn my best dress, albeit from Goodwill. We'd gone to a fancy restaurant. I'd expected to have a wonderful time. But my old "friend" had said something terrible, especially since I'm fighting death. Her words rang in my head despite reason: "I just thought you'd do something with your life."

When doctors have given you an expiration date, you need to die knowing that your life mattered. I guess it "makes the medicine go down."

This happened months ago, and I thought I'd moved past it until I got extra sick. Fevers plagued me for days, making life almost unmanageable. I woke up shaking at 3 a.m. one morning, and that woman's words echoed in the walls of my mind. "I just thought you'd do something with your life."

Why does she think I'm a failure? I started checking off a list of meaningless accomplishments in my head: I've owned successful businesses, managed a newspaper, written nine books in 10 years, purchased a home at the age of 19, attained degrees despite being a single mom, hit the bestseller list on Amazon several times, had over a million views on my blog, managed a medical clinic and its staff... Yet, she'd dubbed me a failure. *Why?* Sure, I'm not the president of the United States, but I'm also not a serial killer. If melanoma specialists don't find a cure—and I'm going to die soon—I need to know why she thinks I'm a failure. What am I missing?

I met Patty in a writing group right before my divorce. She had a Ph.D., a fancy house, a husband you read about in bodice-ripper novels, wit and beauty, a traditionally published young-adult novel, a strong relationship with God, and more money than anyone I know. Our first fight started years ago. She didn't like Mike and insisted on setting me up with all of her wealthy friends. "I am not going out with him again," I said after one date.

"Give me one good reason why. He's stable, older, and settled. You won't have to worry about anything. And he doesn't mind that you already have kids."

"He said I had to kiss him because my dinner was expensive."

"Well, did you kiss him?" she asked.

"Hell no. That's ridiculous. Despite what you obviously believe, I am not a hooker."

Somehow, we got over that fight, and when she heard I had cancer, she seemed deeply concerned. "I'm coming up and bringing you out to eat a nice dinner." Then she drove all of the way from Southern Utah to my small town in Idaho.

I'd been so excited. I got out a black secondhand dress with frills in all the right places. It hugged my body, so I looked like I stood up straight despite not having all of my spine. But when we got to the restaurant, Patty kept talking like I'd already died. Then she said I could tell her how bad it is and be honest about how terrible my life is because of cancer. "But you're happy with Mike?" she asked.

Ring the Bell

"He's my best friend. Don't get me wrong, we've had some bumps, but I can't imagine life without him." I took a sip of my water. "It's crazy because I had an 8-hour surgery. They had to do a blood transfusion—and I almost died. When I finally woke up from the anesthesia, I couldn't remember my own name, but I remembered Mike. I swear that's how much I love him."

She scooted her silverware to the side. "I don't get you," she said. "You sit there, dying of cancer, you have no money because of medical bills, and you still seem happy. I never thought you'd end up this way—in such denial. When I met you, you were getting divorced. And I thought you'd accomplish so many amazing things. I took you under my wing and even brought you shopping and read your manuscripts. But then, you kept doing things that embarrassed me. Like when you mistreated my friend after that blind date. I just thought you'd do something with your life."

I mulled all these details from the past as my fever raged. I even messaged a couple of family members, asking them for advice. My two oldest daughters wrote back such lovely things like, "You are *not* a failure," but it's amazing how one negative comment can stick around longer than it should.

It wasn't until my fever subsided that I finally got some clarity. I'd prayed, "God, please help me get this in perspective. Please help me see that my life has mattered."

It wasn't long after the prayer that I heard this woman's voice in my head again, but I remembered other things; I remembered all of the times she said

64

that I embarrassed her. She'd been "embarrassed for me" before I got my bachelor's degree and remarried. She'd been embarrassed by my small house and unappealing yard. She'd even been embarrassed by one of my other friends. I realized then that it wasn't about my accomplishments or if I'd even been a failure. If I couldn't benefit her in some way by following her plan for my life, then I was an embarrassment. How arrogant of her to think that just because we'd become friends in some dumb writing group, she could dictate all of my future endeavors.

I thought then about what matters. My books, my career, my accomplishments... seemed unimportant. When I die, that's like an ant going up to a human and saying, "Hey, I got this awesome degree from an anthill on the prestigious side of the yard. And I had the nicest hole in the ground." "And I owned a lot of rocks."

Nope. My true accomplishment in life is making a difference — not just for strangers — but for the people who are closest to me day in and day out: my kids, Mike, my extended family, and my close friends. When you strip me down to bare bones, I hope I can be positively judged by the people who really know me.

I look at Patty, and I'm a bit sad. I might be dying of cancer, but that doesn't mean I can't cut other kinds of cancer out of my life too. I've made more mistakes than a lot of people, but at least I'm trying to get through this the best I can. In the end, that's all I can do.

The Irony of Perspective

I know people go to old folks' homes or cancer centers to volunteer, but I decided to play my violin at an inpatient behavioral health unit.

I heard rumors that a woman killed herself there. She'd done it with a sack from the garbage can. Now they don't allow sacks, scissors, or gowns with long strings.

"Follow me," the leader of Music Day said. Watching physically healthy patients walking around in hospital gowns seemed surreal and tragic — but sometimes, the outside doesn't match the inside, and I personally know that. But of course, they weren't there for physical ailments; they'd been admitted for something else. And unfortunately, I've had moments when I've understood this all too well. Long before my cancer diagnosis, I'd get sad about things a man had told me when he said the world would be better off without me. This made me feel like a burden to everyone, but things did get better with counseling. And years after that debilitating conversation, the thoughts only occasionally came back.

The irony is that since my first melanoma diagnosis in 2018, I haven't been plagued by depression much at all. Facing a terminal illness gave me a proper perspective and ignited my will to live.

A director announced that musicians had arrived, so masked patients started pouring from their rooms, coming to a large area where they could hear songs I played with the impressive guitarist.

At one point, a tiny girl raised her frail hand. "Excuse me." She practically squeaked, seeming so nervous about talking. "Can we hear the violin... um... alone?"

"Well?" The guitarist looked to me for confirmation. "Do you feel comfortable with that?" he whispered.

"Absolutely," I said. I remained still for a minute and closed my eyes. I didn't know what to play because I didn't want to make them cry or feel worse than they already did. And then it came to me, something serendipitous.

The strange thing about me and the fiddle is that we're one—like we were always meant to be together. I swear God created me so that I always knew how to play. I remember the first time I held a violin in my hand; it felt like greeting an old friend. So, I played THE ASHOKAN FAREWELL. Rich, low tones swirled up and around, coming from deep in my soul. Tears poured from my eyes, and I couldn't believe the emotion flowing from me.

I prayed the whole time, pleading with God. "Please hear me. Whatever is good in me—no matter how big or small—please give it to the people in this room."

By the song's end, it had turned into something else. Irish melodies came through, happy and lighthearted. And just as quickly, the music floated to a sweet stop. I could've fallen to my knees, suddenly so weak from the cancer. Standing for too long is hard, and my back twisted forward oddly. But all of my problems seemed insignificant when I opened my tear-filled eyes and peered at everyone.

"That was," one girl gasped, "beautiful. But what's wrong with you?" She lost all couth. "Are you okay?"

I'm still unsure why, but I told them everything about fighting cancer and how doctors said I would die from melanoma. The guitarist looked genuinely shocked because he hadn't known either. And for some reason, I think something settled in that room, something I've been dealing with since my initial diagnosis. I believe it was perspective.

Another girl wrapped her arms around me before the medical staff told her we should stay six feet apart. I hugged her hard before they pulled her away. "That last bit—that song... my mom used to sing it to me."

A sob stuck in my throat. I didn't even know what I'd been playing. It just came to me.

As I hobbled from the hospital, I looked into the sky and thought it was the best day ever.

I hoped all of my love would stay with those who had fallen on hard times there. I knew I'd remember them for the rest of my life. That was the last time I got to play for a behavioral health unit when I saw some light come back into a young woman's eyes.

Our insurance company refused to pay $41,000. They reneged like this before—and then, after hours on hold, Mike and I have begged them over the phone, and they've paid. I saw this insurance denial first thing in the morning—and it started my day off poorly. You know those days: Your computer keeps crashing, and your dog gets into the garbage can. You find dirty socks hidden in the sofa, and someone eats all the cookies you *just* baked. That was my day, and I cried. My thoughts revolved around my mom's chicken soup with homemade noodles. If I could have some of that and a kind word from her, it would all be better—even cancer.

Trey saw me crying and instantly pulled out his earbuds. "I'll do the dishes," he said. "And Indy, you clean up the mess on the ground and then take a shower. Mom, go lie down."

"But I need to cook dinner and—"

He cut me off. "Go rest. Now. We can figure out dinner after you rest."

So, I went to my room, shocked that Trey had taken charge like that. I fell asleep for about an hour and woke from a knock on my door.

"Mama," Indy said, plopping down on my bed. She placed her head on my pillow and faced me so our eyes rested only inches apart. "Do you ever get scared of dying?"

My friend said I'm like an otter or a bunny, but Indy is much more like a woodland creature than I am. She has enormous, innocent fairy eyes.

"Yes. Sometimes I get scared of dying," I admitted.

"Me too. It sounds painful. Is that why you get scared?"

Ring the Bell

"No," I said. "I get scared of dying because I don't want to leave you guys."

She bit her trembling lip as we imagined a world without each other.

I honestly can't fathom leaving my family for whatever the afterlife might be. I wonder if we'll remember each other or if I'll quit existing. If it's Heaven... or if I'll become a drop in an endless ocean of energy. "I don't want to be away from you either," Indy cried. "Oh, Mama."

We sobbed together, trying to comprehend what we were going through and how hard life can be. After we stopped crying, I wiped my eyes, thought of something, and laughed.

Indy raised an inquisitorial brow.

"I was so stupid today," I confessed. "I got upset about the dumbest things. Bills. The dogs. That I didn't... get a cookie." We both laughed. "Sometimes I forget to be appreciative."

"What do you mean?" she asked.

"When I used to get upset about dumb stuff, I'd pretend that I'd already died, and God let me come back to live for one single day. If I imagined that, everything bad would seem insignificant because I was so lucky to be 'back on earth.' The day would seem amazing no matter what came at me."

"Would that idea even work with cancer? I mean, would it make you feel better?"

"I think so. It helps me focus on all the things I'm grateful for. Like my family and Noni's chicken noodle soup." I hugged her.

"Mama," she whispered, "what *are* we having for dinner?"

Ring the Bell

"We didn't have dinner!" I walked out of my room, and right after I told Trey how thankful I am for him, someone knocked on the front door. Kim — our neighbor — stood there, holding a big pot of chicken noodle soup. He left after I thanked him for the meal and the French bread. Indy came around the corner as we set the soup on the counter and lifted the lid.

"Homemade noodles," Indy exclaimed.

"Just like Noni makes," Trey said.

But I didn't have words. Instead, I gaped at the soup. How had our neighbor known exactly what we needed?

A Trip to Paradise

My parents must've known that the battle against cancer seemed even more harrowing than before...

"I had so many dreams," I told them both on the phone and then I grew quiet. I had moments when I didn't know if I could continue getting treatments. It just felt too hard. But it wouldn't help to have a breakdown in front of them, so I tried calming myself.

"Remember how you said you wanted to revisit Mexico?" my mom asked.

"Yeah?"

"Well, we're bringing you and Mike," my dad said. "We have everything worked out."

"What about the kids?" Even though Ruby and Sky are old enough to watch Trey and Indy, I still don't like leaving all of them.

Mike sat next to me and smiled. "It's all been worked out," he said.

A short time later, Mike and I flew to one of those fancy resorts that practically has its own zip code. My parents rented me a TURBO scooter that could go over 20 miles an hour, and I felt like a legend. A little kid waved to me after seeing me do a figure-eight in the lobby as we waited for my parents to arrive. My only traumatic event was driving through a Mayan temple at the speed of light. A man kept trying to take pictures of the statues, but I accidentally photobombed them —

waving and everything—and a resort worker asked if I'd had too many tequilas. "Only water." I smiled.

I did throw up our first night there (because cancer sucks even in paradise), but besides taking daily naps, like a 100-year-old, I could hardly wait to make memories with Mike and my parents.

The gritty sand massaged my feet as the sun's heat beat down, masking incessant flu-like symptoms. And as the water repeatedly encased my feet, I couldn't help staring at the horizon. If God can create all of this majesty that somehow balances itself out, I can rest assured that He has a plan even for my life. There's beauty in the mess. There's joy even in the heartache.

"Careful: Turtle Season," a nearby sign read, boasting a gorgeous picture of tortugas—"turtles"— bursting from their shells. I'd seen a documentary once; it said very few turtles make it to the ocean.

As I peered around, I spied bird feathers next to broken eggs. Birds had ravaged a nest, yet little marks etched the sand next to me, and I knew one of the baby turtles must've survived. Sure, it was only one, but that exhibited something powerful: hope.

"Excuse me," a man said, shaking me from my surreal moment in Mexico. "This might sound strange, but didn't I see you earlier? I remembered you because of the scooter."

His wife had come to stand next to him, and Mike sauntered over as well.

Ring the Bell

"My parents rented me this," I said, patting the scooter's handlebar.

They blinked and leaned in as if wanting to hear more.

"I have stage 4 cancer. The doctor gave me two years to live."

"She has a hard time walking long distances," Mike said, "after surgery to remove a tumor."

Their eyes widened.

"My parents refuse to lose hope about my diagnosis, but I know they worry—and they wanted me to have a nice trip." I took in a long breath and sighed. "It *is* good to see the ocean again." I turned to the waves and thought how none of us know when it'll be the last time seeing the ocean, a snow-crested mountain, or the first bloom of spring.

"Well," the man said, "no matter what you're facing, we wanted to tell you that you're positively impacting other people's lives. You waved to us from your scooter on our first day here, and my wife kept talking about how sweet you were—this whole time."

The woman smiled at me so kindly. "You look great," she said. "You'd never know anything was amiss."

"This weather has been awesome for me. I swear I'm sitting straighter and feeling better every day." I grinned.

"It's so snowy back home," Mike added.

"I knew it," the man said. "You're like us— you're from Canada. That's why you're so nice."

Ring the Bell

Mike and I burst out laughing. "We're from Idaho."

"That's close enough," the man said. Then the couple left, and as my parents joined us on the beach, I couldn't get over how great it felt to spend time with them in paradise.

Quarantined Treatment

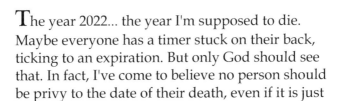

The year 2022... the year I'm supposed to die. Maybe everyone has a timer stuck on their back, ticking to an expiration. But only God should see that. In fact, I've come to believe no person should be privy to the date of their death, even if it is just the year.

I thought about all of this as I arrived at an urgent medical appointment. But the door was locked, and after ringing the doorbell, I simply waited in the freezing Idaho snow. Surely someone would answer the door soon. "The window has a gold star on it," the receptionist told me an hour before. Administration sectioned off an overflow area for people with COVID.

The "gold star" appeared to be a flimsy piece of yellow paper that the wind had played with like a cat. I frowned and pressed the doorbell again. *Several* minutes later, a nurse — wearing garb fit for outer space — stared blankly through the glass. "Why are you here?" Her monotone voice broke through the intercom. "Do you have an appointment?"

"Yes." I shivered, my shoes and socks soaked. "I'm a cancer patient. I have COVID, and I'm having trouble breathing. I need a monoclonal antibody treatment."

She studied me skeptically. "Magagna?" she finally asked, and after I nodded, she requested my date of birth.

Ring the Bell

"Groundhog Day. '83."

"Cute," she said sarcastically, sounding like Darth Vader in her helmet. But, despite that, I knew she'd started to like me.

The woman finally buzzed me in, and my superpower of joy momentarily left. What I saw will always stay seared into my memory.

So many people rested in that room. Painter's plastic swayed, separating the sides of each "station." The cement floors looked more fit for a parking garage than a hospital, and my apprehension grew. It seemed glaringly apparent that this hospital didn't want COVID patients near anyone, they'd become desperate for a location to treat people like me, and they didn't care if it looked like a third-world country.

"Over here." The nurse's helmet muffled her words, yet I still understood. Regardless, I couldn't pull my eyes from the man who looked dead or the bald woman who heaved with each breath. These people... Why couldn't they do more for these people?

"Oh," I whispered to no one except myself. I have COVID, which gave me admittance to this terrible location with the monoclonal antibody treatment. The same room where people seemed to be dying.

I sat on the hard mattress. "Someone's having an allergic reaction to the infusion." The nurse leaned close to me, her eyes red from lack of sleep. "I'll be back."

"Okay." I nodded.

"Hang tight." Then she lumbered away to where another patient spoke frantically.

"I'm still itching," a woman yelled. "Everywhere. And it's even harder to breathe. I thought this would help, not make it worse?"

I leaned back, rested my wet shoes on the bed, and closed my eyes. I didn't mean to listen, but her words nearly broke my resolve. And as I thought about how terrible COVID can be, my thoughts wandered to about a month ago.

"I'm a little nervous about visiting Mexico." I'd typed the text to my friend and hit "send."

"Don't tell me it's because of COVID. You know it's not real. It's just a government ploy."

"Um... It is real."

"You know anyone who's had it?"

"Yes," I responded.

"Anyone who's died?" she asked.

"Yes."

"People probably just said it was COVID. I don't know anyone who's actually had it."

"Did you at least get the vaccine?" I queried.

"No way. Why would I get a shot for something that isn't real?"

"My doctor doesn't want me around anyone who isn't vaccinated. They have a higher chance of getting sick. And if I'm around them, then I can get sick. My immune system is crap right now."

"But you're vaccinated. If you believe in all this stuff, then why get the shot?" she asked.

"I guess the vaccine doesn't work for people who are getting cancer treatments."

"Ha! Figures."

Ring the Bell

"But I need to do what I can to avoid getting it. I'm fighting so damn hard just to live."

We haven't talked after that—both upset. I couldn't imagine her shock at seeing the scene currently around me of the people so desperate for the infusion, oxygen, ventilators... Tears filled my eyes and dripped into my mask as I thought of dying in that cold, morbid community room. Then I heard that woman, "I'm itching. Make *it* stop." She almost growled.

"I'm trying," the nurse said. "We're giving you Benadryl. Everything will be okay."

I wiped my eyes and told myself I was stronger than crying like a baby. Then I thought of a scene in an alien movie, SLITHER, where a lady is enormous, about to give birth to millions of aliens. She says something in a redneck accent that always makes me smile. So, as the nurse approached, I decided to say this line to her.

"Hey... Na-urse. I-ah I-ah thank somethin's wrong wath mey."

She slowly turned to me. Her tough exterior cracked, showing merriment inside. "Ug." She chuckled. "Symptoms?"

"Trouble breathing, headache, dizziness, chest and back pain, sore throat, cough, congestion. A sense of humor."

"Any allergies?" She raised a brow.

"Just aloe vera."

"Perfect. Let's get you hooked up." Then she jabbed the IV into my vein at Warp speed. Resistance was futile. "You'll be here a few hours... Any idea where you got exposed?" she asked.

Ring the Bell

"Mexico." I nodded. "My poor mom tested positive right before I did. I guess my symptoms took a little longer to show. Officials wouldn't let her fly, so my poor parents are still stuck outside of the country."

"Oh, wow. At least you all had a fun trip?"

"The best," I said. "But I'm worried about my parents. They can only leave once my mom tests negative. It's been over a week." I sighed. "Luckily, my dad hasn't gotten sick."

"He got the vaccine?"

"Yeah," I said. She hooked my IV to a bag of clear liquid. "I sure hope I won't get *you* sick." I looked at her pleadingly. "You don't want this."

"Don't worry about me." She sounded surprised. And as she hobbled away to help another patient, I couldn't stop thinking about my friend who doesn't believe COVID is real. What a sad state of denial.

So, I got quarantined to my room; thank God for remote work. My youngest kids thought this was a grand adventure since we communicated through the door like secret agents.

"I love you even though you have COVID," Trey said from the hallway. "I won't discriminate."

I laughed so hard that I started coughing. "I love you too." Then—as the kids went to do their homework in the kitchen—I decided to watch LOST IN SPACE because that's what the nurse's outfit left me craving.

The Barretts

The bookkeeper peeked into my office. "Some guy on the phone says he must speak with the publisher."

"Did he give you a name?" I asked.

"Barrett. Ron Barrett."

"That doesn't ring a bell." I tapped my fingers on the desk. "I'll take it."

Laurie turned around and chuckled. "Of course you will." She always gave me crap for making friends with everyone I encountered.

"Hello, this is Elisa, the publisher of the Morning News," I said.

"Well, hello there, little lady."

I paused. I don't remember names or faces, but I always remember a voice. This happened to be one I'd never heard before. "I don't know you. Care to introduce yourself?"

"I read your articles damn near every day. You have grit, so I want you to join my band."

"Well... sir, I'm already in a band and—"

"Listen, we've both fought cancer. What did you have removed from your wrist—when you worried you might never fiddle again?

"Melanoma," I said. So, he *had* read my articles.

"Well, my wife plays the piano. I play around on the guitar and sing."

And before I knew it, I'd grabbed my coat and headed toward the door.

81

Ring the Bell

"You gotta quit doin' this, Elisa," Laurie—who's practically a sister—reprimanded me. "What crazy story are you covering now?" She'd seen me livestream stories about fires, car accidents, and even a deer that jumped through a storefront window.

"It's not a story this time."

"You're going to meet another stranger, aren't you? Good Lord. I swear if something bad happens to you one of these days... "

"He wants me to fiddle with him in a contest. It'll raise money for cancer awareness."

She just shook her head. "Share your location with me this time."

Over the next few months, some shocking things happened with the Barretts. We won that competition and raised substantial money for the event. Ron gave my daughter, Sky, guitar lessons. And Dottie, his wife, taught her how to garden.

"I have to pay you for this," I said one day because not only had they shown Sky love and generosity, but my kid also learned the value of hard work.

"This is something we want to do," Dottie said, giving me a huge hug. "You don't owe us a thing."

I'll never forget when I told them my cancer came back as stage 4. That tough-old broad quaked a little—I heard it in her voice. And every week for months, Dottie messaged me asking how I was, advising me about what to eat, and sending me things in the mail.

"Dottie?" I messaged her one day. "I haven't heard from you in a few weeks. How are you?"

Ring the Bell

"I have cancer."

"Oh, my gosh... Are you okay?"

She never responded, and a month later, she died.

Sky, Indy, Mike, and I trudged into the funeral home. A family member whispered about "who in the hell" we were. At the end of the service, the pastor asked if anyone else—not part of the program—wanted to talk about Dottie. No one stood. Seconds felt like hours, and my heart began thumping in my chest. Ron looked around.

"Maybe you should," Mike whispered, gently squeezing my leg.

"You're right." I got up, standing much straighter than usual. My black dress was probably too lowcut for a funeral and maybe a bit high on the legs, but I hadn't planned on giving a flippin' speech in front of an entire family of strangers.

"H... Hello." The microphone squealed. "Um. I'm Elisa. And Dottie—and Ron—well, they changed my life." And then I told them everything about the laughter and the kindness. I said how she'd been such a support through my journey. People laughed and cried. "I'll miss her," I finally said, almost sprinting back to my seat.

"Anyone else?" the pastor asked again when I'd finished. Then Sky stood and told her side of the story. I puffed up with pride as she spoke about gardening and spending time with the Barretts. And when I saw Ron, every bit of the whole thing seemed worth it.

Following the closing prayer, Ron struggled to walk, and a woman held onto him as he started

moving toward the back of the funeral home.
"Wait," he said. "I have to tell some people hello."
Then he worked his way over to me, Mike, and the
kids, giving us all such big hugs. "I'm so grateful
you're here and for everything you said."

"If you ever need anything, we're here," Mike
responded.

"I appreciate that. And I'm praying for all of you
every day. Praying that you'll get better, Elisa."

"Oh, Ron. I'm fine. We're worried about *you*."

Then the woman said they needed to leave
because Ron seemed visibly weaker. I couldn't help
wiping tears from my eyes as he hobbled to the
back door. A lady came up to me and shook my
hand. "My mom just loved you guys," she said.

"And we loved her," Sky said.

And when we walked from the building, I
couldn't help feeling like Dottie had seen us there,
and she knew the profound impact she'd made on
our lives.

It's sobering how many friends I've known who
have died since my diagnosis.

A Broken Statue

The statue fell over with a crash. She'd already lost her hand, but now her arm completely shattered from her body. I crumpled, kneeling on the ground, and my first thought was, "I can't take anymore."

The statue has been on my writing desk. She usually stands so elegant and beautiful. And somehow, I'd come to think of her as a perfect little guardian, but now she's disfigured. Like me.

My parents gave me that statue when I became the publisher of the Morning News. They'd been so proud of me as I interviewed senators and a governor. But the newspaper is no longer in business. I got cancer. And a doctor recently called me "disfigured."

I wiped my tears—it's okay to cry sometimes, but I better not make it a habit. It wasn't until I picked up the statue that I realized something. Someone had stuffed paper in the bottom of it.

I pulled out the first note:

"Elisa, I have always been so proud of you." The note from my mother began. I set it down, almost shaking, and read the following note from little Indy.

"I hope that my mom will sleep well and get better and that I'll sleep well too. I love you, God."

The air around felt so heavy. My poor little girl, being so courageous. I rolled the papers and placed the notes back into the statue on my desk.

Ring the Bell

I decided she would remain how she was meant to be—without her left arm.

It reminds me of the word "sincere." My adopted family member, Dee Ready, once said the root of sincere means "without wax." People used to repair broken statues by placing wax in the cracks and then painting over them. The notable thing is that over time, the sculptures that are worth more are the ones that no one fixed. They are who they are—flaws and all. And you know what? Embracing that is a beautiful thing.

If my little girl can find hope and courage by leaning on God, I can do the same—just as I am.

I'd gone to get my taxes done, and after giving numerous papers to the accountant, I studied a photo on her wall.

It's an intriguing picture of five people lying on their backs in a grassy field. Each person is a different race, and the concept of unity seems clear. But I couldn't quite grasp something else about the photo. Each person wore a pair of eyeglasses.

"Wow, you really like that photo," the accountant said at one point as she continued clacking away on her keyboard.

In that instant, I finally found what I'd been searching for. "It's amazing," I said.

"I like it, but I wouldn't say it's amazing." She raised a brow and studied me.

Ring the Bell

"I know this is a common concept, and there are a lot of photos like this, but I just realized what makes this one so different."

"Oh?" she asked.

"If you stop focusing on the obvious things: the people, their clothes, the grass they're lying on, and just focus on their glasses... "

She came next to me and stared at the picture. "Their glasses, huh? Well, they look like regular gla— Wait, I see it. The reflection."

The reflection shone faintly in each of their eyeglasses, but even those faint images were far more beautiful than the obvious picture itself. Greying buildings, lanky trees, and a stormy sky showed itself in the reflections. As if every subject looked at a dry, dying world, ready to be refreshed by a storm...

I almost wished momentarily that the photographer had rested in the grass and taken a picture—not of the people, but up, seeing what had appeared above and around them. Were the people the actual subjects of this photo, or had the artist realized what the reflection told about their surroundings?

"You're right, Elisa. That picture is amazing."

I took my paperwork, got in my truck, and looked through the business window. The accountant sat down where I had been and intently studied the photo.

The whole drive home, I kept thinking about the picture. If we take the time to look at life from different perspectives, we'll discover genuinely amazing things.

Ring the Bell

Lately, I've thought about living with constraints and thriving in different situations.

None of my experiences say it better than this.

When I first started playing the violin in elementary school, my bow arm would fly sporadically as I learned to fiddle and "bile them cabbage down." I thought I excelled until my teacher said I needed to start playing the violin in a corner — with both elbows against the wall where they couldn't be free.

Fiddling in a corner is uncomfortable. I played like that for months, even when I practiced for hours each week at home. Slowly though, I learned to move my right arm fluidly so the bow would stay on the "string highway." My left arm gained proper form too, and the violin's sound changed.

One day, my teacher smiled during my lesson and said, "Elisa, your elbow didn't touch the wall at all. You're playing perfectly."

"Really?" I stepped from the corner and played. At that moment, the sound emanating from my fiddle completely captivated my soul. My violin became an extension of myself. The sheer power and volume, the rich sound, the way the notes cried out with each emotion I felt… All because I'd learned to perfect small things while living under constraints.

We all value individuality and unique endeavors; that's beautiful, but there's also something to be said for obedience and understanding the basics so we can build on foundational knowledge.

This sickness may be a moment for me to focus on the small things so I can excel with complexities.

A Stranger's Kindness

"Tell me again, why are you working as a low-paid security guard?" my mom asked on the phone.

My dilapidated van creaked as I sped to work. It was nearly 11 p.m., and I didn't want to be late for my grave shift. "Something symbolic happened. Remember my dream about a bonsai tree? When the manager offered me the job, she had a bonsai tree on her desk."

Silence... Then, "Elisa, you were offered a job paying twice as much downtown."

"*That* manager didn't have a bonsai tree on her desk."

We said our "I love you's" and hung up after I got to work. Sitting there, I suddenly wondered about the previous summer's strange events.

One week I'd been on TV, talking about my bestselling memoir, THE GOLDEN SKY; the next, a tragic event landed me and my children in a women's shelter. It was a nasty place. I spent almost a month there, sleeping on the floor while my kids slept on bunkbeds—and somehow, my kids found the good in things. That was life-changing.

The grave shift, except for the people, wasn't the best thing ever. Folks kept coming to the front desk where I sat "guarding." Employees couldn't believe I was the new guard: a twig with bright-red hair and lipstick. I looked anything but intimidating.

It seemed monotonous, but I kept glancing at the camera, saving everyone's lives by visually patrolling the facility. That's when I spotted a man in the breakroom. I remember because I noticed his smile. Who knew that a simple dream about a bonsai tree would change my life—and my children's lives—forever?

For Valentine's Day, Ruby tattooed a bonsai tree on Mike, and ironically, this tattoo represents a simple choice that led to Mike being in all of our lives.

While playing my violin for fellow patients at the Huntsman Cancer Center, I spotted a man who seemed hollow and lost. Everyone else listened intently—patients, nurses, doctors, and other medical staff members—but he blankly stared out the window.

Even though I'd been hospitalized for nearly a month, the staff let me play for a gathering of people who also had cancer. I performed in my hospital gown—classy, right?—creating a somber melody that flowed from my tumor-ridden body. I found it ironic that such a perfect song could emanate from someone so flawed. Despite many listening ears, I wondered about the depressed man by the window.

As luck would have it, after my song ended and I packed up, every patient filtered from the area except for the man who drew my attention.

A nurse asked if she could bring me back to my room because using my walker while carrying my violin was awkward. "Actually, can I stay for a while?" I asked, my eyes pleading.

"Um... okay. Sure." She nodded and left me there.

"Excuse me," I whispered to the man, and when he didn't turn, I cleared my throat. "Sir?" Nothing. So, I commandeered my walker—like a Nascar pro—then sat by the guy.

"You have cancer too?" he asked after a moment, obviously puzzled that I'd come to sit by him.

"Yes." Then I shared some of my experience, hoping my offering would cause him to reciprocate. "I guess I'm not scared of death; I just don't want to be away from my husband, kids, family, and friends. Who really knows what the afterlife is like? I'm just scared I'll never see my loved ones again. Does that make any sense?"

"Unfortunately, I understand that too well," he said, and I intently listened to his story. I learned that he'd turned 43 and been diagnosed around the same time as me. We'd both been told our cancer was terminal.

"Our stories are so similar, and we're young. But there is one big difference," he said after a minute.

"Oh?"

"Well, we both have every reason to lose hope—and I think we've pretty much accepted our fates, but you... You're still somehow happy despite everything, and I'm not. Why?"

I remain quiet. I didn't readily know the answer.

"Why?" he asked again, this time with an unnerving desperation.

Ring the Bell

So many thoughts shot through my head. What could I tell this poor man? "I'm still alive." I had to think of something. "And that means there's opportunity."

He snorted. "To do what?"

"To," I glanced at my violin case, "play my violin. To make new friends. To share my story." I thought of all the stupid reality TV shows and America's infatuation with celebrities. "Maybe I can help people stop focusing on inconsequential things. If my body is a sinking ship, the least I can do is tell people to appreciate what they have." He hung onto every word. "Maybe we can help other people find courage, comfort, and joy despite whatever they're going through. If we can have terminal cancer and *still* strive to find the good, that's saying something."

He shook his head. "I honestly don't understand you. You're in hell right now. I know where you are because I'm right here with you."

"And yet, even here, we can take consolation in the positive." I suddenly felt a strange emotion pouring through me; inspiration is the only word for it. "Today, I can be happy because although I'm hospitalized with cancer, I got to fiddle for strangers, and then I got to meet you."

He laughed. "Wait until my wife and kids hear about this."

"They sound great." I paused. "If you have limited time, don't waste it. Find the good."

"You make it sound almost doable." He turned, and I glimpsed his reflection in the window. A huge smile played across his face.

Ring the Bell

Oꞁne of the strangest things on my bucket list is "repurpose a violin."

"What does that mean?" Mike asked a few weeks ago.

"I just want to take a broken violin that's irreparable and make it have a purpose again. Make it look beautiful." I've had this on my list for many years, but it has special meaning now. Often, I feel so broken that I can't "play" like I used to. I don't know what God made me for, but it doesn't seem like I can fulfill that now. And yet, I still want to be worth something.

I thought about this before falling asleep on the couch one day because Mike asked about it again. I'd showed him different ideas and said I'd like to glue gears to a violin and replace the strings with chains and necklaces. "It could be so amazing to make it kind of steampunk."

I fell asleep after that, dreaming about violins that had keys instead of tuning pegs and decorative doorknobs instead of bridges. That's when I heard the door open before Mike's low voice drifted toward me. "Baby, I need you to put these on. I have a surprise."

He'd handed me a plastic sack filled with clothes that shocked me: a mesh white swimsuit top and a white pleated skirt. "This is… nice." I giggled, coming out of our room.

Mike waited as I edged into the hallway. "It's your white outfit."

Ring the Bell

"Oh, yeah? My white outfit." What in the world could he be up to?

"Just wait here for a minute." Then he bounded out the back door and shut it.

I'm not great with surprises. Mike and the kids even hide my birthday gifts days prior because, like an evil genius, I will open and rewrap them.

I put my ear next to the door and heard Mike chuckling.

"Can I come out now?" I stuck my hand through the doggie door and waved.

"Yes, you can!"

The scene shocked me as I took everything in. That exceptional man, Mike, had covered the entire back patio in painter's plastic. I spied cans of paint and a place to sit. He'd set a bunch of gears, yarn, and fabric on a table. Some old metallic odds and ends from his workshop rested amongst other art supplies, and I involuntarily squealed. "Wow!"

I'd never expected a day that started with fatigue and stress over medical expenses to change so drastically.

"You've wanted to repurpose a violin."

"Yeah?"

"I got a broken violin." He motioned to a white fiddle propped on one of our wooden benches.

It didn't stretch very tall and looked so tiny and cute. "Awe! He's a little guy." Even from a distance, I knew this violin must've been a half to three-quarter size.

"I sanded it down and primed it so you can," he handed me a flesh-colored ski mask, "repurpose it. You better put this on." He pointed to the mask.

Ring the Bell

I figured we'd be painting, but I didn't know why I'd need to cover my face. "Okay?" The fabric stuck tightly to my head, pushing my hair flat against my scalp. I only had a small cutout for my eyes, but I still caught my reflection in the house's back window. I snorted. "I look… ridiculous."

"Take my money." Mike held up his hands in mock horror. "Just spare my life." He passed me a pair of goggles. "I figure since your face will be next to the violin."

The situation seemed about as clear as my life expectancy until Mike positioned me on a wooden seat covered in plastic. "Okay. You try to play, and I'm gonna dump paint on the violin. I figure it'll splash around better if the bow is moving."

He set up the camera and dumped yellow, aqua, purple, white, and black paint all over the baby violin. I don't know what turned out better: my clothes or the violin. But part-way through, I realized Mike remained spotless. We eventually switched places.

Onlookers never would've guessed the hardships we're enduring. We momentarily forgot too.

It took a couple of days for the fiddle and bow to dry; we hung them by wires outside from one of our trees. Then the whole family got involved. Mike, the kids, and I invested weeks on that thing. Mike found a knob that resembled a bridge and screwed that, along with a couple of gears, into the top plate. We used chains to look like strings. The kids and I cut skulls and eyes out of fabric and Mod Podged them to the fingerboard and back plate. In the same way my violin magnifies my soul and lets me speak without words, I found beautiful irony in using an instrument to make a silent statement.

"I've been so stressed," I said when we'd finished. "We don't have enough money to keep going on like this. We can barely afford travel expenses. I think we're okay this month but what about after that? I don't think we can afford gas for me to keep getting treatments."

Mike looked at the violin. "You want to sell it, don't you?"

I nodded. "Even if we could make a few hundred dollars, that would get me back and forth to Utah for months. If cancer has taught me anything, it's about enjoying the journey. We made memories as a family. That doesn't mean we need to keep the violin."

"Then I think we should do it."

We took hundreds of pictures and posted a few of our favorites on the eBay listing. "I can't believe you did this for me." I gave Mike the biggest hug.

"You think it'll sell?" he asked.

"I have a feeling it will." And as I went to sleep that night, I felt so happy that we were trying to earn money so I could keep getting the care I needed. In this world, it's so easy to ask for a handout. I know people will help, but they've already been kind enough. I need to feel like I'm contributing too, and I hope the kids also learned from this.

"What are you thinking?" Mike asked as we snuggled into bed.

Ring the Bell

"Just that I married the kindest man in the whole damn world." And I could hardly wait to see if the violin would sell.

A Tumor and the Ukrainian Army

I felt grateful when Sky went with me to treatments but especially that day. I'd just found out that I had a new tumor in my femur. It was easy to act tough for my kids, but without her there, I might've had a breakdown in front of my doctor. Why I'd turned into a tumor factory *still* remained a mystery to me.

"That's it," I told Sky. "I'm joining the Ukrainian army."

She blinked, knowing that I half-joked. "You have cancer. They won't want you fighting for them."

I gasped. "Sky." Then I whispered, "I've heard they're paying $3,300 a month for foreign help—any kind of foreign help."

"Mom, if it were trench warfare, you'd unload one clip and need to nap. You couldn't even get out of the trench." Then, because we both have a ridiculous sense of humor, we laughed like we'd never stop.

"Well, it would suck to carry a gun *and* walk more than a quarter of a mile. Fine. I'll take my chances with radiation."

A patient coordinator walked by during this conversation—which made my infusion more interesting. I flagged him down. "Excuse me. We have a problem," I said, teasing Sky because of her sassiness. "My daughter is cheating at cards. Isn't it enough that I have cancer, and now she's cheating?"

"You want me to call security?" He winked, and I knew he smiled wide under the mask.

"Mama. You're winning by 50 points. If I'm cheating, that's really sad." Then she turned to the man. "And if I did cheat, no one would know because I'm so good at sleight of hand."

We sold the steampunk violin. And when I discovered who bought it, I had to sit and cry...

Roberta is an amazing person. I first met her at Portneuf Medical Center. I desperately wanted to work as the manager of primary care, but even I knew it was a long shot. Yet, over a month after the interview, I got the job and sat in my new office talking with one of the providers: a well-known nurse practitioner named Roberta.

"I wanted you to be the manager," she said, and my heart swelled. I'd recently studied the patient feedback ratings and had already grown an immense amount of respect for this woman. The patients absolutely loved her — leaving comments about her excellent bedside manner. It became evident that each day she changed lives.

Years passed, and our friendship grew. I'll never forget smiling and laughing over falafel or when I had to get a serious surgery in 2018. We went out to eat the day before my hysterectomy, and I got all decked out in what we dubbed my "uterus dress." This seemed fitting since it'd be the last time I went out with my uterus. Even during the tough times, Roberta has a way of making everything unforgettable.

In 2020, when my cancer progressed from stage 2 to 4, my previous coworkers at primary care were some of the first to know. Several of them cried with me and told me they were there if I needed anything. I'll never forget when Roberta gave me a tremendous package filled with various scarves and other things after I lost my hair.

Then the unthinkable happened, and Roberta — one of my heroes — got cancer. I bawled because I know how arduous this journey is. Many people "think" they know what it's like having cancer, but no one fully understands unless they've gone through it themselves. My heart broke knowing the journey my friend would be embarking on.

Despite fighting through treatments herself, she still found time to visit me, bring me a Viking helmet (that matched her own), and play music with me on a day that I needed cheering up. She and her husband both play the piano. My two dogs sat mystified as all three of us jammed. The piano's notes wove together with my violin so well that none of us wanted to stop. "You'd think we'd been playing together for years," I said.

As I opened my computer and realized who purchased the repurposed violin, you can imagine my shock when I realized Roberta and her husband had made the final bid. The genuine warrior who has fought and smiled and brought the best out of everyone despite her own plight... A woman who

101

has hardships and struggles of her own… Yet, she still found the strength to help us.

Looking through the bidding history, I felt amazed to see that the violin got 14 bids. But what touched my heart more than anything was who bought it. It's not just this one action but dozens built up over years of friendship.

The violin sold for hundreds of dollars. This will help us travel back and forth to Utah for months.

It's not that I'm scared to die, not anymore. Pain is far worse than death. I'm just grieving because I want more time with my children, husband, family, and friends. I've had so many good memories that I don't want them to end.

I pondered the past and ended up pulling out a photo book. I smiled over tremendous milestones with my kids, the day I married Mike, book signings, when I held Zeke, moments from my childhood, and so much more. Then my hand fell onto something fortuitous, a picture from my days running a newspaper.

A group had planned to visit the Eastern Idaho State Fair (EISF) from the veterans' home. "One of them just adores Marilyn Monroe," a woman had told me.

I sat at my desk, twirling my bleached blonde hair—you can't pay me to keep my hair the same color for long. "Marilyn Monroe," I whispered and remembered a dress I'd bought at Goodwill. It looked exactly like something Marilyn would wear.

Ring the Bell

So, on the day of the vets' outing to EISF, I donned the dress and curled my hair. I looked nothing like Marilyn, but people could at least tell I'd tried.

I'll never forget when one of the vets saw me. "Randy" asked if he could get a picture with me to put on his wall at the assisted living home. I even sat on his lap with all of the other vets around. I'd tried to do something fun for them but realized they'd done something for me. They made me feel valued and special. And as I wrote a front-page article that would run the next day, I could hardly wait for the vets to read it.

So, that's what I need to do now: make things fun. I know I'll shake it off and return to my regular happy self soon, but I'm embarrassed to say that part of me is still digesting the news.

Although God has put rainbows in my way and I'm grateful to have led such a good life, I don't want it to be over. I'm not ready to give up. It's a good thing I've always liked rooting for the underdog.

Always More and Radiation

Radiation... The last time I had it, they stuffed the lower half of my body—ribcage down—into a bag that they vacuum sealed. I nearly hyperventilated as the bag merged my arms against my body so tightly for 45 minutes that my wedding ring bit into my thigh and left a bruise. This "therapy" is so intense that it kills cells. No wonder brain radiation caused the worst headaches ever, and back radiation created stomach issues and nausea that brought me down to a frail 110 pounds. That's small for my five-foot-seven-inch frame. It might sound dramatic, but at one point, I felt like I'd begun starving. Radiation is one of the worst things I've ever endured, and that's why I abhor hearing that I have a new tumor. I know what treatment entails.

Yesterday, I decided to stop worrying about this tumor. I can only take so much stress. Consequently, I experienced one of the best days with Mike and my oldest daughter.

Shortly after signing a book deal for TWO MORE YEARS, my first cancer memoir, the publisher emailed us. I still felt amazed by this turn of events. I'd had something almost unachievable on my bucket list: have a book traditionally published. And now, I'd signed the paperwork and would possibly live long enough to hold the book in my hands.

So, the publisher suggested that Mike take a picture of me for the cover. That surprised me, and I didn't know what to think about it until I messaged my editor, Robb Grindstaff. "Remember the chapter about the woman with the 'always more' tattoo?" I'd met a beautician who got these words tattooed on her arm after her mom passed away.

"We all have secrets," she'd said. "There's always more to everyone's story." I nodded because I never would've guessed that she'd endured such hardship.

Robb emailed me back, responding with a joke. "Too bad you don't know a tattoo artist," he replied, referring to my oldest daughter, Ruby.

"Ruby," I said after she picked up the phone, "can you do a fake tattoo? Maybe a rainbow feather with the words 'always more'?"

"Yes! This will be so fun." Then, yesterday — her only day off — Ruby crafted a tattoo on my arm so it could be seen while I fiddle. She and Mike took pictures, and I felt so fancy getting worked on in the same chair where Ruby tattoos her clients. She made the experience extra classy. And when they took pictures, I felt beautiful despite the hospital gown or the scarf that hid my short hair.

It's incredible how things work out. When the orthopedic oncologist called today and gave me terrible news, that long-lasting mock tattoo remained flawlessly detailed on my arm. I traced each part of the feather as the doctor spoke. "We've discussed the possible need for surgery to strengthen your femur, so it won't break where the new tumor is."

I gasped despite my normal guarded reactions. "Surgery?"

Ring the Bell

"Well, luckily, you don't need surgery... yet. And if you opt for radiation, you might get away from surgery altogether. It could shrink the tumor. But if you don't get radiation, as I'm told you'd prefer, there's a big chance this new tumor will grow, and you could even break your leg."

I paused, took a breath, and looked at the fake tattoo my Ruby had drawn with so much love. The words "always more" practically glowed as I studied them. There's always more to your future—some surprise to make your life shine even brighter. There's something positive to focus on, even when things appear dim. God brings in the night, but He invariably ignites the morning. Digging deep enough will give you more strength, courage, and hope. There is *always more*... if you look for it.

"Are you okay?" The doctor's voice pulled me from my thoughts. "Elisa?"

"Yes. I was thinking about how grateful I am for not needing surgery. I swore I'd never get radiation again. But not getting surgery, that's suddenly like having my birthday in August."

He laughed. "I guess that's one way to look at it."

I hung up and perused possible book cover pictures. I better buckle up for more rounds of radiation. If the good moments outweigh the bad, then the opposite of femur radiation should be pretty damn impressive.

Too Short Not to Have Fun

Trey finally went to infusions with me — since he's 14, they'll let him into the cancer hospital now. "They're putting that entire bag of medicine into your arm?" he asked, involuntarily shivering.

"Well, this one and then another." I tried putting him at ease. "It doesn't hurt. It's just cold. And then, in a few hours, it makes me tired."

"Anything else?" His eyes widened. "Anything at all?"

"And a little nauseous."

Trey is such a tall, strong kid, but I know he cares far more deeply than he wants to show. "Don't worry about that, though. I want to read your future."

He shook his head playfully. "You brought a deck of cards?"

I nodded.

"I can't believe I even asked that. Of course, you did."

So, after a touch of drama, I pulled out three cards from my regular deck and placed them on the hospital table that spanned the space between us. "These represent your past, present, and future," I spoke in my best British accent. "Your past was fraught with challenges. Oh, my." I gasped. "You've overcome so much. You have a warrior's heart and a saint's will."

At this point, several cancer patients and their families actually stopped what they were doing and

107

looked at us. A male nurse came over and folded his arms. "This outta be good," he said.

I hadn't expected an audience. I'd just wanted to distract Trey from his worries about my treatments.

"Um." I fumbled, and Trey chuckled, realizing how many people watched us.

"Your present," I cleared my throat, "and future are intertwined." I flipped over a four and five of spades. "Oh, no. Not this."

"What is it? What do you see?" he asked, and I wondered if he placated me or really wanted to know.

"A woman."

"Mom. No. Not a girl."

"You're right—she's *not* a girl. She's an older woman. With no teeth."

Trey crinkled his nose, and at this point, the nurse who'd been watching us laughed.

"It's not funny." I joked with him, then turned to Trey. "She will come into your life and teach you many things."

"When?" Trey asked, actually on the edge of his seat and forgetting that he'd been worried about the IV in my arm moments before.

"You'll meet her within a week. And you will learn so much about… math."

Something dawned on him. "Mom, I start high school next week."

"Che Strano?" I said in Italian. I'd always wanted to learn that language and even downloaded a learning app a while ago. But of course, life got in the way, and Italian became a dream I never fully pursued. At least the kids must've remembered something from our foray into linguistics because Trey realized what the words meant, and I giggled so hard. "Beware the toothless, old teacher. Algebra. Geometry. Poor dental hygiene," I said.

A little while later, Trey walked off to the bathroom, and some nearby people told me how cute the "card reading" had been. It's interesting getting infusions because you never know who your neighbor might be and what you might end up visiting with them about — or who might be listening.

"We have to make things fun," I told a fellow cancer patient. "It's hard having to be here so much, but... being silly makes me feel like I have a little control. I get to choose how I respond to my situation."

"I needed to hear that today." She smiled. "Sometimes, I forget to loosen up. Someone once told me to never take myself or life too seriously." She opened her purse and unwrapped a big candy bar. "You're a good mom to that boy," she said, taking a huge bite. "He'll never forget how you made today fun — and neither will I."

I paused. "You're an encourager — and that's such a gift. It's amazing when you meet people who can say just the right things that brighten the day."

"Do you ever get sad about cancer?" Trey asked after we left the hospital.

"Sometimes. Do you?"

Ring the Bell

"Yeah," he responded. "The year you got diagnosed with terminal cancer was the hardest year of my entire life."

I felt so bad. It's tough hearing that something so out of my control could negatively impact my family.

"It really can affect people so differently." I paused, becoming thoughtful. "Cancer has completely ignited my will to live and enjoy whatever life brings. But I know it isn't like that for everyone, and that's okay. We're not all the same, and we each cope in a way that works for us. But for me, losing sight of life—before death even comes—would be way worse than having cancer. Sometimes I feel like I'm trying to make up for how I lived before my diagnosis. Maybe other people already lived to the fullest, and they have total peace about dying. Maybe that's why they willingly give in. It might just be their time."

As we got into our car and I tried to process these deep topics, I got a great idea. "We can't end our visit to Utah like this. Would it be okay if I bring you to meet someone? He always cheers me up."

"He? Um. Sure," Trey said.

So, on our way home, Trey and I decided to visit Layton Funk, a man I adore. Layton has quadriplegia, and he's one of the strongest people I know. Luckily—for me—we've gotten to be friends since my whole ordeal with cancer began. I'd looked for people on Facebook who might be experiencing hardships. When I found his profile, I sent him a friend request and we just clicked.

Ring the Bell

Since my diagnosis, he's said some things that really hit me, especially about not getting mired in pity. He really believes his accident was one of the best things that happened to him. "It saved my life," he told Trey, "and gave me purpose."

After Trey and I left the hospital where Layton lived, Trey turned toward the sky and appeared so grown up. "Today was a good day," he said. "Thanks for letting me be part of all this. I'm seeing a lot that most kids don't get to see. And... I think it's making me a better person, just like Layton."

I'm glad he knows the type of person he'd like to emulate. I want to be like Layton too.

We're All Battling

The girl stared at me in the store, and I felt awkward. I'm walking much better than I used to, but people can still tell there's something "wrong" with me.

Mike and I moved to the checkout line, and the girl followed. "You feeling uncomfortable?" Mike whispered because he'd noticed the girl too.

"Yes," I mouthed back. And as I looked up into his face, his eyes squinted with worry, and his forehead wrinkled; that man wants to protect me from the world.

"Your wife is hot," the girl finally said to Mike.

Was this a game? I hobble around places, and although I have "personality" and funky Goodwill outfits, I'm not what people would call "hot."

"What did you say?" Mike asked.

"Your wife is hot." She finally approached me, her baby-blue dress swaying as her beautiful brown eyes and flawlessly young skin practically glowed. "How do you stay so skinny?" she queried.

"Um—"

"Her whole family is skinny," Mike blurted. "Good genes."

"I want to be skinny like you, though," the girl said, turning back to me.

I didn't know what to say, especially since the whole moment felt incredibly insincere, and I can't abide that. "You look great... but I have cancer," I

112

said. "It's hard to keep weight on when you have cancer."

Her eyes grew wide, and I noticed that a man had begun darting toward us. He studied the girl with increasing concern.

"Dave," she yelled and spun before spotting the man. "I can get skinny if I get cancer."

Mike and I gawked. Dave looked like he might fall over from embarrassment. He glanced at us apologetically.

"You're beautiful just the way you are," I said. "You're gorgeous."

"And you don't want cancer," Mike said.

Dave came closer.

"Do people... get better from cancer?" the girl asked him. She batted her lashes and appeared like a porcelain doll.

"Um, Soph…," Dave said, "cancer can be hard. Some people don't get better." He urged her to come away with him, but she didn't want to go. At this point, I realized the girl had a mental handicap.

"Some people don't get better," she repeated, peering at me with new understanding. So much sadness and compassion filled those beautiful eyes. As if she didn't want to ever look away, she asked, "Why are you sick?"

"It started with a mole."

"It's melanoma," Mike said gently.

"No... but why. Why is this happening? Why do these bad things happen? Why? Why!"

I could've said God has a plan, or I have peace about my situation, but this girl needed something

more. She needed the absolute truth. "I don't know,"
I finally said.

She studied me. "You think I'm beautiful?" she
asked.

"Of course. Anyone can see that."

A cashier called us to her checkout stand.
"Wait," Soph said before we could leave, "you're
strong. Very strong."

"You're strong too."

I knew she didn't know exactly what she should
say. No one knows why sickness, pain, or even
handicaps exist. And I didn't have any more
answers than that sweet girl, but one fact remains:
We're all trying to get through our struggles the
best we can. We're each fighting a battle whether
other people realize it or not.

I'll never forget the compassion in Soph's eyes.
At that moment, *I* wanted to shield *her* from the
world.

A group had asked me to talk to hundreds of
people and share my ongoing experience with
cancer. "Just say something uplifting like your
articles. We all need something good to focus on
right now." This hit me as ironic. It seemed strange
they'd ask someone who's still fighting cancer, not
someone who's already overcome it. But I found
something powerful in that anyway and wrote a
speech about gratitude. I honestly felt really
prepared until the exact moment that the host said
my name and asked me to come onto the stage.

Ring the Bell

That's the thing about public speaking… For me, it always seems easier when you're under the lights because it's hard to see actual faces out there. I like pretending I'm talking to God and He's actually listening. It's what they call "an audience of one." But at this event, there weren't spotlights, and that meant I could see the multitude of faces in front of me, and I froze.

I clutched the mic and sat on the provided chair. But my nerves had completely taken over, and even my weak right leg shook. Instead of talking—like a normal person—I breathed into the damn microphone. And then, hoping someone would help me, a memory hit me…

The woman chuckled. "Speaking advice?" she'd said. "Pick three faces from the crowd and talk to them. There's nothing to it." I figured if Donna thought I could do it, I'd be all right.

So I frantically found three faces. One: the man in the suit coat in the front row. Two: the elderly lady closer to the back on the right. And three: the high school-age kid who looked forlorn and out of place in the crowd.

"We all have problems," I whispered. "Mine just happens to be easier to define. I have terminal cancer. But most of us have something we're going through." My voice had become steady. "It could be marital problems, troubles at work, or maybe even a parent who has terminal cancer." At this, I looked at the third person I'd decided to speak directly to: the teenage kid. He shuffled in his seat, and I knew I'd hooked him.

Ring the Bell

The speech came easy then, and it changed from gratitude to seizing the day.

I shared what I'm going through as a mom and how hard I'm fighting to shield my kids from this. "The doctors initially didn't give me long to live, and I don't know when I'll die." I looked out at the teenage kid and realized he'd begun crying. "But none of us know," I said. And then I told a story about a man who'd been praying for me; I'd been shocked to hear he died that following Wednesday in a freak accident. "I wish I would've been praying for *him*," I said.

"Whatever you take from today, whatever it is, I hope it's to appreciate your life. Don't hold off on doing things—like I did. Do what you want now while you have time and you're healthy. And if you know someone who's sick like I am, tell them how much you care. Don't wait until tomorrow. Spend your time wisely. If you knew you had a year left, a week, a day... What would you do with your time? Really think about it. What would you do in that single day?"

After the speech ended and people started leaving, the teenager waited behind. "My mom's dying from cancer too," he whispered. "It's changed my whole life. I want to be enough for her." Then he peered down at his hands. "How do I know if my life has mattered?"

It took everything in me not to cry. "Can you tell me of a couple of moments when *you* felt like your life mattered?"

He responded, "It's all about the people we love, isn't it? Being there for them."

Ring the Bell

"You're a pretty amazing young man. Never doubt that."

So, as I've thought about this again, I've wondered, "Has *my* life mattered?" And I tried pinpointing five moments when I felt of value.

This hasn't been easy for me. I've bounced back and forth on different memories. Was it the act of giving birth to my children, owning successful businesses, hitting a million views on my blog, landing the lead in a play, or running a newspaper? While nice, stacked against value, each accomplishment seemed hollow and somehow rooted in pride.

"How's your search for value going? Have you landed on your five memories yet?" a friend asked a few days after I told her about it.

"No. I keep thinking of standing before God, trying to brag about my bachelor's degree or being a physician liaison, and it sounds completely inane."

"Elisa, don't downplay your accomplishments."

But she clearly didn't understand.

That night, Mike and I made a fancy dinner with the kids. We laughed and joked. We played ping-pong on the kitchen table and tried the new "Starlight" Coca-Cola. It was the best day I've had in months. Then, when the kids went to bed and Mike sat reading a book about Eastern philosophy, I sneaked downstairs.

I rarely have enough energy to get extra things done, but I knew I could do something small that night—and it would have a huge impact.

My sewing room has a stack of clothes that need patches, buttons, and other adjustments. So, like a little elf, I fixed everything. It didn't take long, and as I sewed, I felt so much love pouring through my tumor-ridden body.

"What are you doing, sweetheart?" Mike peeked his head around the door. "Oh, my gosh. You fixed everything."

He picked up a pair of his pants, and I suddenly felt like I had value. I could hardly wait for the kids to see what I'd done for them too.

"You look tired. But you seem so happy," Mike said.

"It sounds so cliche, but it just hit me. It's the small things." That teenager who came up after my speech was right. It is all about the people we love. "When I stand before God, if He asks me why my life mattered, I'll say it did because I tried to make a difference for the people I love."

Keeping Dignity Alive

I've watched exactly one person die: my son. And it was horrendous.

I've seen numerous other people moments before their deaths because I worked in a burn unit and spent time playing my violin for palliative care patients. I've witnessed people who chose to die with medication on board and others who waived the pain pills. Unfortunately, these memories have surfaced now that I must deal with my fears.

I don't mean to be negative. It's just reality: The glass isn't half-full or half-empty—the damn thing just has liquid in it. If I continue to grow more tumors by this fall, doctors will look into clinical trials because my body won't be able to withstand any more immunotherapy treatments. And *if* those trials don't work, that's the end of the line for me. It could still take a while to die, and who knows what I might expect. Of course, this new bone infusion they're starting tomorrow could be a game-changer. My body might finally cooperate, so I won't get infections and be forced to skip treatments—my literal lifeline.

You might be thinking, "Don't worry about this." "Don't count chickens before they're hatched." But when someone is facing death like this, they can't help but wonder, at least sometimes. And *that* is my reality.

So, I had my second big panic attack last night since embarking on this quest. ("Quest" because it makes cancer somehow better, like I might meet Frodo — screw that, Sam. Frodo's a pansy.) I skipped my nerve pain medicine yesterday. I'm down to only a few pills daily and quite proud of myself. But without this nerve medicine, it felt like someone had punched me in the thigh and back where the prominent tumors are. This became so unbearable that when Mike got home from work, I cried like Frodo.

"Elisa, are you okay?"

"No." I sat in scalding water in the bathtub — the only thing that could momentarily ease the pain. Bubbles gleamed around me. "I'm not scared of the cancer; I'm scared of the treatments. I'm trying to fight and stay alive for you and the kids." I sighed, thinking of how the bone infusions are supposed to hurt excruciatingly. "Tonight, Trey and I played music." Trey plays the guitar, and we love jamming together. "I had so much fun with him. But then, I thought about how doctors said — if I'm lucky — I could have up to 10 years from my diagnosis in 2020. That means, in a best-case scenario, I'd only live to see Trey turn 21. All of the kids will be so young."

Mike nodded instead of saying how they're making medical advances all the time or how I could try this or that.

I reached up, and Mike held my tiny, soapy hand in his large, masculine one. "We don't know where any of this is going. Hell, maybe this bone infusion will be the thing to save my life. But I do need to know something."

"Anything. What is it?"

Ring the Bell

"If we get to the end of the line, and things are terrible, really terrible. If we know I'm about to die... " I suddenly cried so hard that my body shook, sending little tidal waves across the bathtub's water. "I just want to die with dignity."

"You're talking about going to Oregon or something?" he said, his voice shaky.

"Yes."

"Elisa, how would we... would we invite our families over for one last dinner?" Mike's resolve broke. I've never seen such a brave man, so bare and vulnerable.

I blinked back tears. "I think we could. But would that be an option? If we get to that point a long time from now?"

"Yes. Of course, Elisa. If there are no other options and you're just suffering. But we aren't there yet. We aren't even close," he said.

"No, we're not close. But you've just lifted such a huge burden from me. That makes this less scary. To realize if there's no way out, I still have a choice."

So, it probably sounds morbid, and I know many people will not agree with or understand this, but I feel better. I *still* have a choice. And right now, I choose to fight. I want to see my kids grow up and have their adult lives, careers, and babies of their own. I want to grow old with Mike. I'm going to fight for it until I can't anymore. But even then, at least I'll still have dignity.

It is too soon to think about this, yet it gives me strength.

"You're doing better?" Mike asked after I'd donned my PJs and gotten into bed.

Ring the Bell

"No, I'm ready to fight again. You know how my dad's side of the family has Viking blood? Well, cancer picked the wrong broad this time. It's stupid to mess with a Viking."

Mike laughed so hard, wrapped his arms around me, and we fell asleep.

She Felt Heard

Remember how I told you about Ron Barrett a while back? We won that music competition and raised quite a bit of money for cancer awareness. He hasn't been doing very well since his wife died. Just so lonely. "Why don't you call my Aunt Jackie? She's sweet *and* she can cook." My mom's side of the family is Italian, and I love eating whatever they make. They could say they fried up a goat's liver — or brain — and I know it'd taste like heaven. Some people just have the gift; too bad it skipped a generation.

Ron gasped after hearing about my aunt. I didn't expect that. I guess it hadn't even been a year since Dottie passed, and this seemed uncouth.

"Let me call her and see if it'll be all right. Then you should call her."

"Little lady! You mean to tell me you haven't even asked her yet, and you're trying to give me her number."

"I'm not trying to do anything." I giggled. "I'm just testing the waters. I have a sixth sense for this kind of thing. Would it kill you to trust me?"

I called my aunt, and she said she might talk to Ron, but it would be more of a friend sort of thing. They've both lost their spouses, and it could be a way for them to talk with someone else who really understands.

Anyway, Ron actually called, and they've gotten along like best friends on a free vacation. My Aunt

Ring the Bell

Jackie talked with me last night. I've never heard anyone giggle with such happiness. "He saw a picture of me, and he said I'm gorgeous."

"Anyone with eyes and a mouth could tell you that," I retorted.

"Oh, you!" she said, and then she told me all about this exciting new development in her life.

"You should set my sister up with someone," my cousin said after hearing the story.

"She's not old enough. I only have luck if people are at least 70!"

I spotted an elderly lady sitting across from me the other day. My heart dropped as I saw how she watched those around her. A young woman passed and smiled at a middle-aged man. Others walked by, one even nodding to me, but no one acknowledged the elderly woman. It hit me: "Why do younger generations so often discredit older generations, or worse, make them feel invisible?"

So, I stood and took a seat right by the woman. She looked a bit stunned that I'd gone to sit so close. But then I asked her about her day and her life. After a moment, she laughed. And I learned all sorts of things about her childhood on a farm and her husband, who passed away in his 80s. I even learned about her son with Down syndrome.

"Elisa?" someone called.

"Well, it was nice to meet you," I said, and I started to stand.

"Elisa?" the elderly lady asked.

124

Ring the Bell

"Yeah?"

"Thank you for talking with me. I'm still not sure why you came over to visit, but being older, sometimes I feel obsolete. It was nice to feel important, even if it was just for a moment."

Her frail hand came up to rest on my left wrist, the same site where doctors first discovered the melanoma and carved a long scar into almost half of my forearm.

"You're so young and innocent. I hope you won't experience the hardships that I have so you can remain as happy and carefree as you are now."

There were so many things I could've told her. About stage 4 cancer or how she touched the place where it all started. About my son who died or my failed first marriage. But I realized the importance of not placing my burden on someone else. This moment wasn't about me.

"Elisa, are you coming?" the man motioned me forward.

"Yes." Then I turned to the woman and placed my other hand on top of hers. "God bless you," I said before leaving the waiting room.

I realized that sometimes there's beauty in giving people much-needed perspective, but there are other times when the opposite is much more important. I didn't tell her about my problems or hardships. I didn't need to share how exhausted or sick I felt the entire time we conversed. Instead, I let that moment be about her. She felt "heard," which made all the difference.

The Moxie I Needed

"I'd like a mimosa without the alcohol," I said.

"So, you want orange juice?" the waitress asked, a bit snarky.

"Oh, yeah." I turned redder than the walls. "But can you throw some Sprite into it?"

The point is that I'm not the next Princess Di; I couldn't even be Anna Delvey. I can't spot the anise, apricot, or almond aromas in wines. And I don't frequent art galleries spouting about Surrealism or the Baroque period. But I have been touched by art; a specific piece has gotten me through the extra-challenging days of fighting cancer, and it's quite a story.

Several years ago, my brother said if I reminded him of any animal, it would be an otter. Imagine my complete surprise when I discovered a Native American zodiac and that my brother was right. I am an otter. Otters are fun and silly, the life of any party. But the problem remained that I didn't want to be one; I wanted to be a fierce lion.

Ruby, my oldest daughter, loves that I'm an otter; last year, she had one tattooed on her arm, and in high school, she even drew a picture I have on my wall. The one she created looks fun yet wise. But the strangest thing is that he seems a bit perplexed by his own existence and the fact that he *isn't* fierce. Simply put, he is me.

Around this time—when Ruby got the otter tattoo—I finally began embracing parts of who I

126

am. But something was missing, and I realized this after Dee Ready, whom we've adopted as family, came to visit from Missouri.

"I brought something for you," she said before handing me something wrapped in tissue paper.

I gingerly opened it and felt surprised to find a little ceramic lion inside.

"His name is Arthur," she said. " I feel like he's always looked out for me. But now, it's time for him to look out for you."

I gave her the biggest hug. "Oh, thank you, Dee. I know how much this means to you."

I was supposed to get more radiation, and Dee had come to help me. "You know," I finally said, thinking about the horrors of radiation, "sometimes I feel like I can't do this anymore. It's too hard to keep fighting. I'm tired."

"Elisa," she looked at the lion I still held in my hands, "you are an otter, but you're a lion too. And with this journey through cancer, you've shown yourself to be both."

That night after Dee had fallen asleep, I looked at the lion on my nightstand and opened my Facebook page. I felt tired beyond words and extra skinny from constantly throwing up. It had become so exhausting to walk that sometimes I would skip my medicine because getting it meant moving, which hurt too much. That's when I scrolled and saw a piece of art so powerful that it changed my resolve forever.

Artist Daniel San Souci painted what I believe to be a warrior woman by a lion. They both stare ahead as if they are soulmates, twin flames, or somehow the same being. It seemed like a Godwink to see two lions like that in one day (the ceramic one from Dee and then Daniel's painting). It had to mean something.

I studied the woman's resolve and decided to take what Dee said to heart: I *can* be a lion. And I need to be a lion for my children and my husband. Some days it's great to be a fun-loving otter, but on the hardest days, I decided to pull up Daniel's painting to remember to be strong like this woman and her lion.

I've gone back to look at the painting numerous times and prepared to do that last Monday. Oncologists had just explained how I need an entire extra week of radiation; not only that, but there might be even more new tumors, so they're doing a full-body scan to ensure they're radiating all of the new growths, not just one. I opened my computer to visit Facebook and study the look of determination in the woman's eyes. "I can do this," I said out loud. "I can do radiation."

But just before I could toggle to the correct page, my blonde-haired daughter, Sky, blithely walked into the front room. "You got a package," she said with excitement.

"What?" I asked. And after opening the enormous box, I stared in shock. Can you believe Daniel San Souci sent me a copy of his painting? It wasn't just that; he signed it and sent a card. I cried when I read the words he'd written above his signature: "For Elisa, My Hero." That's what meant the very most.

Ring the Bell

There are times in life that transcend words or even coherent thought. I fell into one of those moments as I clutched the painting and stroked the features of the woman and the lion.

So many miracles surround us each day, but through this experience, I'm convinced that our greatest gift is the kindness we can give each other.

I dreamed that I'd somehow found a place that offered death with dignity. It was a small facility, not widely publicized because they worried about the public's reaction.

I met with the doctor — the owner — and signed all the preliminary paperwork. "You don't look sick. Why do you want our assistance?"

"I have terminal cancer," I said, talking far too loudly in the dream.

She looked over the mountain of papers I brought and nodded. "I'll have to confer with your oncologist in Utah and several other healthcare professionals in the area, but it does appear you're a likely candidate. Congratulations."

Congratulations? I nodded sadly, innately knowing this person would someday help me die.

A few months passed, and I found myself back at the facility. They gave me a puce hospital gown, and I placed my regular clothes in a nook, wondering what would happen to them after I died. Would they be donated or get pawed through by a hapless janitor?

Ring the Bell

Soon I wore the ugly gown, waiting for the last time in my life. I opted to die with other people. So, there I sat, with others who could no longer abide the suffering.

A younger man sat on a metal bed to the west of me. He stared blankly as the owner walked around, giving each patient a "gift bag."

"There's a bottle in each bag. Please drink it," she said, pointing to a pink concoction she'd procured. "It'll make you less anxious."

The younger man next to me downed his drink in an instant, then—before I could drink mine—he turned to me imploringly. "Can I hug you?" he asked. "I want my last memory to be... I want to pretend someone cared."

I felt dumbfounded. So, instead of drinking my pink medicine cocktail, I stepped off my bed onto the cold tile floor. I knew there might be germs, but I was finally immune because I prepared to die anyway. I hugged the man, this stranger. It just came to me. "You're beautiful," I said. It's odd, but it resounded so perfectly that the man clutched the gown's fabric on my back, and he cried.

"My mother used to say that. You know... she thought I was beautiful. But she died when I was young."

Soon his eyes appeared droopy, and he got a faraway look. I lost him somewhere along the journey, and he struggled to sit back on his bed. The owner rushed over. "Neither of you should be standing. I need you to drink that drink," she said.

I sat down, telling myself to be brave, but as I studied the dozen-or-so patients in that room, spotting the IV stands next to each one, I realized they'd already lost the light in their eyes.

"Just drink it," she implored after I rested on the metal bed again.

I pulled the drink from my bag but didn't comply. Instead, I watched the doctor hook up various IVs that made the patients close their eyes and then find the stillness of death.

My heart raced. I thought about Mike and my kids—my reasons for living. I suddenly pictured Mike sitting in our bedroom, wondering why I wouldn't let him come. I imagined Ruby, unaware of my choice, happily tattooing a stranger. I envisioned Sky making everyone's day bright as she walked through a local campus. And I saw Trey and Indy both taking finals in school.

I thought of my own test, the test of life, and how I came to the place because I couldn't handle the physical pain. And as I zoned out on a patient across the room, I remembered a strange conversation with Trey.

"I'd walk through hell just for the chance to be your mom."

He gaped at me. "You wouldn't make it through hell."

"Oh, yes, I would," I said. "If it meant I could raise each of you. I'd do it, just for the chance."

His features softened, and a smile surfaced on his face. "I love you, Mama."

The owner shuffled up to me. "I have too many people here. You opted to die with others. I'm facilitating that, but I can't be the babysitter. I need you to drink that."

"I've changed my mind."

"It's too late," she says. "You've signed the paperwork."

"It's not too late." I thought about my children, my husband, and that strange conversation with my teenage son. The woman shook her head. "I should've known you'd be difficult. People like you always are."

My face lit with fire—I felt so angry. And I turned to her. "I want to live until I simply can't anymore."

I donned my clothes and left that place of death and heartache. As I took the bus to Idaho, back home, I still replayed that conversation with Trey in my head. My back ached with every bump. The nerves in my arms and legs turned to fire with each movement. But I didn't care anymore. I realized I'd do anything for one more moment with Mike and my children. I'd fight almost anyone to see them— hold them—one more time. I'd even fight the spirit of death himself. And *that* is, ironically, what I'm doing.

Then, I woke up.

Spirit Animals
Make an Appearance

"I'm so sorry you're going through this," the Jewish woman said, her incredible eyes shining with compassion.

I paused as I thought about exactly what has made this so tough. Yes, it's physically painful, but it's also been difficult for everyone who cares about me. Other things have been unexpected and trying, like the fact that someone anonymously sent a 200-page document with Christian scriptures. The sender claimed this document detailed why I'm sick because I'm not "one of God's chosen people."

I'm unsure why, but I ended up telling Bayle about this. "They must've found out where Mike works from Facebook. Then they sent this document to me, care of Mike Magagna from Mike Magagna." Bayle's eyes grew wide, and I perceived a depth in them that was quite rare. She and her family are exceptional people. The more I've gone to the synagogue, the more they've felt like close relatives. Her daughter is actually our rabbi, and I know I could go to any of them if I ever need someone to talk with. "The whole thing shook me to the core, though. I love God with all of my heart. I can't imagine Him knowing the future, creating me anyway just so He could end up punishing me with terminal cancer because He didn't choose me."

Ring the Bell

She appeared flabbergasted. "The whole thing is bizarre. Elisa, you *are* one of God's chosen people."

"I am?" the words sounded paltry on my lips.

"Well, you're here, aren't you?"

And as her words sunk in, I felt gratitude pouring over me. Many babies don't get to leave the womb alive. Then many children and babies don't grow up—like my angel baby who died in the hospital after two and a half months.

So, the next day, I decided to live life to the fullest. "I'm going to Edson Fichter," I told my family.

"Um. Elisa, are you sure that's smart to go alone? What if you get halfway in and feel too tired to make it back?" Mike looked nervous but willing to help if I pushed the issue.

"I can always bring my phone. Or you can come with me. Either way, I'll be okay. I won't go too far."

But Mike and the kids wanted to tag along, so we went to a local nature reserve where people love using the rope swing to cannonball into the river. This whole area seems forgotten by time, and I love it more than almost anywhere else that I can still go. Trey and Indy insisted on swimming, while Ruby and Sky wanted to take pictures by a clearing in the trees.

"To the fishing pond?" Mike asked me.

"Sure." So we went by the main body of water, and I spotted movement a few feet from us. "Oh, my gosh." I carefully stopped and tried staying quiet. I could not believe the sight in front of us. "Mike," I whispered, pointing to the water's edge. "Mike!" My heart raced. "I just saw two otters."

Ring the Bell

I've been thinking a lot about otters and lions since that award-winning painter sent me the picture of the woman and the lion. I even visited the library to read books about both. But I've never seen something like this in the wild.

"Your spirit animal." Mike couldn't help grinning. I love it when all of his features come alive with mirth. My knees weaken like the first time we kissed. But watching the otters with him that day became one of my cherished memories in recent years.

We sat on the ground. The tumors in my back and hip had begun aching something fierce, but I wouldn't have moved for anything in the world because the otters popped up again and put on a show for us. They jumped and played. One even stole a fish from a fisherman; that made my day but ruined his. They swam in circles, coming close to us and then darting away. I didn't know why they'd picked us to study.

"What's wrong, sweetheart?" Mike turned to me and rested his hand on my right leg. "My God. You're shaking."

"Just the pain. I'm fine. Really. If I can just take the pressure off my hip." I tried readjusting, and Mike came closer, always there to make things better.

I looked at the otters again and realized they must've been mates. They seemed to care for each other. When one got a fish, they shared.

"You know otters mate for life?" Mike asked as he gently lifted me onto his lap. It always amazes me how he can pick me up like I'm nothing. "Is this

better, or should we go?" He'd set me so the
majority of my weight went to my legs and back.

I threw my arms around his neck and continued
watching the otters. "I really want to stay. It's better.
You always make things better."

He sighed and held me tightly. "Elisa, how are
you really? Can you tell me? Please talk to me."

I almost didn't. It's so hard seeing pain overtake
those jovial eyes. But I figure we do need to deal
with this together. It's a future that affects both of
us.

"A doctor told me this week that I'll never get
better, and I just need to face that they're simply
buying me time. But then a different doctor, my
radiation oncologist, said she thinks I might beat
this." I turned to the otters, thinking how surreal
this moment seemed. "Things are good with all of
us for two seconds. I can still move around. All of
the kids are so happy. We have the best marriage. I
just want to appreciate every moment. I wish we
could stay frozen right here… right now and keep
these moments forever."

As we held each other, I knew dirt covered both
of us, but I loved being there by the magical otters
who seemed to know I needed them.

Ruby and Sky just missed the otters, but Trey
and Indy got to see them. We sat at the water's
edge, dumbfounded by the sight. I read a
newspaper article a few days later saying that Fish
and Game had never gotten reports of otters being
at Edson Fichter until that very month. It seemed
extraordinary. I know some people might think

signs are ridiculous, but this felt like a Godwink to me and a lot of other people.

Mike and I went to visit the otters for the next few weeks. On the last day, a whole group of kids clustered on the north side of the water. That newspaper article stirred up a lot of interest.

"He jumped and looked right at us," a preteen squealed.

Maybe being an otter is pretty cool after all. People traveled from near and far just to catch a glimpse at Edson Fichter's fishing pond.

"Now, if we could just see a moose," Mike said, talking about his spirit animal.

"You never know. I feel like I've seen everything now."

Power of Perseverance

Audition day came, and people sat expectantly in chairs that lined both sides of the hallway. Cellists stood with their large instruments. Violists talked about their craft. And everyone stiffly waited, just as serious as I was. That's when I realized that no matter how much I had practiced, I needed something special to stand out.

But the wait lasted forever, and after a time, I overheard some of the parents talking to their kids.

"What if I don't make it in?" a girl whispered to her mother.

"You have to. There's no other option. Our family always gets what we want." The mom wore a fancy creme-colored dress and a look of absolute pride. My skin heated for her poor daughter.

"You'll do great," I whispered to the girl holding a violin.

She went to respond, but the mother grabbed her wrist and then glanced at me condescendingly; apparently, "their family" gets what they want *and* never fraternizes with the competition.

I remained quiet after that, thinking they probably had more money than I could fathom, yet I had what mattered: a mom who cared more about *me* than my ability to win. After all, she'd only brought me since this was my biggest dream.

At 15, I practiced the violin for three hours a day. The notes began resonating with emotion—the accents became incredible. Sometimes my fingers would bleed, and I'd feel like I couldn't do it anymore. But still, I continued. One of my violin teachers—a symphony violinist herself—began taping a thumbtack to the neck of my instrument so that I wouldn't rest my wrist against it. "Try harder," she'd say. "Do you want this or not?" And so, I learned, despite the pain and struggle. Because that violin had gotten into my soul—and no one could tear us apart.

A youth symphony representative finally called my name. I stood and hugged my mother. "You'll do great, Elisa," she said. "Just do your best." I looked into her eyes, knowing I could never truly thank her or my father enough—for scrimping and saving so I could take lessons. I could never explain how much their love and support meant to me.

During the audition, the youth symphony conductor scribbled into a gigantic notebook.

"You're excused," the conductor said with hardly more than a nod when I'd finished.

I trudged to the door, but something rose inside me, and just before I left, I set my violin on a nearby table and faced the conductor.

"Listen," I said. "I want this with *everything* in me. I don't pray much, but I even prayed for this. I've been practicing for several hours every day and am willing to practice more. My heart and soul are in this. If you pick me for the symphony orchestra, I promise you won't regret it. You want a group that can make a difference. You need members who play with their *souls*. That's why you need me."

The air hung thick. I didn't know if she "needed" me—but I told her that anyway.

Ring the Bell

I turned toward the door, but that's when the woman's voice stopped me.

"You're in," she said sternly. "You are in."

I tried not to jump... I tried not crying — or yelling out in excitement. Instead, I told her she wouldn't regret it. And I don't think she ever did.

I thought about this during my last round of scans at the cancer center. I'm stuck in that machine for 45 minutes to two hours per MRI. Lights, plastic, and metal whir so close to my face that I often get sick. Sometimes I think about life. Sometimes I think about death. But this time, I thought about perseverance.

At this point in my life, I'm not sitting in an audition hall trying to earn a place on a symphony orchestra; I'm fighting to stay alive.

All of the tenacity, the moxie, the initiative I had at the age of 15 — I need to remember that passion now.

Who knew a conductor's actions could so vastly impact my life?

For my last performance with that group, I played with the actual Utah Symphony. The woman beside me spoke about passion and how the best melodies could change the world. I told her I made it to the youth symphony not because I was the most talented violinist who auditioned but because I had a lot of heart.

"You know," she said, "you can be extremely talented, but if you're not willing to put in the work — and you don't have passion — it won't matter. In the end, people with that fire in their souls will surpass others. Do you have what it takes not just to be good but to be excellent?" She stared directly into my eyes. "I think you do."

Her words meant so much that they made me cry because she made me want to prove her right.

It's strange looking back because I've played for thousands upon thousands of listeners in various venues where the lights shone so bright that I couldn't see anyone in the vast crowd. I would pretend to play for God alone at the end of all time. Where no mistakes mattered, and the light cleansed my soul.

Maybe that's what brought back these memories, the whirring machines with loud noises and bright lights. It's just a reminder to persevere and stay strong. That's a good thing for all of us to remember, no matter our struggles.

Timing Is Everything

"Elisa," my doctor said, "we've done so much radiation on your back that if we do any more, one of your vertebrae could fracture." They think the cancer in my back is growing—encroaching on my spinal cord. And so, it's sending nerve pain and problems through my legs. "Since the cancer in your back has gotten a little bit worse, you'll most likely need another surgery. They'll remove as much cancer as they can and reposition the cage where your L3 used to be."

Her words struck me harder than a physical blow, and tears filled my eyes to the point that I bit my lip under my mask to avoid falling apart in the oncologist's office. My mother-in-law—who is an absolute legend—sat by me. The last thing she needed was to watch me cry.

I told myself to be strong and play the glad game. I could be happy because my parents decided to visit me in their RV. (I swear they had people in RV parks nationwide praying for us.) I could be glad about surgery because... because...

I thought of the brutal six-inch scar on my back and the five-inch scar on my stomach where they'd pulled my L3 cancer-ridden vertebrae out. Then, for some reason, my thoughts turned to Mother's Day, and I thought of my four kids. How much longer will I be with them? The surgery could lengthen my life and give me more time with my husband and kids. But my choices are between having a serious surgery or letting the cancer take me. During that first surgery, I needed a blood transfusion and almost died. It's hard to fathom all the things I would've missed.

After I got home from my treatments that night, I snuggled into my bed and couldn't stop thinking about my predicament. It's not that I *want* to feel bad for myself; it's just that another surgery sounds almost unbearable. (I had six surgeries in five years—you think I'd be used to it, but I guess everyone has their breaking point.)

I felt so alone. Then a woman who reads my weekly newspaper column, Pamela White, sent me an encouraging message saying she'd asked people at church if they knew about me from the newspaper. I guess people did—and she said many people prayed for me in that town. Just her message and that knowledge wrapped me in so much hope.

That Monday, my memoir, TWO MORE YEARS, came out. It felt unbelievable that in a single day, my memoir hit the bestseller list. A couple of TV stations aired segments about my new book and my battle against cancer. Two newspapers wrote articles about me and the dangers of melanoma, and I can't believe how much I've crossed off my bucket list. This feels like lasting proof that I haven't stopped living.

I can't believe how many wonderful people I've met even as I've battled cancer. I'm so grateful I didn't die in a car accident or have my life snuffed out quickly. Even though this is a laborious, tiring journey, I'm so fortunate to be making more memories than I did for years before my diagnosis.

143

Ring the Bell

I met Ralph several years ago at the Homestead. Mayor Marc Carroll had told me about a group meeting nearly daily for coffee. So, I showed up uninvited. I wore my best dress, pulled up a chair, and sat by them. "How the hell are ya?" I asked.

The men — most of them in their 70s and 80s — looked at each other and laughed really hard.

I became fast friends with all of them, but especially Ralph. We traded stories and writings. I helped him publish his book, SKARR. And then, when I got cancer in 2020, he started coming over to our house quite a bit to make sure my whole family was okay — especially Mike, Trey, and Indiana. Since his family is from Ohio, and we don't have family in the area, this felt like a Godsend.

In 2020, Ralph told me something: "When you get better, I'll let you drive my Mustang."

"Seriously? Heck, yes."

But almost two years later, despite my positive attitude and desire to live for my children, I had not improved. And I told Ralph I was getting worse when he came over. "I go back Tuesday to talk about removing this tumor in my back."

"I'll be here Thursday to check on you," he said.

When Ralph arrived on Thursday, I had no idea what adventure that rascal had planned. He immediately told me I needed to put on my shoes because he'd finally let me drive — the Mustang. I've never driven a six-speed stick, and I could hardly wait.

Ring the Bell

We drove around and talked about music, life, and fishing. But it wasn't until Ralph let me go 80 on the freeway that I felt death would never catch me.

After we returned to my house, Ralph said how excited he was to bring my family fly-fishing later that month. "It'll be great," he boasted.

"Hey, Ralph, why did you let me drive the Mustang today? I'm not getting better," I sighed, "yet."

"Well... " We both knew he didn't want to say things looked bleak. Since the tumor in my back is growing, I can't feel several more sections of my right leg. The doctors said that if it keeps progressing, I might not be able to walk at some point. "Your... your book came out this week," he said, smiling. "We had to do something." Then he paused. "When... do you go back?"

"In a week and a half."

He seemed worried, so I gave him a huge hug. "My family just loves you, Ralph. I hope you know how grateful we are to have you in our lives."

He looked away fast as if something got in his eye, sat in his car, and drove away.

"I'm scared," I told Mike that night. "Even though so much good is going on. My book got published, and there are so many miracles in my life, like our amazing family and friends. But I still get scared sometimes. My leg and back are just hurting so much."

"I'm scared too," Mike said. We remained quiet. "Tell you what, close your eyes, and try to imagine something awesome, something so great it will get your mind off things."

"Okay," I said.

And after a few minutes, I heard Mike's voice again. "Do you feel any better?"

I grinned. "Actually, yes. All I needed was to remember speeding down the interstate with Ralph."

Mike laughed and hugged me. "He's a character."

"Yeah, he is. I still can't believe I got to drive an actual Mustang."

Mike and I talked about Ralph and all of the goodness he's brought into our lives.

Life... Despite cancer and hardships, there are so many good things, like family, friends, and going 80 on the freeway.

I just found out that my friend, Layton Funk, passed away.

After first meeting him, I wrote about the experience, and the story even got published in the Island Park News. Layton nearly levitated with pride when I gave him copies of the publication. He can't move anything from the neck down, but in that moment, you never would've known he had physical limitations as he reveled in the news, saying he was so proud of me. But the truth is that I was proud of him — being his friend made me feel like the luckiest person in the world.

Ring the Bell

And now, as I feel renewed strength to somehow continue fighting, I look back and have to give a bit of credit to Layton. He's encouraged me on numerous occasions when my treatments felt beyond unbearable. I'm so lucky I found him that day as I browsed online... and fortunate he let me be his friend.

"God is looking out for all of us. He has a plan," Layton said one day. "There's a reason you're going through this. Look at what I've gone through. That accident saved my life in a lot of ways. Remember how I told you it gave me purpose? Maybe cancer is the same for you?"

I hated to say it, but he was right. It seemed like Layton was usually right. And he changed my outlook. Now, it's so hard to believe he's gone. Who will I reach out to whenever I need a kind word? No one else seems to understand my plight quite like he did. I took that for granted. I guess after meeting him, I always figured I'd go first.

Tears brimmed my eyes as I thought more about my friend. So, unable to think about anything else, I pulled out the newspaper article I'd written about him.

"I've never met someone that positive and strong. He explained how life can bring the strangest miracles—even if they don't seem *good* at the time. His eyes sparkled when he spoke, and for me, the world changed. I still can't imagine that kind of strength—but I'm proud to know someone who does."

After reading my words, I folded the newspaper and placed it back on its special shelf in my closet.

Ladybug Luck

Ladybugs... I've been thinking about them so much. For work, I recently edited an article about how they bring good luck. This isn't in a usual sense, though. According to legend, they actually remove bad luck and retain it in one of their seven black spots. So, if a ladybug lands on you, it will let you live a "less sorrowful life." Anyway, the thought of lessening someone else's sadness, well, I found that beautiful; it's something I wish I could do, and I hope people will see ladybugs when I die and somehow remember me. This reminds me of something from my childhood.

I was so young. My mom always did my hair, and I laughed later, thinking those tight ponytails could give me a free facelift now. My mom had put me in a darling blue dress because some ladies decided to come over. I loved listening to them talk about adult stuff, so I sat quietly, hoping to be part of the party—and eventually get a cookie my mom had set on a plate. The conversation topics blended until one lady said, "She's so sick." Then she whispered, "You know her mom was sick first." I noticed the woman's spotless shoes and perfect hair.

"I had no idea." Another woman gasped.

"Well." The speaker's perfect shoes tapped under the table. "She always said she wanted to take on her mother's sickness—so her mom could get better. Now her mother is dead, and she's dying too."

148

Ring the Bell

"You don't think—"

"Oh yes, I do," she replied. "I think she took some of her mother's sickness from her, but not all of it. And that's why she's sick now."

My mom didn't say anything; she was always quiet unless she talked about her love for God. I studied her, that beautiful dark hair falling in waves around her face. Dear God, could I please look like her, all Italian and gorgeous, someday?

I smiled at my mama and suddenly wanted to ask her about this mysterious conversation. Sure, I thought some dumb things as a kid—that sleeping with a specific blanket could make me beautiful or that people could get pregnant by touching their boobs to a guy's chest—but even I knew you couldn't take someone's sickness by willing it into yourself. My six-year-old mind whirred. Couldn't they pass it along through their family lines or something?

When I got older, I learned about hereditary illnesses (like everyone else). Still, the humanities always interested me, especially the concept of sin eaters or how people try to hope that one being— even a ladybug—can take away sickness, sorrow, or even sin. People want to define and quantify everything about suffering, pain, or guilt. It's easier to wrap our heads around something if there's a reason—especially if there's a solution.

I know it's foolish (just like my early notions about reproduction), but the other day, I sat on my porch, willing a ladybug to fly over and take my sorrows. I rested in front of our tall "welcome" sign, believing something would happen. Surely God would see me in this time of weakness. He'd do something to help take away the pain or the thought that I'm in a death spiral, fighting until it's time to see my son and friends like Layton in Heaven.

I peered through tears, wondering why life has to be so damn hard. "God," I whispered, "I need help being strong today. It's getting harder the longer I've had to fight. I'm tired."

The wind swept through leafless, barren trees, and a chill came over me, so strong I forgot the pain from cancer. That's when our welcome sign fell over.

"Seriously," I groaned. "Not the *sign* I'd hoped for." But when I went to pick it up, I found something it'd been concealing: a little painted rock. I gaped because that rock went missing over a year ago. After one of my worst bouts with radiation, a nurse came over and said, "I made this. I didn't know who to give it to until now. I want you to have it." I stared at the beautifully painted designs and thanked her—having no idea it was her last day working in the melanoma unit. But after I brought it home, someone moved it, and I couldn't find the rock anywhere.

So, today I held that rock to my chest and sobbed, grasping for hope. How fitting that a nurse who lessened my pain gave me such a sign of lasting peace. I traced the black dots, little eyes, and intricate designs on the painted rock: my ladybug. "Thank you, God. For letting me be alive to fight another day."

Ring the Bell

Who knew that a gift from so long ago would be my miracle for today?

I dressed for the funeral and thought of the strange timing. Do you ever think about that? What were you doing on this day two years ago, four, 10, 20? Some days might be unmemorable, while others have been exhilarating or sad. When life gets tough, it can be difficult not dwelling on some of the more challenging moments...

It's just that my son died on January 30th, and on that same day, I prepared to play at another funeral… for my dear friend, Layton Funk.

How could I feel bad for myself when I could walk, move my arms, paint, and drive a car? A car accident robbed him of everything over a decade before—and now he'd died in his forties. Yet, during his last conversation with me, he remained positive and encouraged me to do the same.

I thought about Layton and my son as we drove to the service. I'd worn my best skirt, something I actually bought new, just in case Layton decided to attend his own funeral. I didn't want him haunting me for not dressing nice.

It's strange how coincidental timing and such can transport you to the past. I remember when my son, Zeke, died during this time of year. I'd been so worried because he was a baby, and he didn't know anyone on the other side. When I get petrified about death, I always envision my best friend, Adam, or my grandma waiting for me. I dreamed about it once: My grandma had on an apron, and she held her arms out, anxious to show me around the afterlife. That woman exuded unadulterated joy.

But my poor son, I had to take him off of life support. When he stopped breathing, I felt like I would die too, like I should never be allowed to breathe again. Mainly because I didn't want to keep living, not in that instant anyway. And I always wondered who showed Zeke around Heaven.

My thoughts turned back to my friend, Layton. It's strange because I'd been practicing my violin before the funeral. I'd played for Layton in the hospital where he lived, and he loved it. But right before his funeral, I got déjà vu and somehow felt his presence, as if Layton listened to me just like that day in the hospital! It probably sounds very strange, but something else happened too. I got the distinct impression that he'd met Zeke.

Anyway, the funeral service for Layton went beautifully. His family is so witty and fun. Throughout the service, they knew when to be serious and when to make it a little bit lighter. They talked about Layton's mother, who died a while back, and how they'd be reunited. And I found myself wishing I could present them with adoption papers since I saw where Layton got his great personality.

Anyway, it came time for me to play. I can't stand long and play anymore because the pain from the tumors in my spine is too bad. And even with pain medicine, it hurts my neck to hold my fiddle. But no one could've pried the instrument from my hands because, at that moment, I felt such power and love cascading through me. The only way to get rid of emotion like that is to play.

So, I sat behind a bunch of flower arrangements because I wanted people to *feel* the music and not get distracted by the person playing. Then I forced out all the sadness and gratitude for Layton's life, love, and friendship. I thought about the people I've lost and the love that I've gained. And I played with all of my soul. I know this might sound far-fetched, but I could've sworn Layton stood by me as I played. And I know he knew how much I loved him and appreciated his friendship.

When I returned to my seat, Trey leaned over and whispered, "I don't know why, but I couldn't help crying. That song you played was overwhelming. I'm so glad I met Layton, but I'm sad he's gone. You know, we went there thinking we'd cheer him up. And he's the one who changed our lives."

"You're right," I said. "But I think he's happy now. I really do." I suddenly felt so much peace that Layton was healthy in Heaven. His body didn't seem broken anymore. And oddly, I got the same reassuring feeling that he'd met my son, and I shouldn't worry about Zeke anymore.

Zeke… that beautiful baby whose soul must've been too perfect for this world. Interestingly, he was on life support, just like Layton, and they almost died on the same day. That seemed a bit ironic.

After his funeral, one of his sisters came up to me. "I hope this isn't too bold to say, but something amazing happened while you were playing."

"Really?" I asked.

Ring the Bell

"I could barely see you between the flower arrangements, but as I watched you, I realized you weren't up there alone. I swear I saw Layton and my mom standing by you. But my mom... she held a baby. It doesn't make much sense, does it? Why would she have a baby? But I saw them by you for a moment, just as clear as day."

"Actually," my voice shook, "it makes perfect sense."

So, as I continued reminiscing about Layton, I didn't feel quite so sad anymore. I felt peace that people die when they're supposed to. Maybe we don't understand it now, but we will someday. I'm grateful people like Layton and my oldest son are enjoying the afterlife. And maybe when they're bored, they occasionally stop by to hear me fiddle.

She Reignited My Passion for Life

One of the people who has changed my life is Dee Ready. We met over a decade ago through blogging; then she edited my young-adult fantasy novel for free—after I paid another editor who never did the work. Somehow, through so many different experiences and visits to see each other across the country, Dee became like family.

I still can't explain how or why certain miracles happen, but I've experienced them frequently. Meeting Dee has been one of those blessings in my life.

In her early years, she joined a convent and became a nun. But because of that, she never dated much, never got married, and never had children. Instead, she became an expert on etymology and Latin, taught at prestigious schools, wrote a bestselling book published by Crown (a subsidiary of Random House), spent time abroad, and amassed rare knowledge. This is always evident when we play Balderdash, and it isn't fun because she already knows *all* of the words that the rest of us are scrambling to lie about. Leave it to an ex-nun.

Dee decided she would come out and see us this May for two weeks, the longest she's ever come. We've made a habit of seeing each other at least twice a year. Usually, I go out there with one of the kids in the spring, and she'll come out here after that to see everyone in Idaho. But this time was different. I'm so sick with cancer and tired. I'm not my bouncy, Energizer Bunny self, and I saw so much concern in Dee's 86-year-old eyes.

We played games and had hilarious conversations, but then Dee shocked me. "I'm excited to get that tattoo," she said, and I almost swallowed a grape without chewing it.

My oldest daughter, Ruby, works at Mad Ink Studios and has garnered quite a list of clients. "Are you serious?" I asked. "Ruby will be stoked."

"Yes."

I studied Dee. I didn't want to be a "stick in the mud," but I don't even have a tattoo—for crying out loud. And sometimes older skin is thinner than it used to be. I didn't want her to get hurt. But I didn't say anything, and that following Saturday, I brought Dee to get a tattoo of Arthur, the same lion figurine she gave me a while ago. She'd gifted me with him after explaining that I'm both an otter and a lion.

"Does it hurt?" a girl asked in the tattoo shop.

"Actually, not at all," Dee replied.

Everyone else paled because some people would cry on the ground while getting a tattoo. Then Dee told stories about the '60s and her time in the convent. It was the strangest conversation I could imagine happening at a tattoo parlor, and I stifled a laugh when the girl getting a tattoo across from us gaped. She said she could hardly believe Dee had been a nun. And as everyone continued listening to Dee's sage words, they appeared inspired.

The excitement of the week didn't stop there. Dee got that tattoo, went on a motorcycle ride with a handsome young biker from the tattoo shop, went on her first date in 50 years — with Ralph in his Mustang! — and somehow reignited my passion for life too.

I'm still unsure why God let me meet Dee, but I am so thankful. It's honestly a miracle, just like those otters at Edson Fichter. Sometimes people pop into our lives right when we need them.

She sat writing the other morning, and I couldn't help studying her. Our dogs and cats ran around the house. Our kids asked her to look at this and that and told her all sorts of stories. Our home is somewhat of a disaster because we have so much going on, but Dee practically radiated with delight, and that made me happy. She's brought so much joy to us. It's because of her that I'm an editor. Not only did I get a friend — she taught me an entire profession. She showed me the ropes. And she never asked for anything in return.

So, the tumor board is reviewing my case today, and a lot of things are up in the air. Results from another MRI came back yesterday, and my back muscles have "severely atrophied" as the cancer has progressed.

But none of that seems to matter.

I had just seen one of the dearest people get a tattoo, drive off in a Mustang, and completely shine with more life than some 20-year-olds.

The point is that we're all getting older. We're all facing some hardship. We all have good days and bad days. Some of us, like me, even have cancer. But like my adopted family member, Dee, we can make the best of things—and brighten other people's lives along the way.

The techs began prepping me for radiation. We'd already done the session where they sent me into the imaging machine and reached in to mark certain areas with a pen. After everything was marked, they brought me out and tattooed each dot mark with a needle. I wished Ruby could've done this because she's a professional artist, and I suddenly didn't trust these people. These techs sent the needle back and forth through my skin in a sewing technique straight from the Middle Ages. After so much radiation on my spine (and brain), I have permanent black tattoo dot marks all over my stomach and lower chest. The other tattoos were much less aggressive than this. Maybe she recently went through a breakup? I bit my lower lip and found something to be grateful for. In that moment, I could be happy because at least they don't use tattoos for brain radiation; instead, they place a tight mask over patients' faces and mark that. Although it's quite terrifying for me, at least it's not a face tattoo. Not to be dramatic, but Mike Tyson is not my hero.

Anyway, I'd completed that session and now gone into a large room for actual radiation—again. They told me to hand them my gown, and I stood shivering with my arms crossed over my fake boobs. Sometimes I've stood there in all my glory. Brave and sassy. But on this occasion, I felt beat down and weak. I'd driven myself down to Utah from Idaho and left around 4:30 in the morning. I'm unsure if it was fatigue or stress, but this whole ritual seemed inhumane. I glanced down at my deformed right leg, where the muscle has atrophied from tumors. I hated standing there in only my panties. At least they could say, "Hey, it's not the best body, but I've seen worse," tip me a few dollars—or something. I guess I'll just have to settle for what they tried to give me: a barbaric cure to cancer. After a moment, I rested in what they call "my nest." This is a mold completely formed to my body. After this, they pulled a big bag over my feet and up to my chest. I can't begin to tell you how awkward this is. It's excruciatingly hard to arch my back since I have my L1–L5 fused. Try shimmying a bag up your body while you're half-naked. I felt like a worm—that a kid had stepped on.

"Why the bag again?" I asked as politely as I could.

"Please put your arms in," one of the women said.

"It gives us up to one millimeter of accuracy," the male tech replied. "We don't want to damage good tissue." He placed washcloths over my breasts to give me a semblance of modesty. Gee, thanks.

They'd hooked a large hose to the end of the bag by my feet, and after something clicked, the hose began viciously sucking the air out like a food saver device. Thank God for the washcloths! I could only imagine my boobs being squished under the plastic for all to see.

159

Ring the Bell

This might sound pathetic, but I felt terrified. I mean, I've done this before. I knew I'd be completely immobilized from the elbows down, but even with practice, it's still hard.

"Wait! Wait. I can't do this," I said.

It's strange being left alone with large metal plates that rotate around. Each session is about 45 minutes, but it feels much longer. I can't even hold a panic ball like they allow in MRI machines. This is a little ball you squeeze to alert the techs that you're "not okay." But during certain radiation sessions, when they even need your arms immobilized, they don't allow the ball—and you have to yell really loud for them to hear you in the next room. That's where they are the whole time, safely operating the machines so they won't be around the radiation.

"The last time we did this, I got so hot. I could feel sweat dripping around my body in the bag." I didn't mean to, but I looked at the male tech because he'd seemed more empathetic. "Why haven't they found another way?"

"They're trying so hard," he said. "But this is the best we have right now. You don't need to be scared."

I had to get my mind off things, so I talked mindlessly. "I got locked in a tiny trailer closet—totally my fault—when I played around as a kid. It took my family quite a while to find me. I thought I'd die." His eyes went wide as he listened.

Unfortunately, telling this story hadn't been the best idea after all, and I'd begun to hyperventilate.

160

Ring the Bell

"I promise to check on you every five minutes." He patted the plastic that pulled my arms taut. "I'll call out and make sure you're okay."

"I know you can do this," the woman beside him said. "You have children and a husband, right? And a great family? Your mother-in-law is in the waiting room."

"She's so amazing." I nodded.

"You need to get through this for them."

"Okay. Yes. I can do this." Their words reassured me. "It wouldn't be too much—I mean, you don't mind checking on me every five minutes?"

"Not a big deal at all."

"We both will," the woman said. "Mrs. Magagna, do you picture anything when you're getting radiation? Some people close their eyes and meditate or pretend they're somewhere else."

"Sometimes I pretend I'm on a dock in Jamaica." That's where Mike and I went on our honeymoon. "Other times, I pretend to be lying on the grass up in the mountains. Anywhere that's big and open."

"Well, I hope you'll envision something good this time," she said, and they left the room.

A Time Capsule

One of the greatest moments of my life happened in Jamaica. Mike and I had both always wanted to visit the island, so we chose it for our honeymoon. He held me tightly as we sat on the wooden dock.

"I love you so much," he said, dangling his feet into the crystal-like waters.

"I love you back." It felt nice leaning into him, and I closed my eyes. A hot breeze swept across our faces, sending my hair whipping to the south of us. As we rested there quietly on the warm planks, I thought of how Mike had become far more than a lover or a friend; he'd become someone I'd fight for, love, respect, and believe in despite anything. I'd finally found someone I trusted with everything in me because I respected who he was. That admiration wasn't demanded or required—he'd earned it like any man who toils tirelessly, constant and sure. Over the past years, Mike had shown himself to be a good man to both me and the children.

Thinking back, I remembered some of our early times together. I had been so scared to kiss him for the first time. "Did you know I would kiss you when we went hiking to that cave?" I asked.

"I had no idea. I thought you just wanted to be friends."

We met at Kellogg's. I was a security guard, and Mike worked as a machine operator. It's hilarious thinking back to when I got that job. I'd needed to do something to keep my house. This was a second job at the time, working the graveyard shift as a single mother of four. "Mike, why did you start coming to talk to me at the security desk?" I sat up and gazed into his eyes.

"Honestly, I was curious."

"But you kept coming after we first met," I said. "That's more than curiosity."

"Because after I met you, you told me about some of the things you were going through and—"

"I couldn't help it though. You were easy to talk with."

He looked at me so lovingly. "You were easy to talk with too. Right off, I knew we'd get along. But I also knew you needed a friend."

"I really did." Although we were on a beautiful honeymoon, my thoughts drifted back to a far less perfect time in my life. "No one knew it, but at points, I felt at the end of my rope. One night I even knelt down and told God that I needed a miracle." I snuggled into Mike's arms even more so he couldn't see the tears in my eyes. We both wore swimsuits, and his skin felt warm against mine. "Mike, I met you right after that prayer. I feel like you're the miracle God sent to me—me and the kids." I tried to keep my voice steady. "I always wanted to think that I could do everything on my own, that I didn't need a man. But I needed *you*. You've made everything better." He continued stroking my hair, cradling me close as we watched the sun set over the sea.

"I'm so lucky to have you." His voice turned low, serious. "I needed a miracle too. You and the kids have given my life meaning. In a way, I was always waiting for you."

We stayed like that, just lost in the moment. I really wished time would slow, for at least a little while anyway. I thought of that morning—we'd had a wonderful day, waking up snuggling under a poofy comforter, holding each other for hours, and eating breakfast on the beach... We'd even opened all the wedding cards that we'd packed in our suitcases. There was one strange thing—an anonymous card with simple, roughly written words and a dirty envelope. "Few people are really good together," it said, "but you and Mike are. I wish both of you the best." I had no idea who the card was from since it wasn't even signed. Mike sighed when he read it and said something about the past finally being in the past. We'd opened the rest of the cards after that and been so elated, talking about everyone's well-wishes.

The rest of the morning passed by in a blur of laughter and excitement until we decided to go back to the room and grab something special. A year and a half before, we'd made a time capsule—a mason jar that contained a special note to one another as well as a bucket list item we'd like to do together. We'd brought the mason jar all the way to Jamaica and planned to open it on the dock. I still remember changing into a new pink swimsuit and then sprinting with Mike to the chosen area, so eager to share this special moment.

"You still want to read the letters from the mason jar?" I asked, loving the warm water on my feet. "I can hardly believe we buried it last year."

Ring the Bell

Mike nodded. The mason jar sat next to us. "All the way from a forest to a Jamaican dock." He washed the mason jar in the oceanic waves that our feet still dangled in, then twisted the lid off. After drying his hands on his swim shorts, he pulled out the letter I'd written to him and the letter he'd written to me.

"You sure what you wrote was nice?" I asked.

"Yes." He laughed, and we both unfolded our papers.

The page was a little faded, and some dirt lined the inside of the letter. I gently blew the loose dirt away and began to read Mike's tiny writing.

Elisa,

I want you to know that I've loved you since the beginning. I remember when we first started talking and getting to know each other. Every day I fell more and more for you. I never wanted to let you go.

Back then, sometimes life encased me like water. But I met you—and somehow, you shared your breath with me and helped me breathe. I felt like I wasn't drowning anymore. If we'd never met, I would've never known *real* love. I would've never felt like, at any second, my heart would leap out of my chest from the exhilaration of being with you.

Everything seems right when you're in my arms. Everything we've gone through has made me better. Every memory will be the best memory because you're in it. And

165

every time I say I love you, that you're the most beautiful woman I know, that you make me so happy... I truly mean it wholeheartedly.

I love you, Elisa, always will.

—Mike

I read the letter a couple more times before Mike finished mine.

"Oh! The bucket list items," I said, remembering that we'd each secretly written something we wanted to do together—no matter what. I unfolded the papers, and my mouth fell open. "We wrote the same thing."

"Go skydiving together," Mike said. "I'm so happy." He put the papers back into the mason jar and jumped into the water. "This is just the beginning."

So that's what I try to picture sometimes while I'm getting scans, radiation, or even preparing for surgeries. I try remembering a day when the whole world seemed ahead of us, and I was the happiest, healthiest woman in the world.

Not the Easiest Thing

I found the bluebird flapping awkwardly, begging me—not for death—for life. Didn't it know what it asked for? It would never fly again, and feathers littered the carpet where our polydactyl cat had played with the bird. Pawing and clawing, enjoying watching it fight for life.

And, of course, I thought about my struggles. It's hard not reflecting on my battle when I see death and suffering. A woman had emailed me and written, "You don't seem to be getting worse, so I won't follow you now. I followed your story to see how long you could stay happy *and* have cancer."

I don't share everything online, and this woman had no idea where I stood in my battle. Although a stranger, her heartless words cut to the core.

I watched the bird, desperately wishing I could fix it. It continued squawking, begging for life—just like me—wanting to be healthy again. To be able to hike with my kids. To go out for more than an hour with my husband... I had to admit that I *wanted* to live. I *wanted* the cancer to be gone. I *wanted* to ring that damn bell in the infusion unit so everyone would know I made it—and they might too.

Yet, the woman who emailed me became the cat, deriving amusement from my suffering. I thought about all this, and tears flooded my face. I honestly had no idea what to do for the bird. Kill it? Try to help it. That's when my cat sauntered into the room, pounced on her prey, and ultimately ended

167

the bird's suffering. I didn't feel sad then. Not at all. I felt grateful that the heartache had ended.

My situation can sometimes seem like a lot to grieve over, even though I agreed to this price: being permanently disabled from surgery, so I can live.

Luckily, my rabbi, Sara Goodman, once messaged me about moments like this, and I'll never forget her words. "There is a wonderful Jewish folktale," she wrote. Then Rabbi Goodman explained that a man had a dream about the king and immediately went to tell him.

"You climbed a ladder," the man said, "but when you reached the middle of it, I woke up." The king felt so delighted by these words that he gave the man a bag of gold. Walking home, now rich, the man told his neighbor about this good fortune, but the neighbor became jealous and devised a plan. He could also visit the king and tell a story.

"I had a dream too," he said to the king the next day. "But in my dream, you climbed the ladder and reached the top." To his dismay, the king didn't appear happy at all and immediately asked the guards to bring the man to the dungeon.

"Why?" the man pleaded.

"Because," the king replied, "your dream prophesied my demise. There was nowhere else to go!"

"Elisa," Rabbi Goodman wrote, after sharing this story, "your outlook on life and your commitment toward living every moment of every day to its fullest is a gift and an inspiration. For you, every moment is a rung on that ladder, and you cherish each one. Most people resolve to live life in this fashion, and we believe that we do. But in reality, our lives are simply a garage full of many small ladders we endeavor to reach the top of and then put away. Goal met, done! This is very different than living every moment to the fullest. It's not a bad way to live, just different. And not how we tell ourselves and others to live."

I paused while reading this and stared at my front yard. Before receiving her message, I'd been sitting on a bench, watching Trey and Indy chase each other in the grass. Their laughter brightened even that sunny day.

"So, when people meet you—in person or through your books," Rabbi Goodman continued, "we are hit with the realization that we're not living in the way we thought we were. It takes a lot for a person to be able to say, 'Okay. I'm actually not where I thought I was, and I'm completely okay with that.' So, thank you, Elisa, for inspiring me to live my life in a fuller way."

A river of gratitude poured through me. Rabbi Sara Goodman is one of the kindest women I have ever known. To hear this validation from someone like her, someone who is so innately good...

"Are you okay, Mama?" Indy asked, and both she and Trey ran over to either side of me.

"I just received the sweetest message," I said. "I'll never forget it." And I never have.

Since I first got hospitalized in 2020, I discovered peace in Judaism. But when I found our local synagogue, I finally understood where I belong: with people like Rabbi Goodman and her mother, Bayle. They're true examples of altruistic, uplifting women, and I can only hope to be more like them someday.

It goes to show that words have the power to hurt or heal. But it means a lot that people like Rabbi Goodman believe in me, saying that I truly appreciate each rung in the ladder.

I qualified for permanent disability — which everyone says is terrific — but I guess that's just not what I planned for my life. Indy and Trey walked into the room during a moment of desperation, and I'm so embarrassed. Despite how honest I've been throughout this ordeal, they hardly ever see me cry. So, I rushed into the laundry room and shut the door. They know I'm fighting for my life, but they don't hear about the crippling pain or how terrifying it can be for me. I'm not scared of death or suffering. What I fear now is being unable to see my children grow up. Not holding Mike's wrinkled hand as we hobble along for our 50th wedding anniversary. Not being remembered well and not making a positive impact on my loved ones. Not showing my children that cancer, sickness, and even death will never rob me of who I am. And if they see me cry or watch my pain, I think that's placing *my* burden on them. Life is hard enough; the least I can do is shield them from my grief.

Anyway, at that moment, I listened through the laundry room door. All of my kids are hilarious, but my two youngest are always teasing each other and pulling pranks. It started young too. Trey would give Indy candy if she'd open child-proof drawers for him so he could access all of my Tupperware. And now that they're older, their schemes have grown more sophisticated. One distracts me while the other cooks insane concoctions. One watches a romance with me while the other hangs up heavy metal posters on the wall. And even though I act dumbfounded, I secretly love all of their antics, and they usually keep my sadness about cancer at bay. But two weeks ago, that particular day felt hopeless.

Mike burst into the laundry room. "What can I do?" He looked desperate. The family isn't used to me falling apart quite like that. "I don't know what to do." Tears filled his eyes. "I hate this so much."

"A bunch of things feel off," I said. "I know they said there's a chance they might be able to keep the cancer stable at some point. I could have years and years. But I'll always be... disabled. I don't mean to sound ungrateful, but this feels like a Herculean task."

Tears flooded my eyes. Mike is so young and full of energy. I just felt like a lead weight around his neck. How must he feel dealing with this? He's only 35.

"You could be with anyone," I said.

"And I want you."

Looking into his kind face tore me apart. I can't be exactly who I want to be, but at least I can do better than being a bawl baby. After I'd stuffed a bunch of towels into the washer, I grabbed a piece of paper and told myself to "get it together." Then I made a list of everything that was bothering me. I wrote about how I rarely do my makeup and hair because I tire quickly. I wrote about wishing I could do things with Mike and the kids like we used to. I also wrote about how I want to visit Italy someday. I read it at the end and realized that every sentence started with "I can't.

Mike left for work, and Trey and Indy confessed that they knew I wasn't okay.

"Mama, what's going on?" Indy asked.

"I just wish I could do more things. I can only walk a quarter of a mile. I want to bring you hiking and on epic fishing trips again."

"But there's so much you *can* do. We can go fishing in places that are close to the car. And you can hike to the bridge up Gibson Jack." And later that day, Trey and Indy helped me make a new list of things they wanted to do. Every sentence started with "I can." Fish at Edson Fichter. Hike a quarter mile to the bridge where we can eat Lunchables. Float the river where it doesn't require much rowing, and Mike can help me. Visit Bear World. And the last crazy thing on our list? Go to Italy.

It's astounding switching a mentality from "can't" to "can." My kids helped me realize that there are so many possibilities. The world awaits— and maybe someday, Italy does too.

"That's why I believe there's something after this. I mean, we go someplace after we die," Trey said.

Ring the Bell

There's something quite exceptional about Trey. He's almost otherworldly. Even as a tiny child, he would say tremendous words and understand things he shouldn't. If reincarnation were real, he lived previously as a philosopher. And if anyone is innately good, it's him.

"Trey's special because he's the only son you had after Zeke—your first son—died," a friend once told me. "God gave him to you."

"*All* of my kids are exceptional," I said.

Trey brought me back to the moment. "Even though you have cancer, and all of these bad things have happened to you, you'll always believe in the afterlife, huh? Because of what happened to us?"

"You're talking about Adam?" I asked, and he nodded.

Adam. Now there was someone too innocent for this world. I never expected it when we dated at 15, but I began to realize when he reached his 30s. The man had faced more hardships than Job, yet he refused to don armor. I cried hearing about some of the things he'd experienced. My stomach twisted in knots because the hardships were one thing, but the way he stayed resolutely unchanged mystified me. Instead of getting angry with someone who almost killed him... instead of getting bitter with his bride who got pregnant with someone else's child... instead of letting the world destroy him, he fiercely loved everyone. And then...

We always stayed in touch but grew a closer friendship after my divorce. It felt devastating when I realized he'd gotten back into drugs.

Ring the Bell

"I can't have that around my kids," I said. "We'll talk again when you're sober."

But we never talked again. And several months later, I received a message from a mutual friend. "Did you hear about Adam?"

"What? No. What happened?"

"Elisa. Adam... is dead."

We all took it hard, especially Trey, who'd called him "Uncle Adam."

Months and months passed. We didn't talk about Adam much. I didn't want to upset the kids. Then, one day I walked into my bedroom and felt like Adam was waiting there. I honestly thought I was losing it. And even when I sat at the edge of the bed, it seemed like Adam sat next to me. You know how you feel around different people: the smell of their perfume or cologne and how they make you think about yourself?

I sat there for a minute, then walked out of my room and into the hallway. Trey stepped from the bathroom at that moment. He was only five or six at the time, a tiny guy with a quiet resolve. "Mama," he said, "something weird just happened."

"Oh, yeah?" I asked.

"Yeah," Trey said. "Uncle Adam came and said 'goodbye.' He told me he was sorry he had to leave early. I guess he just wanted me to know."

I stood in shock. Dumbfounded.

It's been so many years since this happened, but every once in a while, Trey still talks about it.

"So, that's why you believe in an afterlife?" I asked Trey.

174

Ring the Bell

"Yeah, and with you being sick, it's helped me a lot. It's nice to have that memory to hold onto."

"For me too," I said. And whether it was a coincidence, String Theory at its finest, or something divine, it doesn't matter. That moment still gives my son peace. And for me, it keeps my sense of wonder alive and well.

Lifechanging Lesson for
Five Bucks and a Quarter

———

"**H**e didn't have enough cash on him," the cashier said to everyone in line at the Wendy's near our home. "He'll be right back. Thanks for your patience."

Moments before, an older man—who looked delightfully like Mr. Magoo—had darted from the counter and rushed to his car.

"I'll pay for it." How could I not? To buy a meal for Mr. Magoo felt like an honor. "Whatever he got, I'll pay," I said, and both Trey and Indy lit with excitement because our day was about to get interesting.

"That'll be $5.25," the girl said.

"Well, that isn't much." Magoo should've ordered more. "That's less than some people spend on a coffee."

I'd wanted to pay and leave the register before the man returned, but unfortunately, it didn't work out that way. Instead, he burst through the doors and dumped a bunch of change on the counter. "I'm sure I have enough now," he said.

"No worries," the lady said. "This woman paid for you."

He turned to me, concerned. "I don't take handouts. Please let me pay."

"I've been wanting to do something nice for someone *all* day. It helps get my mind off of what

Ring the Bell

I'm going through." He went to protest, and I'm unsure why, but I felt like mentioning the fact that it was almost Father's Day. I turned to that small man and looked kindly into his eyes. "It's Father's Day weekend," I said, then I reached out and went to rest my hand on his, where he still clutched at the coins. "You're a father?"

He nodded sadly as if a long, tragic story rested behind those eyes.

"Well, I felt almost inspired to tell you something. Happy Father's Day. It's not much, but it's a free meal." And then I winked.

Magoo teared up and looked far more grateful than anyone should over five bucks and a quarter.

After a while, the cashier came and talked with me and said this started a chain of people wanting to pay for each other's food. I guess it made her day, and before returning to her post, she whispered, "You said this helps you get through your struggles? If you don't mind my asking, is everything okay for you guys?" She looked from me to Trey to Indy.

Indy bit her lip.

"I have... " I exhaled. "I have cancer. Doctors initially gave me two years to live, but now I might have more. We just don't know. I keep telling almost everyone I meet to be grateful for what they have. It might sound cliche, but life really is short."

It seemed as if she'd stopped breathing. "But looking at you, you're the picture of health. You have cancer?"

I nodded. "Life is a crazy ride," I said. "You know, seeing how happy that man got over a simple meal someone paid for made my whole day shine. That kind of gratitude is beautiful."

"For me too," she said.

We were just about to leave the restaurant when the manager came up and announced that they wanted to pay for our entire order: three meals. "We were running behind—which is very uncharacteristic of us—and what you did for that man was so kind. Here's your money back," the manager said, handing me cash.

"Put it toward the next person's order," I said, and his smile slowly lit his face.

"Okay." He shook his head in disbelief. "We will."

After we got into the car, Trey and Indy kept talking about how exciting our outing to Wendy's had been.

"Talk about instant karma." Indy giggled. "I can't believe they tried to pay for *our* meal."

"Wow. What a day. That's the thing with kindness... " Trey said, obviously thinking out loud.

"What?" I asked.

"I rode my bike to the gas station once, and a guy paid for my drink. He told me never to forget it and to do something nice for someone else. Every time I'm kind, I think about what that man said. I'll never forget it."

I nodded. "But how do you think that relates to today?"

"It's just that... " He paused as if trying to choose his words carefully. "It's great what you did, but what means more is all of those people paying for each other's meals. And the cashier, I know she'll never forget us or our story. We showed her that hardships haven't gotten us down and that if we can rise above what we're going through, no matter what other people are fighting, other people can overcome their struggles too."

I had to look out my window. I didn't want Trey or Indy to see me cry. I was just so proud of them. Cancer can be devastatingly brutal, but the lessons we've learned are worth their weight in gold. Who knew you could buy all that for just five bucks and a quarter?

Watching the Earth Come Alive

Today I tried to pick a favorite memory with my dad, and I realized just how many we have. From watching THE GREY at a theater (laughing that we paid to see a survival horror movie) to deep-sea fishing in Mexico (catching more tuna than the boat could hold and spotting humpback whales to the side of us), we've had some pretty amazing times. But the one that stands out the most for me today is one of our hunting trips.

He woke me up even earlier than farmers rise and handed me a thermos that held shepherds' coffee. I quickly realized the value of drinking that stuff slowly—to avoid a gut full of grounds.

We four-wheeled over toward a ridge my dad had scoped out with my Uncle Wayne the day before. "We're trying to blend in," my dad whispered, then placed a finger to his lips.

It took a while for the two of us to combat crawl toward the edge of a cliff. Then we waited for a long time...

It was slow at first, but I started to feel the earth's pure energy—the heartbeat. The wind played the most beautiful melodies I've ever heard, and, as if calling them to life, oranges and yellows streaked across the sky—making a symphony for those lucky enough to see it.

The earth's skin ached to shake off the cold and darkness as a tumbleweed popped from the ground and rolled along, fighting his way through this world, just like the rest of us.

And then it happened: The sun burst from a mountain range and started highlighting the tips of everything. The trees ignited with life. The ground heated with excitement and joy only brought by a new day. My strawberry-blonde hair whipped in front of my face and turned to fire. And my dad, well, he grinned in a way I've never seen. He looked every bit like a majestic mountain lion, wild and free.

Not long after the sun rose, we spotted two does resting under a massive tree across the valley. My dad and I worked all day to get within shooting distance, but when we were almost there, the does stood up and bounded — as fast as lightning — to the exact spot we'd started from *across* the valley.

After that, we gave up the charade and talked freely. I relayed how surreal it'd been feeling the earth wake up like that, and my dad imparted the value of always finding beauty in life.

We ate fancy potatoes that my Uncle Wayne and Aunt Judy made that night. I heard hilarious stories that shocked me, and I remember feeling the warmth of the campfire as I looked from my parents to my epic aunt and uncle. The four of them have always been true legends; just being by my dad and Uncle Wayne is like meeting Butch Cassidy and the Sundance Kid.

Over a decade later, my dad had a stroke. I couldn't get a plane ticket fast enough, so I hopped into a car with Ruby and sped through two states to be by my dad's side. "This means so much to me —

181

to us," my mom said. "I can't believe how fast you got here."

"That's what you do for the people you love," I said. And as I squeezed my dad's hand and told him I loved him, I just knew he'd fully recover like he did.

I never lost faith that he'd get better because I'd seen him on that ridge many years ago. I'd seen his fighting spirit and the beauty of his soul. And that's an incredibly valuable thing he's passed on to me: the courage to fight even when all the odds are against me.

Life Will Surprise Ya

Indy had no idea I'd begun feeling nauseous on this shopping trip. She'd waited days and days for the outing, and I didn't want it ruined—especially because of cancer; it's taken enough from us. "Mike, you'll help her get some stuff?" I whispered. "Make it fun?"

He nodded. "You go rest in the car. I've got this. She'll have an awesome time."

Indy seemed happy to shop with Mike, which made a big difference for me. But after I stepped outside, a wave of fatigue hit so strong that I couldn't take another step. I placed my hand against the exterior brick wall and then slumped to sit by the garbage can at the store's entrance.

So many people passed. One fancy woman studied my pale face and stick legs, tipped her nose, and walked on. This continued until I willed Mike and Indy to burst from the store. I couldn't stand people's judgment anymore, but I needed help getting back up.

So, instead of letting pity hijack the moment, I pulled my phone from my pocket and saw a new Facebook message. "Remember how you paid for that man's meal at Burger King? You told him to have a nice Father's Day?" a man named 'John' wrote.

I studied his profile, but he'd used a golden Lab for all of his profile pictures, and I didn't recognize his last name. "Yes," I wrote back. "The story about that got published in a local newspaper. That man was so kind."

"At Burger King, well, I thought it was you," he wrote back. "I watched your story on the news a while back and started following your posts on Facebook *before* you even paid for my meal. I didn't ever comment or message you. It just helped reading about your days. I thought, 'If she can get through life — with cancer — then I can get through my stuff too.' But when I actually saw you in person, and then you paid for my food — it seemed unreal. Here's this person I was following who bought me a meal. And then, you wrote about it!"

I could hardly believe this turn of events. "Wow," I wrote. "*You* are amazing. This is such a Godwink."

"I got to be one of your Godwinks?" he wrote back. "I've heard about them, but now I *am* one!"

I couldn't help giggling.

"You must get so scared in your situation," he replied. "Sometimes… I get scared."

"We all do," I wrote back. "Because we're human. I hope you'll find whatever will help you fight the fear. But I guess acknowledging it — in my situation — became a step toward not being quite so scared anymore. For me, I want to see my kids grow up. But realizing everything will be okay, no matter what, that God is looking out for them and me — for all of us... That made all the difference."

Ring the Bell

Although this was just an online message, I felt that somehow a quiet understanding settled there.

"Thank you for this," he finally responded. "I really needed to read that today. I'm so glad I got to meet you at Burger King."

"You too." My heart filled with such contentment. And even my stiff back and upset stomach couldn't ruin the moment. I still remained outside of the store, waiting for Mike and Indy to finish shopping, but after messaging John, I gazed at the luminous sky. How could I have missed its beauty before?

Cirrus clouds spread to the edges of the mountaintops, framing the sun quite perfectly, and I thought how ironic it is that I love feeling sunshine on my face even though it's what doctors say probably gave me melanoma.

The 'Bell' Police

He rang the bell, and everyone clapped, but the patient looked tired, and then he cried.

My journeys to the infusion unit started in 2020, and I've seen several people ring the bell. Some look ecstatic, while others appear deflated.

"What does it mean?" I asked a nurse after witnessing this a while ago.

"They've finished treatments. They're done."

At first, I thought this meant they were in remission, but after almost two years, I've realized otherwise. It doesn't always mean they've beat cancer; sometimes, it simply means they've ended this leg of their journey. While some head to a happier cancer-free life, others—like the man I saw yesterday—are wheeled away to palliative care.

This journey has been excruciatingly hard, and since 2020 I've desperately wanted to ring that damn bell.

They call it "a bell," but it's actually a Zildjian gong. You can't put something like that in front of a musician and expect them not to touch it. But it's harder to reach than the treasure in RAIDERS OF THE LOST ARK. So many nurses swarm around it, and their queen (the charge nurse) hardly ever leaves its side.

That's why yesterday seemed so surreal. I went to leave the infusion room, and my path to the "bell" was free and clear. I sneaked up to it, probably looking like Gollum because of my back surgery, then swiftly lifted the mallet... When I finally prepared to hit that coveted thing, a nurse saw me.

"Excuse me, ma'am," she said as Sky snagged a couple of pictures. "Is today your last treatment?"

"Well... No," I said to the bell police. "But a girl can dream, can't she?"

She broke out laughing. "You'll get to ring it someday. And it'll be wonderful."

So, I set the mallet down very slowly and left.

Later that day, a medical specialist said my labs looked almost better than they have since I started this journey. "Don't lose hope. You could beat this, Elisa. We're getting more scans in July. It seemed impossible before, but you're such a fighter and so positive. I think you have a chance. You could beat this."

I'm not sure if she should've told me this. Everyone else keeps saying this is what I'll die from. Despite my reservations, my heart soared. When I got home, Sky and I looked up the etymology of the word "hope." She's enrolled at a local university in town, and she loves studying anything and everything.

"Hope," I said.

She flipped to the correct page. "It says we have to research the root of despair."

"That's weird." And when we found that entry, I pondered those words for a long time.

"Hope is a late word," Sky read. "It says despair comes first, and then hope follows. There is no hope without despair."

I read the rest of the entry about how once a rat is cornered, it only fights because it hopes to escape.

Ring the Bell

The text explained how soldiers fight because, at some point, they hope to live and put an end to the suffering.

"I guess I do need hope," I said to Sky.

"We all do." She looked at me with sudden tears in her eyes. "Mama, you've got to keep fighting. We all want you to beat this."

And we hugged for the longest we have since I'd rock her in a rocking chair when she was a little girl.

So, I didn't hit the gong, but I did hold the mallet in my hand — and it felt *awesome*. But what felt even better than that was holding Sky in my arms.

Singing the National Anthem at a Semi-Pro Baseball Game

"**W**ould you like to sing the national anthem at a semi-pro baseball game?" she asked, and it felt as if the woman had reached into my soul and found one of my deepest desires. In bold letters on my bucket list, it even reads: sing the national anthem at a baseball game.

At the age of five, I sang the lyrics to the national anthem so many times that my mom woke up singing them one morning. "Wow," she said, "I must be hearing this a lot." And we both laughed.

But my stamina isn't what it used to be, and I honestly worried, wondering if I could do this. So, I dressed up like a pinup girl because if anything says America, it's: apple pie, 1950s cars, baseball, and pinup girls. My kids were so excited to support me, and many friends showed up at the ballpark.

I'll never forget standing under the stadium lights on the pitcher's mound. Thank God I brought my cane because it felt like my sole friend, trusty and reliable. But then, as I heard other songs playing on the speakers, I forgot the STAR-SPANGLED BANNER's melody. To make it worse, I couldn't remember the key I needed to sing in—a cappella.

I started shaking and felt like I could fall over. Then the announcer walked up and handed me the microphone. It was my turn. I felt so weak and dizzy. But somehow, I miraculously began singing, only to forget the second set of words.

I stared out at everyone: friends, family, throngs of strangers... My breath caught in my throat. That very moment was such a metaphor for my life. I always end up having an Anne-of-Green-Gables moment, and things are never perfect.

I apologized into the microphone: "Sorry." I looked out, and people cheered, hoping I would have the gumption to continue.

And then, like it often does with life, the melody returned to me. I instantly thought of ice skaters and how when they fall, they better pull off a triple axel at the end. That's when I decided to go for the high note. My kids had helped me practice, and Sky — who's the best singer I've ever heard — told me not to try for the high note if I got nervous. But what could I lose now? So I sang with everything in me. I still shook a little and held my cane tighter for support, but I pulled off the high note — and then an octave above it.

Afterward, a well-known local photographer took pictures of me, and a reporter even did a story on me and my will to persevere despite hardship.

I met the owner of the baseball team and got to see so many friends whom I hadn't visited with in years. But I must admit that I cried pretty hard because of my mistake. It wasn't until I got home that I realized it was a good thing.

"You cried?" my kids asked, shocked.

"But, Mama, you don't cry about stuff like this. People will remember your strong voice and that you actually got out and did this even though you have cancer," Indy said.

"Yeah, most people wouldn't even try," Trey said.

Sky and Ruby gave me the biggest hugs. "We're so proud of you," they said and that meant the world to me. So many tears filled my eyes. Hearing this from my kids had more import than I can describe. No matter how hard things have been, we now have all of these memories to look back on. It's not the terrible things we've gone through that matter; it's how we handle them.

Trey cleared his throat. He's 14, but he is so serious when he's been thinking hard about something. "It's like with everything else," he said, pausing, "if you have a hard time, you just keep going, Mom. You showed everybody out there what you're really like. Life can be hard, but you don't let that stop you. None of us should."

My Shitty Attitude Is in Remission

My leg started shaking and then gave out on me. "We need to buy a wheelchair," I told Mike, defeated. We'd borrowed them at airports and other places where they were available, but now I needed more than that.

I'd planned to bring my violin to a wellness complex where I could set up a blanket far from everyone and play without anyone hearing me. But I knew it would be too difficult to walk that far. I couldn't even hold my violin in its case for that long.

"Let's go to the pharmacy. I've actually worried about this. I've been putting money aside in my account. It's for a wheelchair, but I didn't want to say anything."

Somehow Mike is always one step ahead but not too pushy. He knows what to do yet understands there's a time and a place. I'm ready. I hugged him so tightly. "I'm glad you waited for me to say this instead of suggesting it. It's taken a long time for me to get to this point."

"We can buy the wheelchair and come right back. It's not too far away."

So, we drove to the pharmacy. "I don't think I'll need it permanently. Do you have a rent-to-own option?"

Ring the Bell

The man smiled, "Absolutely." And Mike loaded my new friend into the car.

We went back to the wellness complex. It's a big area complete with a pond for fishing, basketball and volleyball courts, picnic areas... I soon sat down in the wheelchair and set my violin on my lap. After my emotions finally calmed down — since change can be hard — I looked around and realized that some people were unhappy. Sure, maybe all of them aren't battling a terminal illness like I am, but they each had their challenges: some easier and some much worse. A couple sat on a blanket, blankly watching anyone around them who seemed remotely happy. A woman tried wrangling her young children but turned red as if she might burst like a teakettle. An elderly man sat on a bench, so lonely and sad.

"I want to do something fun," I told Mike. "Are you in?"

This was a silly question because Mike is *always* in — and he smiled, a bit too eager to push that wheelchair as if it were a racecar. "I want to play my violin as you push me around. I think people will get a kick out of it."

"What are you gonna play?" he asked.

"ORANGE BLOSSOM SPECIAL." I beamed. "Since it's supposed to sound like a train, it just fits."

So, I played that as we chugged around everyone we could. The place goes in a loop, so we just circled around the whole Portneuf Wellness Complex. And as I studied everyone's faces, the happy people got even more exuberant and the others transformed from boredom to excitement, confusion to wonderment, and sadness to joy.

After we "parked" with my wheelchair at a picnic area where we could spread a blanket under a tree, Mike and I chuckled about our shenanigans. I thought I might laugh so hard that soda would come out of my nose.

For the second time this month, I saw the power of bringing joy to others no matter what we might be going through ourselves.

Mike planted several different kinds of flowers in our front yard. I'd seen them at the store where they looked beautiful, with bright futures. I bet some hoped to be planted in a botanical garden while others longed to be in a nature preserve. Yet, the poor ones we purchased ended up in our pathetic flowerbed. We do our best, but most things we plant out front die.

Last year I studied the perennials and thought, "If doctors are right, these flowers and I have something in common; none of us will see next year."

At that moment, a truck pulled up. Braydon stepped out with his dad. Braydon is one of the coolest, nicest kids in the whole damn world. He feels like an adopted son, and we all adore him because he's such a great person.

He lived with us for a bit in 2019 and 2020. It's funny that we initially just wanted to help him, but what he did was help us. He came into our lives right when we needed him.

I had never met Braydon's dad, Shane, before that day. And I could hardly wait to shake his hand and tell him what an exceptional son he has.

After I introduced myself and hugged Braydon, Shane whispered, "I hear you're fighting cancer." You can tell he's a conscientious guy who didn't want to bring up the topic if I didn't want to discuss it.

I nodded.

"Well, I… " He paused. "I brought you something." And he dug into his pocket and handed me a coin.

I raised a brow.

"This might not seem like something special, but it's lucky. I've even won thousands of dollars when I've had it on me. It's kept me safe when I could've gotten hurt. And now, I want you to keep it — just until you get better."

"But what if I don't get better?" I said reluctantly. "Shane, I can't take this."

"Hey now, you are gonna get better. Because you need to give this back to me."

I laughed, and so did Braydon.

"It might seem strange, but I felt like I should give it to you — and it's the best thing I have to offer because I know it'll help."

I glanced over to the flowers Mike had just planted, and that saying came to mind: Bloom where you're planted.

I held the coin tightly. Blooming where you're planted means always doing your best — no matter where you are in life. This kind man wanted to do something for me despite my circumstances and offered me this unique gift—a token he always carried. I had to take the coin.

"Okay," I said. "I'll give this back... when I get better."

Time passed. And when I've been at my lowest or thought I might never be cancer-free, I've held the coin in my hand and thought, "I need to get better. I made a promise to give this coin back."

Anyway, today I got home from my three-day marathon of hospital visits this week. I had the coin in my pocket the whole time, even as I pulled into my driveway and realized the perennials Mike planted last year had come back to life and bloomed.

I'm gonna bloom right where I'm at. Sure, life didn't go exactly how I expected, but I've become a better person because of the soil and conditions God chose to plant me in.

Dreams of Italy

"It's like Make-A-Wish, and you've been selected."

I paused, a bit dumbfounded. I've been nominated for a few things since my cancer diagnosis, but this is the first time I'd "been selected."

"Think of something you want to do with your family, something really big."

My first thoughts revolved around Italy. My biggest bucket list item has always been to visit Italy — especially where my mom's family is from in Calabria. Going there with Mike and the kids, well, that would be a dream come true. But I didn't want to ask for something so huge. Instead, I said, "Maybe they could pay for us to go to Lava Hot Springs. The day passes cost under $20 a person, and we love going there." I figured this was something fun but not extravagant.

"Are you kidding?" the woman said on the phone. "That's not nearly big enough. You need to think of something big."

So, I thought about it for the next couple of days, and when I called her back, I had thought of something enormous. It was beyond going to Lava Hot Springs. Beyond going to Italy. Beyond landing on the moon. "I want to meet Oprah," I said.

She snorted with laughter before trying to calm herself. "We can't help you meet Oprah, Elisa," she said.

Ring the Bell

And I immediately felt my skin heat to the temperature of total embarrassment.

"Go look at our website and see what we can do. Go look at what other people have asked for."

I saw that they built ramps to go into people's houses. They've paid for big vacations to different states. They've bought people old cars.

But I still felt mortified, so I called one of my best friends to vent. "Oprah? How utterly stupid?" I said, pouring my guts out to her.

But instead of instantly consoling me, she laughed and laughed. "Come one, Elisa. This story is hilarious. You have to admit. It *is* a little funny."

She is an incredible person, pretty well off, but it hasn't ruined her. I remember talking with her about wealth once. "It won't bring the people we love back," she said. And I knew this was a close-to-home subject since she's had family members die from cancer. Maybe that's one of the reasons we've gotten closer since my diagnosis. She understands what I'm going through.

"So, what are you gonna do now?" my friend asked.

"Well, I've decided to call the lady to tell her to give the money to someone else—maybe a kid or something. I think someone else could use it more than I can."

Months passed, and I didn't hear from that organization again. I hoped the representative found someone who could think of an appropriate wish, something that would change their lives. "I wonder what *they* picked," I told my friend one day, and she said it was interesting I brought that up because she had a surprise for me.

"It's not just me," she explained. "I've gotten together with a few other people about this. Don't get too excited because we're just covering the plane tickets. But... "

I held my breath.

"We're buying you and your family tickets to Italy."

I nearly dropped my phone. "What?" I stared ahead blankly. "You can't do that. That is so much money. And I'm still so sick. I don't know how long I'll live." I was trying to be realistic.

Silence. Then finally, "Elisa, I just read your book. You remember the man you met—the one who said he got better for a few years, but the cancer came back? He said his advice to you would be to live to the fullest if you ever had the chance because you never know when it might come back."

"I remember," I said.

"I have so many family members who died of cancer. They didn't get to live out their dreams. But you... *You* have the chance. And I want to help give you and your family that opportunity. Take a leap of faith."

I became a blubbering mess, and I wondered how I would ever pay this person (and the other contributors) back.

"Just promise me," she said, "I want to remain anonymous, and so do the other people who pitched in. Just have a great time and promise you'll write about it. All of us read your stuff."

Ring the Bell

Mike and I booked the tickets almost a year in advance. This really was being optimistic. Even though one provider said I could get better, several other oncologists confirmed, once again, that this advanced cancer is terminal.

I felt several odd emotions and kept thinking someone else deserved this more. Plus, I didn't know if I'd live long enough to see the trip come to fruition. And what if I did miraculously get better? People would probably feel bad they'd donated.

"Are you kidding?" Mike asked when I told him about my worries. "Everyone wants you to get better. These people love you. Just let the worries go and enjoy their kindness."

I thought about one person who confessed that they'd donated to this trip as well. They're a fellow cancer patient who is on palliative care and can no longer travel. That was so humbling. "I'm so happy for you," he said. "I've been to Italy. And now I want you and your family to go before it's too late."

It's odd to think that so many miracles have happened since doctors diagnosed me with terminal cancer: I got to sing the national anthem for a semi-pro baseball game. My memoir got published by a real publisher and became a bestseller. I went skinny-dipping with Mike—even though he seemed a bit worried I'd get swept away in the current. And now we planned to visit Italy. The wheelchair would help so much too, since my stamina remained low. But that was a small price to pay. Someday we'd be going to Italy—I just needed to stay alive long enough.

Like a Character in a Novel

"Stop living like you're in a novel," a guy said after bringing me on a date. I'd just told him I wouldn't go out with him again. "But I can give you *everything*," he protested.

I shook my head. "I don't think so." I paused, trying to explain, but I wasn't sure how. There have been certain things in my life that I've just known I was meant to do... like playing the violin — as if destined. I always *knew* God created me to play the violin. When I was three, I saw a violinist on TV and begged my parents daily for a fiddle. Once I hit kindergarten, they finally acquiesced and let me take lessons.

We found a wonderful teacher: Atalie Cook. I remember her beautiful blonde hair and kindness even when I pleaded with her to teach me new songs. "This one," I said once with so much excitement. "EL SHADDAI."

I practiced for hours upon hours because it felt like those Hebrew words and alluring notes drifted through the ceiling and connected me directly to God. His love would wrap around, and nothing else mattered. When that hollow, wooden body sang, so did my soul. At age eight, I learned that specific song so well that I even got to perform at an unforgettable place I called "Andrew and Terri's church" — instead of the real name, New Life Ministries. But, from a young age, I found my passion, unaware of how rare that was.

201

Ring the Bell

"What are you looking for?" the man asked at the end of our date, shaking me from my thoughts. "I'm young. I have a ton of money. Women have said I'm handsome."

"But with us, the important things are missing." He appeared perturbed.

We lacked what I'd found even as a young child with my violin. "Excitement. Adventure. Passion."

"You're looking for something that doesn't exist—a man who isn't real. I'd be good for you and your kids."

Sure, he looked good on paper.

I smiled a bit sadly. My children had been through enough with my first marriage. Unless I found the perfect person, I would never remarry. Plus, I loved being a single mom and didn't need to teach my children how to gamble.

"Best of luck to you," I said.

"You really should stop living like you're in one of those stupid novels you read. You'll never find happiness," the man told me. "Ever."

"But I already have happiness… with my kids." I said goodnight and walked into my empty house. My four kids had gone to be with my ex-in-laws for a couple of days, and the hours always dragged without them. I knew they'd have a blast because the kids' grandparents always make things fun for everyone. They cook, paint, play music, and sew. It makes things a little easier, knowing the kids are having fun. But as I drank a glass of wine and slouched in bed, the man's words replayed in my head: "You will never find happiness. Ever." What a manipulative man. Thank God I'd learned how to dodge that bullet.

I haven't thought about this for a long time, but for some reason, the memory came to mind this weekend as Mike drove me and the kids to a book signing in Helper, Utah.

Mike and Trey brought several boxes of books into the coffee shop and set everything up. And almost instantly, people began pouring in. I saw relatives and friends. I visited with some of my favorite people on earth and new friends who drove miles and miles to meet me. "I used every extra dime I could to hitch a ride here today," an elderly woman said—and it blessed my heart more than I can say. "My daughter died of cancer." Her eyes filled with tears. "I drove hours to meet you. I read everything you write."

I gave her a huge hug and a free book—it seemed to be the least I could do after she'd traveled that far. As we've been at several signings now, I've felt humbled by such encouragement and love. At these events, I've now met people from Idaho, Wyoming, Utah, Washington, Montana, Arizona, and Nevada. It's unreal.

Toward the end of the signing, a familiar-looking woman walked through the door. "Atalie?" I gaped, completely dumbfounded. "Atalie." My very first violin teacher had come to my signing. We hugged each other, and tears filled my eyes as she spoke to me.

"I've been following your story. Even when you were a little girl, you inspired me to try new things and embrace life." She looked me up and down.

Ring the Bell

And I wondered what she might think because cancer has taken my ability to stand straight or hold myself up for too long. But instead of mentioning any of that, she commented on something else. "I always knew you'd grow up to be an amazing woman. And you did. Look at you now."

I'm unsure what it was, but her words hit me, meaning so much. My growth is what matters, not any of that other finite stuff.

I caught sight of Mike then, shaking hands with someone across the room. "You can't believe a word she writes about me," he said, his voice always carrying. "She wears rose-colored glasses when it comes to me." I had to giggle because he's so perfect in my eyes—my exceptional, wonderful, goofball man.

Indy talked with someone nearby, explaining how cool it is to be in an "actual book," and I spotted my Uncle Bob and Aunt Kathy smiling at me with so much love.

"You're gonna make it through this cancer business," my cousin, Jesse, told me. "I just know it."

As we drove home the next day, I thought about how strange it is; no matter how hard life gets, if we can look for the bright side, beautiful moments follow.

Cancer has brought me closer to my family and helped me appreciate everything. I've realized what I've always wanted...

At different points in my life, I felt like my overarching plot is a romance, a comedy, a mystery, or even a tragedy. But right now, my book is truly an adventure. And I'm proud to say that the rich guy I dated was wrong. My joy isn't something that comes and goes. It's rooted in gratitude, and it blooms even in adversity.

"You need to be grateful. All you think about is food." Indy's little voice trailed from her room and drew my curiosity.

I'd called in sick to work, which is extremely hard for me. And I'd been lying in bed moments before, feverish and dwelling on the fact that I've been sick every day for over two years. Luckily, Indy broke me free of my unhappy reverie.

"I'm serious," she said to her cat.

Indy had her back to me, and her curls and the big bun on the top of her head bounced as she talked. If you're ungrateful, it is my fault because I'm your mama. You need to see an example — I should show you how grateful *I* am." Indy pointed to an apron that was proudly displayed by her dresser.

"You see that apron?" she asked her cat. "It represents hours of hard work. I made that with fabric from Norma Furniss! It was tough to make, but you know what? I won first place in a contest for that thing. So it helps me remember that I can do anything if I put my mind to it. And I'm grateful for that."

Nova, Indy's tortoiseshell cat, just meowed as if she didn't have a care in the world.

Ring the Bell

"Now, tell me something you're grateful for," Indy prompted, but Nova simply flopped on her side before licking her limp paws.

"Don't you give me those Puss-'n'-Boots eyes?" Then Indy giggled. "Tell me something you're grateful for."

Nova finally sashayed over to her dry food. She sniffed at it, stuck her nose in the air, and placed her paw on an unopened can of wet food.

"Oh, Nova. I just said all you think about is food." Indy paused, deep in thought. "But... at least you have something to be grateful for. It is a start."

Indy stood and prepared to turn—but I didn't want her to know I'd been snooping.

"Mama?" she asked as I tried to dart past the door, but I can't move as quickly as I used to. And I kind of hobble-limped.

"Oh. Hi, Indy," I said, nonchalantly peeking my head in. "What are you up to?"

"Just trying to teach Nova how to be grateful. Boy, do I have my work cut out for me?"

I laughed and nodded. Little did Indy know that she'd said the exact words I needed to hear. It's always a good time to be grateful—even if it is for wet cat food.

Belinda's Advice

Thirteen years ago, something drew me to the little fabric shop tucked away into the back corner of Main. I trudged toward the dilapidated door and then paused.

Why was I there?

"Belinda's" remained the most expensive fabric store in town, and—to be honest—their selection wasn't great. Yet, there I stood.

After stepping inside and being blasted by the aggressive air conditioner, I sidled toward some watermelon-print fabric near the register. I couldn't really concentrate on that fabric, though, too distracted from my dreams the night before. I'd fought with my husband at the time. We both went to sleep angry, and I'd dreamed about my ex-boyfriend from high school.

"What's wrong?" the elderly lady at the register asked, pulling down her glasses and studying how I absently pet the watermelon fabric.

I set the cotton down. "Just a long night." A sigh left my throat before I walked toward the exit, deciding to go. I didn't make it far because the woman belted, "I'm bored. And I love a good story. Mind telling me yours?"

She positioned two stools across from each other at the register and selflessly listened to how guilty I felt about dreaming of my ex. "Why would I have a dream like that?" I nearly sobbed. "I feel terrible. It's been forever since high school. I told

207

one of my friends, and she said this isn't normal at all."

The woman laughed and rested a wrinkled hand on my shoulder. "Listen. I'm 85 years old. And what you're going through is completely normal. Do you have time to hear my story?"

I nodded, pretty enthralled.

"My husband died five years ago. We were married for nearly 50 years, but like you, whenever we had problems, I started thinking about—or even dreaming about—my old beau from high school."

"Woah! Even after 50 years?"

She looked down and nodded. "Yeah. So last year, I contacted my old beau. Things seemed great at first, but guess what happened... I finally remembered why I broke up with him in high school. He'd never changed. We split for the same reason a lifetime later, just being the same core people."

I felt utterly stunned.

"My point is: I spent all that time regretting not being with a man who wasn't right for me. I remembered the good and forgot the bad, only to realize I broke up with him in the first place for a reason. All that time wasted... wondering 'what if.'"

We hugged each other before I left, and she gave me a red sucker—even though I was a grown woman.

Thirteen years have passed, and I know I'll never forget that woman and her story. Although I'm happily remarried, there are other life choices I often look back on with regret. Since I have what doctors are calling "terminal" cancer, I've assessed my life in greater detail than if I would've died suddenly.

Should I have traveled? Spent more time with my kids? Cleaned less? Regretted less (irony)? Worked fewer hours? (Who gets to the end of their life and wishes they'd worked more?)

But then I realize that woman's advice still stands, and maybe Katherine Anne Porter said it best: The past is never where you think you left it.

If you're like me and you've ever struggled after ruminating over regrets, I'll leave you with one more quote: The grass is greener where you water it.

The only thing we can change is the present.

The squirrel bounded onto the freeway, and I stopped breathing. The car in front of us sped onward despite its tiny obstacle, and when the squirrel resurfaced again, its back half had turned into goo while its front paws frantically clawed at the ground. At that terrible moment, the creature faced me as if staring directly into my soul.

"Oh, my... " I clutched the car's dashboard as Mike drove over the squirrel.

Mike looked horrified. "Is it...?" I asked.

"I think so," Mike said. We both stared into the rear-view mirror. "I couldn't dodge it. It was too late."

The words hit me. "Too late," I repeated. Oddly, the situations that strike me now — things that generally wouldn't have haunted me before my cancer diagnosis—plague me for days, weeks, and even months.

I thought of the squirrel, now glued by death to the unforgiving freeway, and for some reason, it brought back a traumatic memory from 10 years ago.

I drove down I-15 in Salt Lake City. The day seemed bland, and I didn't expect something irrevocable to happen. Then, out of nowhere, a distant car—a Cadillac—in the fast lane swerved, slamming into the median. It pinballed across the lanes a couple of times, miraculously dodging traffic.

At 80 mph, I approached at an alarming rate and seemed to be the one who wouldn't get away. Within moments, the Cadillac slid sideways as if floating across the freeway until it totally faced the *wrong* direction. Then time stopped.

An elderly couple sat in the car directly in front of me. The woman's shoulder-length gray hair drifted out a bit to the side, performing an underwater ballet, and the man's eyes flew open so wide he looked like a grasshopper. They both stared at me as my eyes darted from one to the other. And instantly, the terrifying thought came to me that one of them would die that day.

I slammed on my brakes, hoping to escape their car which still faced me but continued sliding sideways.

I'm unsure how, but we must've missed each other by inches—so close to death I felt a suction-like wind pulling my vehicle just as their front bumper cleared mine.

Ring the Bell

My foot shook as I shoved the gas pedal completely to the floor and somehow got away when their car lurched into the next lane.

Within seconds, a gut-wrenching smash jolted everything, and I turned to witness the worst wreck imaginable. The elderly couple who'd been driving the blue Cadillac hit an SUV head-on. Metal flew everywhere, and glass crunched.

All the traffic behind screeched to a sickening stop, and the accident became a broken cog, binding every gear of Salt Lake's southbound freeway system.

I'd pulled over in the distance, rubbernecking in complete shock. But I couldn't bring myself to get out and go back. I saw heroes rushing to the scene, talking frantically on their cell phones, and screaming in disbelief. But I knew I couldn't stand the grisly nature of such an accident. So, I put on my blinker, got back into the fast lane, and sped away.

That night when I watched the news, a peppy newscaster talked about a horrible accident on I-15. "One fatality has been reported," she said, her blonde hair staying hair-sprayed in place despite animated movements. "Another person is in critical condition, and several other people were injured."

I wondered then about the two people in the blue Cadillac. The catastrophe had seared their faces into my mind. And I kept thinking how strange it was that I might've been the last person one of them ever saw. Or how I might've been the one to hit them head-on instead of the SUV. I could've died. And how sad that someone had. It was beyond sobering.

So that's what I thought about after the squirrel ran onto the freeway the other day. Everyone says that life is short, but on some days, life feels long. I guess what I'd like to keep in the forefront of my mind is that life is unexpected—and it's not guaranteed.

I hope whoever died in that accident realized what's important *before* that horrific day... After what I've gone through with cancer, I can't imagine death without warning. Doctors keep telling me that despite some good news (about a few of my tumors not growing), I still know what I'll die from. I just don't know when.

Meeting Doug Sayer

I've met some legendary people in my lifetime: some who I knew would significantly impact my life and others who have changed the world. It's incredible to meet both kinds of people, but there's something extraordinary about seeing a world changer up close. They have this energy about them that instantly builds excitement and innovation. And even in a few moments, you can catch that… "Non so cosa"—in Italian, that means, "I don't know what." I remember feeling this when I met Stephen Covey and later stayed at his home while fiddling as a homeless street musician in Hawaii. And I also felt that while visiting with Douglas Sayer.

Many of you might recognize this name, especially if you're from Idaho. Doug started Premier Technology with his beautiful wife, Shelly, in 1996. Since then, it's accomplished the unthinkable: streamlining processes that have helped industries across the globe, creating cutting-edge technology that genuinely improves the world, and finding solutions that were once unthinkable. Yes, this company boasts over $100 million in annual sales, but that's not what impressed me most about Doug. What impressed me is his kindness.

Let's back up a minute. In 2021, I cried at my computer. Months before, doctors had given me two years to live, and I found writing to be one of my best outlets. But sometimes, even writing can be

213

devastatingly hard. And so, feeling even more sick than normal, I thought about quitting writing. "There's no point," I said under my breath. And I thought then that if God wanted me to share my story, He needed to give me a sign. If (and that seemed to be a *big* if) my writing benefited others, I needed someone to say so... that day. To say: Keep Writing. Honestly, that's all I needed, those two little words.

I posted a story and got several lovely comments, many about people praying for me. And while these meant the world, they weren't what I'd asked for. I turned solemn, thinking it had happened; my time to retire my pen. Then, just when I'd nearly given up hope, I received a comment from Douglas Sayer — thee Doug Sayer. And he, of all people, sent those two words I'd asked for hours earlier: "Keep Writing."

You know, life is astonishing sometimes. I never told Doug what his words did for me that day; I didn't know how. Anyway, time passed, and he continued commenting on some of my other posts. I told my son, Trey, about this one day. "That's the kind of guy I want to work for," he said.

"Huh." I smiled. "I think they do tours."

So, I reached out to Doug, and when I asked if they provide tours, he said "yes" and offered to show us around himself.

Trey and Indy got more excited than I'd seen them in a long time. Indy changed her outfit three times, and Trey wrote down a few questions he'd ask if he got brave enough. We arrived, and Trey looked at me with wonder. "I can't believe he bought some books from you."

"Right?" I said. "Trey," I tried remaining calm, "the books he bought... I really needed that money for trips to Utah so I can get the new radiation treatments." I swallowed the lump in my throat. "I just want you kids to remember how good God is." We've definitely seen miracles since I got sick.

After entering the building, Trey and Indy pushed me in my wheelchair, and Doug gave us a comprehensive tour. I asked some of Trey's questions (since Trey got nervous), and then I threw in a couple of my own. "I'm just full of questions." I giggled. "You can tell I used to work for a newspaper. But I wanted to ask... you said the most important thing you've found in business is to 'look ahead' to always stay above the competition. But what about life? With everything... " I paused. "With everything I'm going through, I've been thinking about the meaning of life, wondering, 'What's the point?' So, what's your best advice for life?"

He appeared thoughtful. "I guess my advice would be the same: look ahead. I always compare it to throwing a football. You know that the football and the shadow will meet at some point. I'm like the shadow, trying to keep up."

And as he spoke, I nodded, thinking how ironic it felt that this advice fully embodied what he'd done for me with the words "keep writing" years ago. He shared that at a time when I felt like no longer making goals or achieving them. Sometimes it's so easy to give up and give in when you're told you're dying from cancer. But his sage words, both in 2021 and today, hit home.

On the ride back to Pocatello, Trey tapped the steering wheel. "I told you he's the kind of guy I'd want to work for."

"Why do you say that?" I asked.

"You can just tell the kind of person he is, how he took time with us to ensure we all felt important. It means a lot right now."

"That whole thing was amazing," Indy said.

Trey nodded. "I'll never forget what he said about looking ahead. I know it's important to plan, but something about his words—I'll never forget it."

"That's because you just met a world changer," I said, and I didn't even have to explain further.

"I guess so." And that was the end of the conversation.

Chicken Murder and Aunt Jackie's Spaghetti

A book club read my memoir and invited me to one of their meetings. It became one of my favorite nights of the year.

"You can't go to the book club," Trey said because now he's extra darling, overprotective, *and* my boss. "You seriously can't go — you had a fever this week. You need to take it easy."

"I know you're worried, *Doctor* Trey, but I can't stop living because my body thinks I'm over 100." So, I hugged everyone and hobbled off to the book club.

On my way there, I hoped I'd quickly get everything in perspective: at least I'm breathing.

I wondered what these ladies might ask. Would they wonder about Mike and the kids or one of my many Godwink moments? Maybe they'd want to discuss cancer or staying positive despite hardship.

The real excitement started after everyone arrived, and we went out on the deck.

All of them seemed quite cordial, but I just hoped something would happen to break the ice. That's when we heard it — the scream of a dying child. I thought it was a child, but then it screamed and almost gobble-gurgled.

None of us knew what to do. You know the scene: we're all sitting there, eating fancy fruit, and then something dies.

Ring the Bell

"What?" someone asked delicately, setting down a piece of fruit. "What is that?"

All of those fancy ladies stood and peered over the railing. That's when we spotted the host's dog, full-on murdering a chicken. I mean chicken *is* delicious—and I know where it comes from—but this was a bit National Geographic.

Soon the dog held it by the neck, and we discovered from the host that this white chicken had been one of her favorites. The chicken soon flopped uneventfully, and when the dog spotted her owner, she dropped the chicken and bolted like an armed robber.

I felt so bad for Danielle, the host. You could tell she loved that chicken (and not in the same way that I love McDonald's chicken nuggets).

"It might still be alive, right?" Ashlynn said.

"I don't think it's breathing," Crystal whispered as Danielle approached it. Plus, half of the feathers had been plucked from its neck, face, and left wing, leaving a bloody pulp that I have never seen at the grocery store.

Danielle squatted and placed her hand on its back. All of us held our breath and then jumped. Can you believe the chicken shot up at that moment—basically coming *back to life*—and started walking like a drunken sailor? "It looks terrible." That was the understatement of the meeting; it looked like Jonah after being puked out by that whale!

Ashlynn went down and selflessly edged closer to the murder scene, just wanting to help.

Ring the Bell

"You said you grew up on a farm?" I said to her over the balcony. "Maybe if you grab the chicken by its head and swing it around, you can break its neck and put it out of its misery."

She simply looked up at me.

"So you can do that, right?"

Ashlynn could light up any room, and her response to this made us both break into laughter. "I grew up on a farm, Elisa. Not a ranch."

"I think he might live," Danielle said, inspecting the chicken. I'd learned moments before that she is a physician's assistant, and if anyone held the fate of this chicken in their hands, it was either the PA or the farmer. Danielle explained that she could put the chicken in a particular area where it would be safe from the dog under the deck. And after a minute, she came back to her seat. We were all quiet, not knowing what to say. I had to do something.

"When you laid hands on that chicken, did you pray?" I asked. "Because if you did, I think you should pray for me."

Everyone laughed. "Oh, my gosh," Tasha said. "This is just like something that would've happened in your book." Tasha is the one who made this whole thing possible. Her husband works with Mike, and that's how the group heard about my book.

"Are you going to write about this?" Mysha asked.

"Heck, yes. I am."

And that seemed to be the beginning of so many jokes and a great conversation. One lady talked

219

about the white feathers in my book, TWO MORE
YEARS, and how she found strength in that story;
my mom said if you see a white feather, it means an
angel is looking out for you. Another woman
peered over the balcony and said, "Well, there are a
bunch of white feathers down there if anyone wants
to take one home."

Every once in a while, the chicken would make
a deafening noise under the deck. "Do you think it'll
make it through the night?" Mysha asked.

"If it doesn't, maybe you could eat it," I said.

"But what about all of that stress hormone?" a
lady said.

"Well… I mean… You could massage it as it
dies."

I will never ever forget that night. Those ladies
helped me momentarily forget about my hardships;
they made me feel so special.

"I can't believe this all worked out, and we got
to meet you," Tasha said.

"Honestly, I've had the best night. And cancer
doesn't seem like a big deal right now. I'm just so
glad I'm not that chicken."

I have an extraordinary family. I know everybody
says that, but when I say it, it's true.

My uncles are the stuff legends are written
about. They've cornered mountain lions and
probably choked them out with their bare hands.
They've gone fishing for Alaskan salmon, and
instead of catching fish, they caught bears. Some

can fly, build tennis courts, ride Harleys, cook steak, and more. One thinks 40 hours a week is part-time. Another is part Greek—part Chuck Norris (probably).

My aunts, well... they're classy *and* sassy. One was a homecoming queen and a fantastic writer. One has the best taste in the world. Another makes the fanciest jewelry known to man, and the others are some of the most hilarious people I've ever met. If they aren't hittin' you with glamour, they might be laying on some thick wit that you'll be mulling over for days.

This goes for *all* of my aunts and uncles, but the one I'd like to highlight today is the myth... the legend: my Aunt Jackie.

Do you remember how I told Ron Barrett to call my aunt after his wife died? Well, he started calling her every day at 7:30 a.m. for morning coffee. Then, he called her each morning during coffee and at lunchtime too. And when a few months passed, they talked during dinner as well. Somewhere amidst all that coffee and food, the two fell in love over the phone. And I enjoyed hearing about it whenever I could.

"You gotta set Jimmy up," a friend said after hearing about "Uncle" Ron and Aunt Jackie's romance.

"I keep telling people," I replied. "I'm only good at setting people up if they're over 70. Tell Jimmy to come back in 20 years."

Well, Aunt Jackie and Ron have never actually met in person, so when she came up with my cousin, I vowed to make it happen. "Maybe I won't meet him while we're up here," she said. "What if he doesn't like me in person?"

"He's seen a picture of you," I said, and my cousin nodded in agreement. "Of course he'll like you. He already does."

"That's not why we're here anyway," Aunt Jackie said. "You know why we came up." I must've smiled so big because she laughed and laughed. We've been planning this for years, but we live in different states and that can make things hard.

I have a lot of wild things on my bucket list. For example, my birthday is Groundhog Day, and I've always wanted to see the groundhog up close. I'm glad I didn't go this year because when they pulled the groundhog out on my birthday, he was dead. Talk about a bad omen.

Anyway, the biggest items on my list are skydiving with Mike and going to Italy. We're working on the Italy thing—I just need to live that long. But another huge item is learning to make Aunt Jackie's homemade spaghetti. I didn't know if I'd have to steal the recipe or what. But this has been a lifetime goal.

You see, she's a phenomenal cook. She makes pickled eggs that are actually good. She's half-Italian, and 100% awesome. So, imagine my surprise when I got a message from my beautiful cousin, Jeana, saying she'd be coming to see me with Aunt Jackie.

"We just have to see Ron while you're in Idaho," I said.

"But he's an hour away, and it's hard for you to go places."

Ring the Bell

"I don't care how sick I might be. We need to do this."

Aunt Jackie is brave and hilarious. I didn't know she was scared of anything until we took that drive. Then when we stood in front of Ron's door, I almost held her hand to give her strength. But when he opened that door, I watched something so magical unfold.

They couldn't keep their eyes off each other. I swear Ron's eyes filled with tears, and he held her to him. "You gorgeous woman," he said. "You're even more beautiful in person."

I've seen love in my life, but what I watched that day was something special. It was almost as neat as finally getting that coveted recipe!

Things Look Different from Here

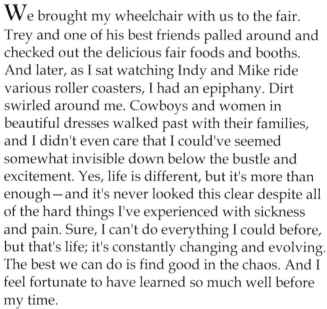

We brought my wheelchair with us to the fair. Trey and one of his best friends palled around and checked out the delicious fair foods and booths. And later, as I sat watching Indy and Mike ride various roller coasters, I had an epiphany. Dirt swirled around me. Cowboys and women in beautiful dresses walked past with their families, and I didn't even care that I could've seemed somewhat invisible down below the bustle and excitement. Yes, life is different, but it's more than enough—and it's never looked this clear despite all of the hard things I've experienced with sickness and pain. Sure, I can't do everything I could before, but that's life; it's constantly changing and evolving. The best we can do is find good in the chaos. And I feel fortunate to have learned so much well before my time.

When we got home, I realized my joy isn't always derived from being the active participant who's front and center. Instead, I'm content with seeing the happiness around me and still being able to watch my family enjoy our world. When it comes down to it, I would give nearly anything to see them happy, to spend one more day with them, and to see their smiles in person.

I know I'm lucky to be here. So many of my sweet friends at the cancer center have passed away since I met them in 2020. I know it must've been their time, but they fought hard to stay... They were cheerful and strong. They *wanted* to live, but cancer is a merciless, incompetent judge—and it doesn't care how much someone deserves to keep breathing. When I hear people taking their health or lives for granted, it almost seems unfair to those who fought hard to stay and still died young.

I wish it wouldn't take hindsight to see things this way.

Needing a wheelchair has opened my eyes; everything looks different from here.

I felt scared, like my impending doom loomed right around the corner. Despite calling this appointment "urgent," the providers were all busy, and I remained in the waiting room for almost two hours. They needed to take new scans and labs to see where we're at now.

"We'll be with you shortly." The receptionist came over, looking terrified to hear my response. "I am so sorry about this."

I told her not to worry about it and that I "had all day." But truth be told, I hated sitting there with my own thoughts, and after a while, I actually prayed. "God," I thought, "my entire body is falling apart to the point that this is insane. Not to be dramatic, but you took some of my spine when I felt like I'd just grown a figurative backbone. That's too ironic—even for me."

I sat there for so long, staring at the clock on the wall, freaking out. Tick. Tick. Tick. And that's when I fell asleep...

Ring the Bell

My consciousness floated in an area without gravity or sound. I didn't know how I could possibly think in a place that felt void of *all* energy. I couldn't see my body or anything. I could just sense an all-encompassing purity around me. A purity that just... was.

"Why did it take you so long to pray that I would heal you?" The words enveloped me, and I realized I felt them more than heard them.

"You're God. What's the point of praying for what *I* want? You'll do what you need to anyway. You know a heck of a lot more than I do." I paused. "Plus, who am I to ask for something if it goes against your plan?"

Nothing happened, and I remained, waiting for a response.

"I trust you." The words finally came from my consciousness, more gently this time. I already had cancer; the last thing I needed was God's wrath.

"Do you? Do you really trust me?" The words didn't feel punitive, but they did seem contrary. "You thank me for things, but you rarely ask for what you want. Why?"

"You know why." I didn't mean for it to sound angry, but it did. "When Zeke died, I begged you to heal him. I got down on my knees and cried. I spent hours upon hours talking to you, asking you to fix my son. And then — when I took him off life support, I kept thinking that somehow, some way, you'd heal him. But you didn't. Some lady even approached me at his funeral and said my son would've lived if I'd had more faith. Well, the joke was on her. I had enough faith it should've moved mountains. That's when I realized how futile it is to pray. You'd do what you needed to anyway—I mean, you're God. And after Zeke died, I did finally come to a semblance of peace. Nothing would ever bring him back, but I could see that maybe you had a plan. That we can find good even in harrowing situations. That Zeke was only meant to live a little while. Everyone—including me—became better just by knowing him for that short time. And I learned to find joy despite the heartache. Life is hard; there's no point in making it even harder by depriving ourselves of potential happiness that we let pass by during tough times."

"But you finally asked me to heal you. After all of this time. Why?"

"Maybe there's power in surrender."

"In surrender? Or in acknowledging pride? Elisa, be honest with yourself; you didn't want to ask me in case you aren't healed. You're worried you'll finally put faith into this and be let down again—like you were with Zeke."

I thought so hard about this, stumped. "I… didn't want you to know that I'm finally breaking, that maybe life is getting the best of me."

"And you thought that your actions showed strength. That it would somehow impress me. There are so many humans, so many creatures, so much creation—"

"You're right. And compared to everything, God, I'm almost nothing. And so, yes, I realized my pride no longer mattered. I don't care if you think I'm weak. I finally begged you to heal me the other day because this is hard. Because I want to see my kids grow up. Because I'm tired of seeing everyone who cares about me struggle because they hate seeing me so damn sick all the time. And because... I can feel myself breaking on some days. Constant suffering seemed doable the first several months, even the first year. But after almost two years of this — without an end in sight except for death — to think that life will never be the same as before my diagnosis. Yes, I prayed for you to heal me."

"You need to stop trying to win my love."

"But I'm not—"

"Stop trying. I know who you are. I made you. You are flawed. You're a mess. You're chaos. But you are also joy. I made you to be joy."

A strange kind of love washed over me. I felt such truth in those words. I've always wondered who I am and what my root is, but to get this confirmation, even in such an odd venue. It just rang true.

"That's why you see joy in so much — it reflects your true nature. The good people see around them; that's who they are. The good you see is *joy*. But it's time to see strength in unexpected places as well. Where you make joy out of hardships, strength can be found too. In weakness, there can be strength."

"Everyone's heard that, but what exactly does that mean?"

"It took strength to acknowledge that you're weak. It takes strength to truly admit to pride. Pride can eat people alive without their knowledge, and it can be *much* worse than any cancer."

"Even melanoma?"

Ring the Bell

"Yes." I could almost hear the mirth. "Even melanoma. Acknowledging faults is not a weakness or a sign of brokenness. That's finding room to grow as a person. You found strength in admitting that you feel weak. Your body might seem like it's failing you, but as it fails, you are growing in the ways that really matter."

"But... God. Is it too much to ask for both? Can't you heal my body too?"

"Elisa? Elisa!" the nurse's voice woke me. My head had slumped to the side, and my neck throbbed from where doctors have said another tumor is located in my thoracic spine. "We're ready for you."

"Okay." I straightened, then I followed her through the doorway. I wanted to be present for the moment, but no matter how much I tried, I couldn't stop thinking about that strange dream where so much truth laced the conversation. An illusion or not, I hoped I'd never forget those words.

Turning a Corner

My doctor ordered new scans, and something shocking happened. All of the tumors have started staying the same since the last scans! They said if things continue this way, I can possibly stop treatments in October and go on "observation." This won't mean I'm in remission, but it's the next best thing. It means they'll try to keep me "stable" for as long as possible. I'm supposed to be cautiously optimistic, but this could be a long time. *This* is a miracle.

I told my family, and some of them cried. Despite all the enthusiastic responses, the message that totally floored me came from my 12-year-old, Indiana. She messaged me these words: "Mama is going to be okay."

I cried after reading that because I just got the greatest gift: more time with the people I love.

My parents went to my treatments today. We all took a nap, and I woke up and cried a little bit at one point. I'm thrilled to be turning a corner, but I wish we all could improve at the infusion unit. Maybe I have to remember my first thoughts: It's important to rest in the hope that God will take everyone when it's their time. I thought all this as the music therapist started singing during my infusion. The words to DON'T STOP BELIEVING hit extra hard. "Some will win; some will lose."

All of us have won something in that place because we've grown through the journey. Some appreciate life more than ever before. Some have started finally pursuing their dreams after years of achieving what others wanted for them (instead of what they wanted for themselves). And people like me have grown closer to their families. But… I want everyone to "win" and get to ring that bell because they're cancer free. I want them to feel as good as I did at that exact moment.

I've been skydiving before when I was much younger. But this idea landed on my list again because I wanted something different. I wanted to go with Mike — and our kids — if possible. But I always wanted to jump from the wing of a plane: a puddle jumper.

We thought about it, but life and work got in the way. I kept thinking I'd do this or that when the kids got old enough. I saved everything for "tomorrow." And then time stopped. I've tried to settle into the fact that there are things I can't do anymore. Doctors don't even like it when I fly because I've had so many blood clots. Can you imagine if I went up in a plane and then purposely fell out of it?

But then something fortuitous happened. Sky told us she wanted to skydive with the family for her 18th birthday, and I wanted to go. So I called several places around Pocatello. A woman in Utah made me cry. "You have cancer. You could put the instructor in danger." She even went on to use the word "selfish."

Ring the Bell

I tried changing the subject. "Oh. Well... No worries. Um... I won't go. But how much is a down payment for my two oldest daughters and my husband?"

She wouldn't drop the subject. And I finally interrupted her monologue. "Enough," I cried, sobbing almost uncontrollably. "I'm still f-f-fighting cancer. I don't need this. You have n-no idea what I'm dealing with... or what my exact situation is like. I already told you I won't go." And I hung up the phone.

It took me a few days to calm down. Then I tried one last place: Sky Down in Caldwell, Idaho — almost four hours away.

"We help people with cancer quite a bit," the woman said. "It's a pretty common bucket list item."

"I'm worried because my right leg doesn't work well after muscle atrophy. And I'm always so nauseous from cancer treatments. The last thing an instructor needs would be throw-up hitting their face at terminal velocity."

"You'll be fine. We have instructors who are trained for everything." The lady on the phone, Denise, was so kind. She even assigned me to an instructor who's helped many people with special needs, and when we got there, he explained everything. He would bear the weight of my legs and roll with me if anything went wrong so that neither of us would get hurt.

"What if I get nauseous?"

"You won't." He laughed. "But it might surprise you how much I get thrown up on."

I balked. "Seriously?"

Ring the Bell

"You know how people throw up on rollercoasters? I guess it could be compared to that. But you won't. I just know it."

He'd strap me tightly to him, and we would land sitting. I couldn't believe it. My dream of skydiving with Mike would come true, but more than that, we would experience this with our two oldest daughters, Ruby and Sky, while our two youngest kids cheered us on. It would be incredible.

And it was. Skydiving a second time was different from the first because I enjoyed it with Mike and the kids. I basked in their joy as we watched each person land and while Indiana and Trey hollered for everyone, even saying, "The Sky is falling," when Sky did her jump.

Unfortunately, my right leg unexpectedly gave out when I tried to lift it before landing, and several seconds before hitting the ground, my right leg drooped at an angle, caught on the dirt, and forced us to pitch down. Fortunately, the instructor— rolled to keep us safe.

"Are you okay?" I asked the second we stopped moving.

"Are you kidding?" he said. "I'm totally fine. I do this for a living. I'm just worried about you."

After we returned to the hangar, when everyone had completed their jumps, I talked with Denise and heard stories about the people they've helped accomplish their dreams despite having disabilities.

I gave Denise a huge hug. "Thank you so much for making this a reality for me." I looked over at the skydiving instructor and the pilot of the plane.

Ring the Bell

"You've given all of us a memory we'll never forget for Sky's 18th birthday. You've made it so special."

As Ruby smiled, talking about how much she loved free-fall, and Sky glowed, looking at how they caught her $E = mc^2$ tattoo in a photo of her plummeting next to the moon, I couldn't help feeling the happiest I've been in a long time.

Who cares that I didn't stick the landing? I got to go skydiving with some of the best people ever. Sky had the birthday of her dreams, and we all *lived*.

Too Good for Our World

"I'm scared to die," she said.

I hadn't realized how sick she'd become in the last few months. "I think everyone is."

"Really?"

"Yes." I paused and thought about what I've seen throughout my journey with cancer and all the people I've met who are close to death. If people claim they aren't scared of the unknown—not at all—they've either never directly faced the dragon, or they're lying to themselves. Fighting death reminds me of skydiving. You might feel ready when you prepare to jump, but that doesn't make it less terrifying. I know I'll fall into death's embrace someday, but the thought of my body breaking beyond repair, unanimated without my soul... Well, it seems unfathomable.

The fact that she remained honest through her journey has been humbling. "You're so strong," I finally responded, thinking about some of our experiences together. "Whatever the future holds, you've got this."

Ashley exuded something special. She modeled in her younger years and could make any conversation interesting just by being part of it. In her 20s, she crafted visionary cakes that could've been featured on television. It wasn't enough that she completely excelled as a mother and wife; she could master anything.

235

Ring the Bell

Sometimes in life, you might encounter someone and immediately feel a... "non so cosa," but the details of it won't become apparent until time has passed. That's what happened with me and Ashley up in the mountains.

Our husbands are best friends — like brothers — so several years ago, when Ashley and Garrett invited us to camp with them, I could hardly wait. One day, Ashley sat by the stream, gazing wistfully at the water. "I can't explain it," she said. "I just feel so alive." Ashley loved it up there: the looming cliff-face, the refreshing steam, the pure power and majesty of nature. And instead of returning home, like the rest of us, she stayed with her kids in the mountains for days and days. I talked with her on the phone and ended up chuckling. That was her "something special," her own "non so cosa." She seemed ethereal — like some mythological creature, always meant to be wild and free. So that's how I picture Ashley now. She's sitting by that stream, saying how beautiful everything is and how alive she feels even though she's not alive at all — and she had to leave us too soon.

"There was no reason to be scared," she says, probably making an elaborate cake for God. Then I picture her sending love to her husband, kids, and mother. She died on her second-oldest son's birthday. That might seem devasting, but there is something good to find in the heartache. He'll always have a beautiful guardian looking out for him forever. Always protecting and fighting for him, his siblings, and the rest of their family. The day he first met his mother now marks the anniversary of when God deemed her too perfect for our world. Ironically, my son died years ago, and his viewing landed on my birthday. I thought I'd never like that day again, but now it's a chance to remember someone I love.

So, at this very moment, Ashley might pause up in Heaven while mixing ingredients. And nod about these words because we understand one another.

"I love your writing," she used to say. "It somehow gives me hope." It felt nice hearing that from a person I knew was so strong.

The point is that even though she died in her early 30s, she showed me what truly gives a life meaning. Instead of flaunting her talents and exceptionality, she brought out the best in everyone else. She made people believe in themselves. Ashley got it. She lived purposefully.

Looking back, I'll remember our time in the mountains when she looked like a nymph of the forest, and her gratitude for the simple things in life changed my view of everything.

Alzheimer's and Dementia

"**O**h, my gosh. Mr. Smith," I said.

He looked at me blankly, waved, then continued placing items on the conveyor belt at the grocery store.

"I'm Elisa," I went on. "You remember me? From the newspaper?" He called me with news tips; we laughed and joked. One day he called about a moose that ran around town. So many memories, but now he looked at me again... bewildered. "Mr. Smith?"

"I don't know you. But you seem like a nice girl." He smiled, looking much older than his 70-plus years.

Studying him, he had the same light in his eyes and an unmistakable touch of mirth to his smile. But something felt off. "Well, anyway... It's wonderful to see you," I said, so surprised that he didn't remember me.

A woman came from behind us and stood by him. "Excuse me. Do you need something from my husband?"

"No. Not really." I shook my head.

After a moment, Mr. Smith and his wife finished checking out, and he headed toward the door. "How do you know him?" his wife suddenly returned and asked when he'd gotten a few feet away.

"The newspaper. He'd always give me tips."

Ring the Bell

Her expression turned a bit softer. "Oh. You're that Elisa girl. You had the EC Stilson column, right?"

I nodded, excited she remembered me. It suddenly felt so essential to be remembered.

"He loved talking with you." Then she paused, constantly watching her husband as he approached the store's exit. "I'm so sorry that he didn't recognize you. He's... having some memory issues. It's been hard on all of us."

"I can't even imagine what you're going through. He's the nicest man."

"He really is." Then she explained that she had to "go after him," and she darted out the automatic doors after waving goodbye.

When I got home and put my groceries away, I sat on my front porch and waited for the kids to get home from school. The wind licked my face like a dog, and I felt so happy to be home. Birds whistled, sending cryptic messages through the trees. And I closed my eyes and felt every bit of "life" seep into me.

Sometimes it's hard not dwelling on the tough things in this world—how people can lose their memories and really their stories, and how fast one can lose health, relationships, status, and so many other things on a whim.

But as I felt the wind lighting my skin on fire with insight and the birds trilling above me, I remembered Mr. Smith's eyes and how he hadn't changed. His spirit is still the same, filled with the jovial mirth and sense of play he always showed everyone. He made people feel important and unique — and I bet he still does.

It's sad when you lose that tie to a memory, though. I can tell people what it was like when he called about the moose and other things, but now I'm the only one who carries those stories around. And when I'm gone, that experience will be gone too. No matter how much I talk or write about it, that will disappear. Like everything we know here on earth. Everything — I believe — except love.

Yet, sitting on the porch, none of life's heartaches seemed to matter because I felt the true beauty of change. If I were a conscious observer of life, I wouldn't want to freeze time and stifle everything; I'd want it to flow through me: the good, the bad, all of it.

The kids got home, and I gave them enormous hugs. "You coming inside?" Trey asked.

"I'll be there in a minute," I said.

So, I still don't know how I feel about poor Mr. Smith, but I hope to see him and his wife again. Sure, he might not recognize me, but I'd love to offer a kind word that will hopefully brighten his day like he always brightened mine.

Preparing for gallbladder surgery isn't a big deal for an average person, but I guess I'm not normal anymore. We just discovered that cancer treatments did something bad to my gallbladder, and I need to get it removed as soon as possible. So, I stayed at the hospital for hours, undergoing various tests, including extensive labs, an EKG, and much more. I'm sure the surgery itself will be straightforward. I've been through worse. But as I waited for the surgeon, everything suddenly felt insurmountable.

"Are you doing okay?" the doctor asked right after entering the room.

"I'm happy today," my voice shook as I forced a smile onto my face, "because you guys have upped your game. Can you believe they gave me free soap to use the night before my surgery?"

He laughed. "You know, *that's* why you're doing so well—your sense of humor. I read your chart." He paused. "Do you realize how lucky you are?"

"What do you mean?"

He donned his glasses. "Most people would've given up by now. That's one thing, but sometimes it doesn't matter how much people fight. Once melanoma enters the brain, it's almost unheard of for the cancer to stay the same size or even shrink. We don't like to tell patients that, but it's true. You're probably one of the luckiest people I've ever met. You're still here, and you look great."

I'm unsure why, but tears flooded my eyes. "Oh... I don't mean to cry."

"Hey, you're okay. You've been through a lot. I have a couple of extra minutes. What's bothering you?"

I couldn't believe he even said that. Most doctors are busy going from patient to patient, but this guy seemed to care. So, I gave him a brief synopsis of my situation and said I didn't know if I should continue getting treatments. "Am I just prolonging the inevitable?"

"You are fighting for more time with your husband and kids, right?" he asked, and I nodded. "So, even if you are prolonging the inevitable, at least that means you'll have more time with your family. And… I honestly think you might beat this. You are stronger than you think."

After he left, a nurse came to tell me I could go. "I heard you had a bad week?" she asked.

"Yeah, the surgery I can handle, but this journey with cancer isn't easy."

"Can I tell you something that might brighten your day?" she asked.

I studied her face, curious. "Sure."

"The nurses were all talking about you earlier. We think you look like a Disney princess. We would've never known that you're fighting cancer — especially such advanced melanoma."

I snorted — actually snorted. "Imagine Belle or Snow White or Ariel with cancer. That is a strange thought," I said.

She nodded. "But somehow, they'd make it look good."

So, I left the hospital to get approved for that upcoming surgery. The medical staff made such a difference for me; they renewed my strength.

It had been a rough week but a good one too. I got called a Disney princess despite having cancer. I know life could be better, but you know what... I'll take what I can get.

When Dreams Become Reality

"**Y**ou see the world weird," the girl said from the hallway. I sat in the elementary library, reading a book instead of going to recess.

"Lindsay, that's not very nice," the librarian said, but Lindsay had already darted out of sight.

"Mrs. Campbell," I said, putting a bookmark in ANNE OF GREEN GABLES and turning to the middle-aged woman. "Do you think I'm weird? I don't have many friends. And I'm usually either reading or hanging out with my cat."

She laughed so sweetly that her voice almost sounded like little bells. "No, Elisa. You're just you. And you see beauty in everything. That's not weird. You're just lucky."

I remember the first time Lindsay called me weird. We each had to use figurative language to describe the ocean. I'd closed my eyes and pictured it like liquid glass. I thought about how to crack the surface and see a new world of creatures and excitement waiting below. It felt magical—just like the library. Except at the library, I could "see" more than just the ocean. I could visit Shannara or Middle Earth. I could learn from people like "Anne with an 'e'" or Mr. Hyde.

Plus, other incredible things happened at the library too. My mom had brought me to an event there once, and a newspaper reporter asked the head librarian, "Is there a specific kid we should take the picture of? Someone who comes here often?" And of everyone there, they picked me: an unimpressive elementary kid. I even got to be on the front page. Yes, I had a big scab on my forehead from falling out of a gigantic tree, but I still got the glory—forehead scab and all.

"What do you want to do today?" my mom would ask on Saturdays.

"Anything?"

"Well... within reason."

"Can you drop me off at the library? Just for a few hours?"

She'd chuckle because that was almost always my answer.

I devoured books, row after row. The librarian even gave me THE GREY KING because I read it so much. "Just take it, sweetheart," she said. "We have an extra copy."

I wrote my first book in sixth grade—most of it at the library. It was 90 pages, about a hamster that ran away from its owner and embarked on a grand adventure. After I wrote that "epic saga, based on a true story," I noticed a change. When I visited libraries or bookstores, they didn't feel the same. Instead of many adventures waiting for me to discover, each book felt like someone else's dream. I couldn't imagine getting a book published or having other people read it. All of that seemed farther away than Narnia.

My first real job was at a library. I could hardly wait to work there and shelve dreams. I'd long outgrown worrying about people like Lindsay; that validation held little value. I cared more about people like the heroines in Austen's novels,

Melville's Ishmael, or even Margaret Mitchell's Melanie.

And years later, when I'd become a closet writer, I would bring my kids, nieces, and nephews to the library and bookstores. Every time I brought them out, they knew I'd buy them a special book from a specific Barnes and Noble. And the whole time they perused, I'd dream about getting a book published and having people read a few words that *I* wrote.

"It's a pipe dream," an elderly relative told me. "Do something that makes money. Do something that makes sense. Don't try to be an author."

But I kept trying anyway. And nearly two decades after writing my first full-length manuscript of 90,000 words, I finally had a book published by a real publisher.

"Can we go to Barnes and Noble?" Indy asked last Saturday. We'd traveled from Idaho to Utah for a bridal shower. Unbeknownst to Indiana, she'd asked to visit the exact store I'd brought all of the kids to years before.

"Do you think they have your book?" she asked.

"Probably not. But we can look," I said with a bit of longing.

So, we found the nonfiction section. I let my hand trail along the spines of many great books like NIGHT and ANGELA'S ASHES. And then, my breath caught in my throat. "Oh, my gosh," I said, trying to keep my emotions in check. "It's. Actually. Here."

I gaped, just staring at my dream manifested. I could hardly believe what it felt like seeing

245

something I've wanted so badly and fought for against all reason. Something so many people said would never happen. My dream sat on that shelf, proving that sometimes the impossible is possible if we keep trying despite sickness, heartaches, and setbacks.

Indy's reaction made the moment even better. "Hurry, Mama. Take a picture. I'll do my 'look of surprise' for you."

After I snapped the picture, she peered at me quizzically. "Are you okay?" she asked.

"I just wanted this moment with everything in me. And it was so hard to write while I've been fighting cancer. But now look. It was worth it."

"Mama," she held my hand and swung it, "that's cool. But if I'm good—I mean *really* good—can I get a book today?"

"Yes." I giggled. And I brought my smallest daughter to the kids' section, where she bought a book about a child who has few friends, owns a cat, and loves the library—she bought something remarkably like *herself*.

At Least Today Isn't Yesterday

Many people have asked about Sky, especially after reading TWO MORE YEARS.

"I just really relate to her," Heather said. She'd called to see how I fared after yesterday's surgery. "I finished your book and loved it. I thought that might brighten your day a little bit."

"You're right! And you're the best. Thank you for reading it."

"It *is* weird knowing all of you, though, because I could hear your voices throughout the whole thing. But Sky is so real and much like I was as a teenager." Then she whispered, "My mom had cancer when I was young too."

"She did? I remember you saying she died a while ago. Did she die from cancer?"

"Yeah," she whispered.

It does seem like everyone has been affected by cancer. And I'm shocked by the number of people who've died from melanoma. I might feel like telling someone my story—they could be the cashier at a grocery store, a waiter at a restaurant, or someone sitting by me at the DMV—and they'll know someone who died from melanoma.

"So… How *is* Sky?" Heather asked, bringing me back to the moment. "Is she still having a hard time with everything in her life?"

"Actually, no. She's been doing amazing."

I thought about my beautiful, vivacious Sky. She's my rainbow baby. That means she had a sibling who died right before her. And I always thought God sent her down at that exact time to ease the pain somehow. And she was just a ball of blonde-haired, giggly fun. She made it so hard to be anything except happy around her. I should've named her "Joy."

It's hard to explain what our relationship has gone through the past two years because we've been through the fire and come out stronger for it.

Sky moved to Utah her junior year—smack dab in the middle of my diagnosis when doctors gave me two years to live. She visited us a few times, but nearly six months later, that's when things changed. I remember her look of worry as we played board games and talked about life. "I miss you, Mama," she said.

"I miss you too."

And we both cried.

All of my kids have grown up in their own ways and have been exceptional throughout this experience: whether it's swooping in so I won't have to do dishes or cleaning hard-to-reach places in the bathroom. Trey and Indy do things "just because" now. And Ruby has bought groceries or taken me out on mom-daughter dates more times than I can count.

But Sky has changed in her own ways too. She rearranged her schedule numerous times to go with me to treatments. She held my hand as the medicine dropped into my veins.

"Every time I have a cold, and I want to call in sick to work," she said one day, "I think about how tough you are—and how you're sick all the time—

and yet you hardly ever call in. You've even worked from the hospital room."

Then she took it a step further and changed her entire schedule so she'd work the same time as me — early mornings. We now had the afternoons alone together. Those are times I will always treasure. Whether we ate fancy cheese, drank bougie coffee, played 31 or SkyJo, or waxed poetic, that year warmed my heart.

"You kids and Mike are like my best friends. I'm so lucky."

She got a little teary-eyed. "You too, Mama."

Heather waited, probably wondering why I hadn't said more. "She's in Montana right now, working for a hotel in Yellowstone for a few months. And she's grown up so much. I'm proud of her," I said.

"You must miss her, though."

"I do, but the job ends in a few weeks, and she'll be back soon. Plus, she comes to visit and sends me these videos every day. They are so cute." I told her about Sky's adventures and the wonderful people — and even animals — she's encountered.

"Elisa, is this ever hard for you? That you can't do things you see everyone else doing? I know you wanted to travel. And you loved hiking. Sometimes it makes me sad because we think things are going better, and then you need stronger treatments, more radiation, or even that stupid gallbladder surgery. Everyone loves you so much, but it hurts me thinking of all the things you used to enjoy — but you'll never be able to do again."

Ring the Bell

I glanced away, nostalgic, because my life has changed so much. "I did love those things, but what's even more extraordinary is seeing life's beauty through my kids' eyes. Sky called me the other day so excited about epiphanies I had at her same age, and I could hardly wait to hear her talk about her renewed joy in life. Ruby brightens every day, showing me the latest tattoos she's done—she's extremely talented. And Trey and Indy are so cute, raving about the songs they're writing together and hoping to perform onstage someday. I'm living it up—in my own way. Happy just seeing people enjoying life around me. It's not about what I'm missing but what God has allowed me to be part of."

Later that night, I clicked one of Sky's videos and watched it for the hundredth time. In it, she talks about how much she's learning and enjoying everything about Montana.

Tears filled my eyes, and although I feel like I have raised the most brilliant and accomplished kids in the world, what really matters most is that they get "*it*"—they understand life is not about what we can gain, accomplish, or conquer. The point of life is simply to spread love and appreciate that we're lucky to *even be alive*.

Penitent Man Will Pass

I love Indiana Jones so much that I named my youngest daughter Indiana. But I can't shake one of the scenes from my head today. Do you remember when Indy crosses that "invisible" bridge? He takes his first step of faith by talking about how "the penitent man will pass."

I've seen several people ring the bell: those who've decided to stop treatments so they can begin palliative care and others who've actually beat cancer.

I dream about this all the time—beating cancer. More than having a book published, visiting Italy, or going skydiving, I just want more time with Mike and the kids. Yet, as I strive for this goal, I find myself in a bizarre middle ground: cancer purgatory.

The cancer in my body stayed the same size for months. "We never say that people with stage 4 melanoma are in remission," an oncologist told me. "Unless you have a freak accident, you still know how you'll probably die, but we have bought you time."

So, my dear friend, Kara, and I left that office with Mike. The three of us trekked to the infusion clinic for my treatments. "Two long years of immunotherapy," I said somberly. "That's all doctors said my body can take. I just have to hope and pray that the 'stable cancer' won't keep growing if they decide to stop treatments." Then I paused and glanced at Mike. "I would've written my life differently," I told him. I don't mean to be irreverent, but I am an author, and this plot line could be skewed as a tragedy. I want to be in an adventure at the Temple of Doom with Short Round.

"That's not the point, Elisa," Mike said, and I wondered what he meant.

"Elisa," Kara interjected, always trying to make things better. "You're such a good friend. I just wanted you to know."

"I don't know about me, but you definitely are." She raised a brow as we continued, finally reaching infusions. "It's just one instance, but don't you remember my wedding day?" I asked.

"I didn't do anything special."

"Are you kidding? What you did was unreal. You fixed my hair so it stayed in place. You made sure my makeup never smudged. You took shots of Kahlua with me in that barn so I wouldn't be too scared to walk down the aisle. And you single-handedly made sure I could take my vows. It's just an example of the kind of friend you are. You made me feel beautiful, like I was worth something."

"Of course you're worth something." She paused. "I don't remember doing anything extraordinary. Isn't it funny what sticks out to people? You know what sticks out about you?"

I shook my head.

"Your positivity. I never told you this, but last year after I went to treatments with you once, I realized how negative I'd become at work. I watched you fighting so much pain. But you still asked how the nurses were and worried about everyone else. You stayed so damn positive. And I thought, 'If Elisa can be this positive — with everything she's going through — I can try too.'"

I bit my lip, and from the corner of my eye, I saw Mike smiling with what might've been his I-told-you-so face.

"I started a positivity board at work because of you," Kara continued.

"Really?"

"Every day, I add something to it for everyone to see. It's gotten pretty big — and I haven't taken a recent picture, but here's one from a few months ago. And it all started with me going to that one treatment with you."

I could hardly believe it. Kara is a director of composite at an elite manufacturing company. She even got featured as one of the top 100 "Utah Women at the Forefront" — a *huge* honor. It felt hard to comprehend that anything I'd done had even remotely impacted her.

"That's what I meant earlier," Mike said. "That's the point of your story. It's not about how to beat cancer. It's about appreciating what you have right now."

I decided Mike is right — the point of my life isn't to show people how to be happy *after* overcoming hardships. It's about finding true joy and remaining happy regardless of your situation.

Ring the Bell

Idaho has some pretty unique places. Island Park is known for its amazing residents and beautiful scenery—especially since it's close to Yellowstone. Sun Valley is known as a celebrity haunt. Boise is now known for its flood of Californians. Atomic City is... well, Atomic City. And Pocatello is a bit peculiar.

One of the main elementary schools is located at "666" Cheyenne Avenue. The police station is on "911" North. Prominent locals have striking or ironic names like Black or Craven; an OBGYN (who should've been a urologist) is named Dr. Cox, and there *is* a urologist named Peter. Many other hilarious names almost sound fictitious, but I'll stop there.

Plus, those aren't the strangest things. Pocatello High is internationally famous as a haunted building—and paranormal investigators travel thousands of miles to visit the place. On top of that, the funeral home (Downard) across the street from Pocatello High School got shut down for some pretty horrific things. What kind of town is this?

Downtown Pocatello has other oddities that many people find intriguing, and when I heard it boasts—not a palm reader but—a toe reader, I wanted to check her out.

"This is your intuition toe," she said, explaining how the length signifies my intuition with myself and others. She went on to talk about trust and hardships, among other things. "See this crease? You endured something really terrible in the middle of your life so far."

Ring the Bell

My eyes widened. That's when my first son died. But I didn't want to tell her anything personal, so I shut my mouth. This was getting strange.

"Do you mind if I touch your feet?" she asked.

"Go ahead," I said. I'd gone to see her more out of curiosity than anything because I'd never heard of a toe reader. I believe in pressure points in our feet and things like that, but I didn't expect her to talk about hardships. Then she said something I haven't forgotten for months...

I thought about this the other day after my friend died from cancer. I'd just been so sad, facing her fate and what will probably be my own.

My parents had asked me and Ruby to breakfast. I didn't tell them about my poor friend who died, but I thought about her as we drove to breakfast. We passed the 666 elementary school, the haunted high school, and the 911 police station. That's when I finally piped up. "It was bizarre," I said. "I went to a toe reader, and she said something I'll never forget."

"A toe reader?" my dad asked. My dad is a big, strong cowboy. This reaction was quite hilarious, and Ruby turned to me as if she'd burst into laughter.

But my parents are so sweet. It doesn't matter if we're talking about my latest art obsession, a recipe I just tried, or a toe reader; they always seem genuinely interested. "What did she say?" my mom asked.

"She said she could tell I haven't been doing well for about two years. And I hadn't told her anything about cancer. Not a word."

"Really?" Ruby said. "I'd like to go see her sometime."

"You should," I said. Ruby is so much fun. She's extremely free-spirited and full of life. It's been surreal to watch her business grow. When we go out, at least one person will recognize her as "that talented female tattoo artist in town." She's booked out until next year, and I couldn't be prouder of my baby. It's been fun watching such a tiny person do gnarly tattoos on anyone from housewives to burly bikers who would intimidate anyone but my girl.

"Well, what else did she say?" my mom asked.

"She asked if I feel like I'm paying off some type of debt by being sick."

I thought back to the meeting and figured I'd probably gaped at the woman, shocked during the interaction. "No. I don't feel like I'm paying off a debt," I'd told her. "But I am sick—and you're right. It's been two years. I have—what doctors call—terminal cancer."

"Are you sure you don't feel like you're paying off a debt?" she said almost gently. "Are you being honest with yourself?" And then I started crying. Because I *have* felt—somewhere inside myself—that if I'm sick long enough, God will see my suffering, His heart will be softened, and He'll forgive me... for everything.

"I've made some *huge* mistakes in my life," I'd responded to her. "And I keep thinking God will forgive me if I endure enough... " Forgiveness would be even better than being physically healthy.

She explained how I can be so strong because I embrace life—even the bad things—but I need to realize that it's okay to have good things happen too. "I want you to repeat after me," she'd said. "I am worthy of receiving goodness. I am worthy of being healthy. I am worthy."

I'd repeated the words, even if it sounded silly. There I sat, crying, getting my *toes* read, saying that I felt like my terminal illness could forgive my sins.

I told my family all of this on our way to breakfast. "I honestly don't know why I'm telling you this story," I said as we pulled into the diner's parking lot. "I just felt like I should."

My mom looked at me. "I'm so sorry you're going through all of this, Elisa. It breaks my heart."

We got out of the car, and my dad hugged me.

"I am worthy of receiving," I thought to myself as we waited to be seated. What a strange thing to say.

"Pocatello is such a weird little town," I told Ruby as we walked to the table. That specific diner slips customers their bills in classic novels. Patrons never know which book their bill might come in. Last time I got STRANGE CASE OF DR. JEKYLL AND MR. HYDE. Hilarious since the diner isn't too far from Hyde Street.

"It's kind of a different place." Ruby nodded. "Almost like Salem, Massachusetts."

So, the waitress took our drink orders, and I kept thinking how easy it is to embrace the bad because at least I won't get hurt from being let down. But maybe the toe reader was right. My friend just died, and I need to hope for health, embrace the good, and realize the obvious—that I'm not paying off some stupid debt. It's okay for me to be vulnerable and hopeful. It's just hard knowing the odds are against me, and—unlike a hand of poker—what I stand to lose is my life.

That's when the waitress set down all of our coffee cups. Everyone got a different cup with unique colors, but words shone on mine alone. I turned it around, excited to read what it said, and my breath caught in my throat. "I am worthy of receiving... " The words sprawled under a bright rainbow. I showed Ruby and my parents, completely dumbfounded right after telling them that story. "It's what the toe reader told me."

"*That* is weird." Ruby's eyes widened, making her look even more like an ethereal pixie.

"It really is," my mom agreed.

And so, after breakfast, I left the diner reaffirming that Pocatello is a bizarre place—and that the oddest things happen here.

An Unexpected Tragedy and Sorrow for a Dog He Hated

A friend recently experienced a horrific tragedy. Her little boy, under the age of two, drowned. I don't think anyone can hear this and not feel devasted over such a loss. But it's even more tragic when you hear how precious this boy was—his love language was food—or understand how incredibly kind his parents are.

I first met Tasha a while back. Do you remember that book club when the chicken got attacked by a dog—and consequently died?

Well, after discovering I'm a local author, Tasha kindly selected my book for the large group's monthly read. Each member purchased a copy of TWO MORE YEARS and read it over a short period. What made this miraculous to me is that unbeknownst to Tasha, I'd been considering ending treatments before she contacted me. This could've been devasting since shortly after this, some of the cancer stopped growing.

I'd just felt that my cancer journey had become too challenging. And although this would mean death, I didn't know if I could take any more. Doctors kept saying this road would end at one of two places: Either they will tell me they've run out of options, or I'd no longer feel strong enough to continue pursuing treatments.

Ring the Bell

A layman with no cancer experience called me during a terrible moment of weakness. He explained that if he were me, he'd be strong enough to accept death instead of getting infusions. "Death is natural," he said.

We'd worked together a long time ago, and I listened, not wanting to seem disrespectful. Then the conversation took a dark turn. "Too often people think about quantity, not quality." He sighed. "Do you have quality, Elisa?"

"Yes," I said. "Right now, I do."

"Really… " He paused for effect. "Well, other people — not you — continue getting care for the wrong reasons."

I cried after the call, but ironically, that's when Tasha contacted me. "We all read your book. We love it — and all of us want to meet you."

That book club meeting changed my entire outlook. And even months later, I found myself praying for them, hoping their kindness would come full circle. Those ladies made me feel like I should keep fighting for my children, Mike, and even a few people outside of my little world.

Anyway, time passed, and I got the devastating news about Tasha's son. At the funeral, before she walked into the main room, the irony of the moment tore me in two. She'd given me one of the best days of my life, and there I stood witnessing one of the worst days of hers.

"I want to tell you about a dog," a speaker said shortly after the service began. "I hated that dog because it was annoying." My brows furrowed as I wondered where this speech could possibly go.

Ring the Bell

Everyone else must've thought the same thing because the room got so quiet that I heard the second-hand ticking on a nearby clock.

"I got a call that this dog had been hit by a car," he said. "So, I ran out to see if the dog was okay, but it had already passed away. And… I felt horrendous. Even though *I* didn't like that dog, this was a huge tragedy. Plus, I knew so many other people had gotten joy from him." He sighed and tapped the pulpit with the fingers of his left hand. "Just to see him there, lifeless. Without his spirit. That was so… so terrible. I've been thinking about that for days. And now, hearing about James… To think that I'd felt so much sorrow over a dog—one that I didn't even like. Imagine how tragic it is to know what happened to such a precious little boy."

Of course, this made me think about my little boy, Zeke, who died at two and a half months old. I had to take him off of life support. And it seemed like over a decade before I began to recover emotionally. I still carry scars that will remain with me for the rest of my life. That being said, this is nothing compared to what my friend, Tasha, experienced. I can't imagine loving a child for almost two years and then tragically losing them. Yet, both situations might make you wonder, "Why? Why didn't they live?"

The speaker did say something that profoundly impacted me. When he talked about the dog that had died, I realized: That dog's value was bringing joy to people.

With every hardship, I've wondered, "What do I add to the world?"

Ring the Bell

I know it's important to tell people to see their dermatologists, so they won't endure what I have… But isn't there more? Maybe that's why the story about the dog resonated with me.

That dog brought people joy. My friend's baby brought so much joy as well. And, remarkably, that's exactly what I think would bring value to *my* life. When I'm gone, the greatest thing anyone could say at my funeral would be, "She made me happy." "She made people feel good about themselves." "She saw the best in me."

Joy. It's pretty simple.

A couple of people approached me at the funeral and said they felt sorry for how sick I've been. Their words struck me because I'd just been thinking about how lucky I was to still be alive.

"**W**e… have something for you," Ruby said gently, standing next to Sky. Sky's back from working in Yellowstone, and she's planning to live here until she finishes her anthropology degree at Idaho State University.

After making breakfast for Trey and Indy, editing for a few hours in the morning, and then sending Mike off to work, I usually visit with my two oldest girls around ten every day. "What are you two up to?" I smiled.

Then they both handed me a piece of paper and a beautiful vase with flowers in it.

"What?"

Ring the Bell

"We're just really happy, Mama," Sky said. I love how she still calls me mama after all these years. "You made it longer than doctors expected. You did it, Mom."

I blinked, totally stunned. They must've been keeping track of the approximate date when doctors gave me two years to live.

I opened the first note—from Ruby—and read her words out loud. "Thank you for being the most wonderful and magical mom out there. You're my best friend" When I finished the note and looked up, Ruby appeared to hold back tears. This is a rare sight from my tough tattoo artist daughter. Ruby is normally stoic and strong. In fact, when she dates guys, we don't worry about her. We pull the guys aside and explain they're about to get crushed. She's 100 pounds even after going to a buffet, and her spirit animal is probably a honey badger. Yet, seeing this softer side of a young woman who didn't want to lose her mother... It both broke my heart and filled me with humility that God let me live to see this day.

By the time I got to Sky's letter, I sobbed pretty uncontrollably. "You've taught me to be strong and to appreciate the beauty around me. Watching you go through this *has* changed me. It's made me a more empathetic person and helped me discover who I am and who I want to be. I'm proud of the woman you are and how you've handled literally everything with such fortitude. You're the strongest person I know, and if I could emulate anyone, it would be you, Mama. I love you."

Ring the Bell

I held my two oldest daughters so tightly and took a mental snapshot of the moment. I just wanted to remember that exact experience so I could pull it out of my mental Rolodex any time.

"What made you want to do this?" I asked.

"Now you have something special to remember you made it past the two-year mark," Ruby said.

"You love writing about us. We wanted to write something for you."

After they both left to work, my eyes wandered to the trees outside of our window. I spotted what I've seen dozens of times, but it seemed somehow changed. All of our trees hung thick with leaves: some mint-colored, emerald, or orange. But winter finally came before the trees could prepare, so each leaf cradled a burden of snow.

The leaves weren't ready to fall, though. And so, they cupped their treasure of glistening flakes as if solely existing for this honor.

Sometimes I feel like those trees, totally unprepared for the winter of my life. My leaves haven't fallen, and I'm only in my 30s, yet I'm carrying my burden, desperately trying to make this hardship look like a weight of diamonds instead of something cold and unforgiving. Something that threatens to steal my life…

But it's like three words Sky wrote in her letter to me: *Appreciate the beauty.*

Getting up every day to cook for Trey and Indy is such a gift. Spending even a second with Mike is the best thing ever. And getting letters from my oldest daughters meant so much more than words on a page. It's proof of a bond that I know is stronger than time... stronger than death. That bond is one of the most powerful things in the universe: the tie a mother has with her family.

Looking out that window, tears blurred my vision for just a second. Those trees were so damn beautiful. Although winter came before they expected, they're going out with grace.

Greatest Heist in History

I really wanted to do something to help a stranger, but I've lost so many of my previous abilities. I'd been mulling this over when we visited the synagogue that week, and they discussed this exact topic. "Everyone is capable of doing a good deed — or what we call a 'mitsvah.' Even the poorest person can find something to give. And we should *all* do what we can, even if we're experiencing hardships."

An older man talked about the Tzedakah box in his home. "We put money in it for charity. Even our grandkids put something small into the box. Everyone gives what they can, but we give with a joyful heart because we're excited to help others — we want to see everyone succeed."

"What can *I* possibly do?" I asked one of my Jewish friends after the Shabbat service ended and we'd eaten challah. "I don't have much to give, and I don't have the stamina to shovel someone's driveway, mow their lawn, or clean their house."

"There is so much you can do," she responded. "You're playing your violin at our services now. That's a big deal to us."

I gave her a grateful look. "You are such a sweetheart. I love playing, though. That's a gift you've given me." A sigh left my throat. "I want to… do something more. Something that doesn't benefit me at all. You know? I wish I could do something for a stranger."

266

Ring the Bell

"The perfect opportunity will present itself," she said. "I just know it will."

Mike and I went to the dollar store a couple of days later. We had $20 to spend on *anything* we wanted, and I could hardly wait to peruse their new items. As we looked around, that suddenly seemed like all the money in the whole world. A little bit goes a long way at that store. But after we'd been there for a few minutes, a man's voice carried over the aisle.

Mike and I glanced at each other. We didn't mean to eavesdrop, but I figured we heard the man for a reason.

"I don't have enough money right now," he said into his cell phone.

"He's the tall man who walked by us earlier and said good morning?" I asked Mike, whispering. "That sounds like his voice?"

"I think so." Mike nodded.

"I can pay you a hundred right now, but that's all I've got today. I'll have the rest in two days. Please don't turn off our power." His voice frantically ascended an octave. "We have a baby. We need the power to stay on." Then his voice went a little quieter. "Don't shut us off because we're $20 short. That would be absolutely cruel *and* ridiculous."

"It's our chance," I nearly squealed.

"But we don't want to make him feel bad," Mike said, almost laughing at my excitement. "That could be embarrassing if we just hand him money."

I remembered seeing the guy shopping a few minutes before. He'd appeared so meticulous, weighing each choice and only getting essentials like baby supplies and toiletries.

"I have an idea." I giggled. "This'll be like pulling off the greatest heist of *all* time."

"Um... okay?" Mike appeared to be bracing himself for impact. "Are we helping or robbing this guy?"

"Helping. We'll have to put our stuff back, but what's more fun than a heist? This'll be perfect."

Mike and I knew $20 wouldn't be much to a rich person, but it might help the guy keep his power on. "I'm gonna pass him," I whispered, "and then—like a badass—I'll drop this cash on the ground behind him. After that, you'll saunter—like you do—and say, 'Oh, no... Sir, you dropped some cash.' But act super surprised. Okay?"

"Sure. But—"

And before Mike could back out, I started down the aisle and passed the man who pled over the phone with the power company. The man forced a smile onto his face when he spotted me limping near him, and then he turned, whispering into the phone.

Perfect. I could drop the money and get out without anyone knowing.

At that moment, like the star of OCEANS 11, I threw the cash behind the man. *Yes!* But he seemed suspicious of my lingering presence, so I continued away as fast as I could and then went to hide behind the end of another aisle.

All right, Mike—it's your turn. I willed him to do something. Anything. But where was Mike? Finally, waiting longer than a virgin in the 16th century, Mike entered the main aisle at 12 o'clock, looking genuinely confused. That's when I realized the money had somehow partially slid under a display.

I can be an idiot. Plus, why is it so damn hard to be kind? No wonder people don't do it more often.

"There," I mouthed, doing my own version of sign language. But Mike's lip- and mind-reading skills are weak. "*There,*" I whispered, my mouth staying in a giant "O" before cinching together in agony. I did a butterfly signal that swooped toward the ground and under something.

Mike played it cool and ignored me completely—what a legend. And just as the unfortunate stranger ended his call and turned around, Mike seized the cash.

Thank Jehoshaphat.

"Oh, hey... weird. It looks like you dropped some cash, man." And he said it with this hilarious tone that would disarm anyone.

That. That's why I love him. A friend told me, "You have to look out for the funny ones." One minute you're laughing; the next, you've been married for years.

Anyway, the tall guy looked utterly confounded. "Wait. No... What?" I continued peeking, so giddy.

"You did. You dropped it," Mike said. "Anyway, here you go." Then he handed that man the cash, and the guy's eyes brimmed with tears.

"Oh, yeah. I guess," he said as if suspecting our plot, "that must be mine. I'm so grateful it... is mine," he said as Mike walked away.

Ring the Bell

Mike and I left the store, and I felt so capable and relevant. "We can't give a lot," I said, "but we still can give something."

"And it was exactly what he needed." Mike grinned at me.

Moments like that make life shine so bright. My friend at the synagogue said the perfect opportunity would present itself—and it had.

After the enormously gracious acts of kindness we've seen over the past two years, it felt nice doing something for someone else.

"What do you give us on a scale from one to 10?" I asked Mike. "How smooth were we?"

"I mean, I don't think we're gonna successfully rob a bank or anything anytime soon."

I broke out laughing. "We weren't that bad."

"Well," Mike said, "considering we almost lost the money, and you were doing gang signs from across the store... "

I shook my head in disbelief. "Honestly, I give you a 10. And me a two because I probably looked silly, almost throwing cash *at* him."

Bam!

Despite sickness, pain, and all the hard things this world can hold, we helped lighten someone's load, and in the process, we also made the day exceptional for ourselves too.

The crowd pressed in.

Ring the Bell

I looked about five times my normal size because I'd worn two sweaters, a jacket, and a couple of coats. Idaho is cold, but cancer is colder.

A man bumped into me by accident, and I almost fell. We crowded like cattle to see our children perform, sing, and play instruments. But the staff hadn't cleared a place for the extra flood of parents, and we bottlenecked at the back of the gym.

I prayed that Mike would come in soon since he makes everything better. But poor Mike dropped me off at the school's front entrance because I can't walk far. And as I stood at the back of the gym, I felt bad for Mike, walking a couple of blocks in the freezing air, his beard swaying in the wind and his brown coat zipped up to his neck.

Then so much pain pulsed over me that it banished any other thought. Tears rushed to my eyes as my legs shook from standing too long. I cussed myself then for pridefully *not* using my wheelchair. A woman must've heard me groan because she flicked her hair and glared at me. "People should stop complaining," she said to a man whom I assume was her husband, boyfriend, or admirer of women with heavy makeup.

I wanted to tell her why I groaned. Fighting cancer is exhausting. I'd just gotten over another infection, and on some nights, I cried myself to sleep because of debilitating pain. But I didn't say any of that. Instead, I bit my lip. I wasn't there to confront some judgmental blonde. I'd come to see my little girl play the bells and sing. So, I somehow weaved through the crowd without falling and asked a teacher if I could sit somewhere since cancer has eaten so much of my spine and my right leg.

"Oh, my." Her eyes weighed with worry. She quickly gave me a stool outside of the gym.

People gawked, their eyes ping-ponging between me and the stool. They knew I was a parent, so why did I sit there? And although I looked like a marshmallow of padding, I'd painted color onto my face, *and* I looked deceptively healthy. But still, every person who rushed toward the gym took a moment to stare at me quizzically. A man whom I know stopped and squeezed my wrist. "I'm so glad you're feeling better," he said. "Wait 'til you're in your 50s, and then you'll know what it's like to experience aches and pains."

I plastered a congenial look onto my face, but it took effort because his comment was completely thoughtless. "Thank you," I mouthed as he bounded away. Will I even make it to 50? Unlikely. And then I felt tears coming to my eyes because I'd stooped to pitying myself. Yes, mere aches and pains are so much worse than terminal cancer. You bet.

Most of the other parents there seemed near my age. Yet, they could walk around and jump and play. They could run up stairs if they wanted to. They could skip away from senseless conversations. They didn't have some expiration date circling their heads like a vulture.

I shook it off. Maybe I was being too sensitive. Who cared that I was the only adult sitting on a stool outside of the gym? Who cared people didn't know what to say — or became relentlessly curious about anything they didn't understand?

At that moment, I spotted a row without people. It stretched behind a group I knew would never judge me, and for that reason alone, I wanted to be there more than anything — by the kids with handicaps. So I lumbered off the stool and over to those amazing kids. I struggled up the stairs and slid into the row, hoping the "parent seating patrol" wouldn't see me. Some parents started to follow, filling up that section as I snuggled into my layers of clothing, so happy to rest my aching joints. Plus, it felt nice being by a group of kids that wouldn't say I'm sick "because of my sins" or that if I "could have more faith, I'd be healed" or if I "could eat the right things, it would cure cancer."

Mike came in and lit up the gym with his infectious grin. He spryly shimmied into the seat next to me, but his coat felt so cold that I leaned in, willing my warmth to transfer bodies.

Right after he sat down, a tiny girl in front of us smiled and waved to me and Mike. Honestly, her simple kindness held so much power. With a single wave, that kid with Down syndrome resurrected my mood.

The assembly started, and I remembered why I fought so hard to attend this crowded event. My youngest daughter, Indiana, shone as she played the bells and then sang several songs with the choir. I felt so proud that I could hardly stand it. The pain seemed inconsequential. The self-pity and sadness faded. And only joy remained.

Ring the Bell

The choir director asked the crowd to help the kids sing one final song. I harmonized, hitting all the right notes along with some stranger behind me. Sometimes, when we're sad about what we've lost, it pays to remember what we still have. And although I could no longer run or even speed walk anymore, I could still sing.

The tiny girl in front of me looked back again, and I winked. Her eyes sparkled as I sang along with the man behind me. Her genuine happiness grew as the words and melodies transported all negativity far away from the gym. The girl clapped and hugged herself with such enthusiasm, and I thought that maybe—in some small way—I'd made that kid's day a little brighter.

Right after the performance, Indy gushed, telling me and Mike all about her big debut. "Did you see that...?" or "Did you hear when... " Then, at the end of her questions, she asked, "Can we go to a victory dinner after this? Because I did well."

"Yes." Mike and I looked at each other, loving every minute.

"A victory dinner?" Mike asked as Indy ran to put chairs away. "That was darling."

As Indy continued cleaning up, Paul and Natalie Bitton came over, and I couldn't wait to say hello. They're one of the cutest couples I've ever seen, so happy and in love.

"I can hardly believe we met on that airplane, and our kids are friends in school," Paul said.

"Right? It's kind of unreal." I smiled at Mike. He always says the strangest things happen to me. "Your son, Ammon," I turned to the couple, "he's helped Indy so much. She's been nervous to be in advanced band, but he's helped her practice for tests and everything. She's needed someone to be kind like that, especially with everything we're going through. I just thought the two of you should know. He's made a big difference in her life."

They both seemed moved. "We think he's pretty great, but it's awesome to hear that from someone else."

I held tears back because band class and choir had become lifelines for Indy, something positive she could dive into and work on. I know she worried about me, but at least she had outlets for when she needed to get her mind off of things. Ammon, the band teacher, and other students helped more than they probably realized, especially since some of them didn't even know about my fight against cancer.

After the Bittons left the gym, someone else came over to me—Ashlynn from book club.

"Ashlynn! How are you?"

She gave me the biggest hug, and we talked until Indy came back over.

As we drove to Indy's "Victory Dinner," Mike chuckled to himself.

"What are you laughing about?" I asked.

"You just have so many new friends. It's neat to see."

"I'm the luckiest person in the world."

"So am I," Indy squealed from the back seat, "because we're actually going out to eat. It's gonna be the best day ever."

Ring the Bell

"Who does that sound like?" Mike raised a brow at me, and the three of us laughed.

I've decided to start weighing things lately by asking a quick question: "Is it worth worrying about?" If the answer is "no," I better move on and just enjoy the moment.

I Refuse to Give Up

Remember how I set my friend Ron up with my Aunt Jackie? After they started dating, things went so well that I called him "Uncle Ron." He acted like a teenager, raving about how beautiful and unique my aunt is. She did the same. "Doesn't he have the greatest voice?" she asked one day. And I loved... seeing them in love.

"I never knew I could feel this way," Ron said. "I've told her things that I couldn't tell anybody. The greatest highlight of recent years was the surprise of falling in love again and getting to know such a fine woman."

Ron has always been so generous, and a few weeks ago, he said he had something for me. I could hardly believe my eyes when I spied the brand-new purple fiddle. "I wanted to learn how to play, but I'm not feeling so well," he said. "So, I decided to give 'er to you."

I knew Ron had felt sick for a while, but I had no idea how serious it was.

I phoned him days later and left a message, gushing about the violin. I don't know if he ever heard my words, though.

My Aunt Jackie called a few days later, crying. "Elisa, I don't know how to tell you this. But... Ron died," she said.

"What?"

"He... He died."

Ring the Bell

I have no words for how hard life can be. I cried today, telling Mike that too many people I know have passed away. "It feels like once a month, someone I know ends up dying."

He nodded, and then he just held me.

"This is how the elderly population must feel, watching all of their older family members and friends die. People should be nicer to old people. They have it rough."

I know this is the one thing that's guaranteed with life: all of us will die, but sometimes it's hard to stare this reality in the face, knowing that whenever I talk to anyone, it could be the last time...

I'm so grateful for the memories and the good times. Ron wouldn't want me to "wallow like a stick in the mud," so instead, I'll pick up that purple fiddle and play my heart out, hoping my song will reach Ron in Heaven.

"I love seeing you this way," I told my grandma. We sat on a semi-modern couch she'd just designed in her green room. "Other people have had dreams about you too." I fumbled with my hands in my lap, letting them fall over one another like water. Several of my cousins have had similar dreams— with shocking similarities to mine. "Well... I'm glad you're doing okay. It's nice of you to keep in touch."

She laughed, even happier than when she was alive.

Ring the Bell

"With how often I dream, how come I hardly see Zeke?" I repeated the same question I'd asked her numerous times.

"It would be too hard for you to see him. If you knew how amazing it is here with him and all of us—without pain—it might be hard for you to stay where you are. It's surreal what happens once you see the big picture. It makes everything worth it."

"I read something strange the other day." I studied the clock on her wall and realized it remained stuck at midnight. "It said the reason life is hard is so we can fully appreciate the afterlife. That bothered me."

"Why?" she asked.

"Well... I don't like when people try to justify the pain. Maybe that's like trying to justify nature. Isn't it fair to say that some things just *are*? We all die. Pain is just our mind's way of keeping us alive and healthy for as long as possible—so we don't accidentally hurt ourselves and die from an unintentional wound that we can't even feel. Does pain really make us more appreciative of the afterlife? Maybe pain doesn't exist in Heaven because we no longer need a mechanism to prolong our own deaths."

She went to respond, but my alarm resounded, and my grandma... vanished.

Since my battle with cancer began, sometimes it's strange waking up. I don't always expect to be sick or in pain, and some days the pain blindsides me because I want cancer to be the dream, not the reality. Today was different, though, and for the

279

second day this week, I felt "normal" for a few hours. Maybe even healthy.

"It's so weird," I told Mike, "remembering what it's like to feel *okay*. I almost forgot."

"Are you doing anything different?" he asked.

"The doctors just switched my medications. Maybe that's it. How strange, though, to feel like this today... It's like some gift. You know it's Zeke's birthday?"

"Oh. That's right."

My first son, Zeke, would've been 20 years old today. It's unreal to think two decades have passed since his birth. "I can't believe that at 19, I'd already had two kids... It was so hard to take Zeke off of life support."

"I'm sorry, Elisa." Mike hugged me. "I still can't even imagine what you must've gone through."

"It was harder than anything. No one wants to see their child in pain. And no one wants to face ending life support for their own kid."

I thought about how much life has changed in the last 20 years. A good word for these decades would be "perseverance" because there have been some tough times, but somehow, we've always made it through, and I've tried so hard to remain strong for my children.

I wonder what Zeke would think about everything. How I published that book about him, THE GOLDEN SKY... How I've tried so hard to tell his siblings about him... How I've missed him *every* single day since he died...

I always felt that he had a front-row seat to my life, watching my choices and rooting for me. I know he does the same for the rest of our family too, because he knows how much we love him.

I kept thinking about Zeke on his birthday, wondering what he's thought about my journey, especially with cancer. I wonder if he could give me advice, what it would be. It's just been so hard to keep going. Many times, I've contemplated stopping treatments. Even now, understanding that in addition to everything else, I require specific infusions for my bones several times a year... the reality of my new life can be daunting. Yet, when I have mornings like I did today when I catch a glimpse of health, I'm so happy to hang onto that feeling, even if it's only for a moment.

As I thought about all of this, my eyes fell on a gift a friend gave me earlier this week: affirmation cards that I've already begun using daily with my kids. Every day we pull a card and read it to each other. "I am strong," Trey read the other day, then turned to Indy. "And you got 'I am unique,' Indy. That really matches you." Indy blushed at her brother's words.

So, after feeling somewhat prompted, I grabbed the deck and wondered what kind of advice Zeke would give me about cancer. I shuffled, thought hard, then held a card toward the bottom of the deck. I had to shake my head in wonder when I turned it over. It didn't say, "I am strong" or "I am unique." Instead, it said something I've quoted to myself several times. I might not be the bravest, wisest, prettiest, or most talented person, but I have tenacity. And I keep going even if I'm crawling along the ground, with everything against me except the complete desire to quit. I read the words repeatedly: "I refuse to give up."

Maybe that's what he would tell me if he could: to keep fighting. If so, I got the message loud and clear.

A Letter to My Future Self

Hands shaking, I pulled the crumpled letter from my purse and read the words on the lined paper. "You'll know when to open this."

The handwriting inside looked jagged, exhausted, and as if the author wanted to give up.

To my future self or whom it may concern,

Life is terrible right now. I can't tell anyone, though. They have enough on their minds, and adding my weakness to it would be too cruel. The doctors have said I'm dying. But I don't want my family to worry anymore. So I'm acting brave... putting on a show.

It's true that when you're at the end, you start remembering everything. But my life isn't flashing before my eyes in an instant. I've been processing everything from a forlorn hospital room, thinking about my childhood, youth, kids, and Mike.

Hospitals worry about COVID, so I can hardly have visitors. That's why I'm writing this letter. I don't have anyone besides the clergyman and nurses to talk with. The clergymen are more interested in talking than listening. And one of the nurses gave me an enema.

Anyway, the doctors have given me two years to live. If you're reading this, it means I either didn't make it and you've discovered this letter, or I've lived longer than oncologists expected. I'm obviously hoping for the latter.

"So why am I writing this to my future self?" you might ask. It's because I want you to remember.

The pain is terrible, beyond unbearable. Medicine barely touches it, but I couldn't live this way without pain medicine. Can you imagine feeling like an alien is eating away at your spine, devouring the bones, ingesting the marrow where it's burrowing to make a home? That's what melanoma feels like—as if something is eating me alive.

So, I'm writing this to tell you to be appreciative. Elisa, if you're still alive, remember where you were at the beginning of this when doctors said you'd die. Even if you're on hospice or barely hanging on, remember where you were and why you've fought so hard or continue fighting. If you're someone else reading these words, I want you to appreciate your health. Realize what you have. Stop complaining about the little things: your kids didn't pick up their backpacks, your spouse didn't do the dishes, or you're having a bad hair day and tired of your job.

They always say bad things happen to someone else—disaster strikes another home. Well, I never thought I'd be 37 years old and someone would tell me I'm about to die. They won't let me out of the hospital right now, and I've even been meeting with a hospice group. It's terribly sad listening to people who are about to die. But now the doctors say I'm one of them, and it's tough to believe.

So, don't let life pass you by. Don't put things off until tomorrow. Take that trip, try a new hobby, and shoot for the stars.

We never think bad things could happen to *us*. But death comes for everyone, and no matter how much we try to distract ourselves with unimportant things, what we should be doing is appreciating every... single... moment.

Take it from me: Life should be lived. I'm stuck in this hospital, and I may never be able to go home.

When it comes to the end of things, when you're looking at life in the rearview mirror, things seem different. It's not about fancy jobs, riches, or accomplishments... I guess at the end of everything, the greatest thing I could've done is make my loved ones know how much they mean to me.

It's crazy how simple things look at the end. So, Elisa, if you're still alive, I hope you haven't forgotten what matters. And if you're someone else who chanced upon these words, I hope you're living to the fullest.

From a woman who wishes she could get out of this hospital and conquer the world, please enjoy the moment,

Ring the Bell

I folded the letter and placed it back in my purse. It seemed crazy how hard I'd fought through hospital stays, surgeries, blood transfusions, radiation therapy, and infusion treatments. I almost died several times before that moment, but somehow — miraculously — I had lived.

I read that letter because… I. Got. To. *Ring. The. Bell.* Just before our trip to Italy, my biggest dream came true. I felt so excited about the vacation that our friends gave us, but it came in second to this. My heart flooded with happiness, and I staggered, completely stunned. I had no idea this would happen when it did.

Doctors decided to do one big scan before our vacation, and it showed the cancer hadn't grown since the last scans! "We still need to be cautious," my doctor said, "but I think this is a good sign. Just go out and enjoy life while you can. Live to the fullest, Elisa."

"But I thought you didn't want me to go on a plane?" I asked.

"And then you went skydiving!" We laughed so hard. "Just enjoy your trip." After that, she explained that my nurse, Susan, had sent antibiotics to the pharmacy for me. "The last thing you need is to get hospitalized outside of the country. If you have any side effects — like the last time — give me a call. It might be a sign that you'll need to take these. Okay?"

I nodded with tears in my eyes. "Okay!" Then she and Susan both gave me massive hugs and told me to stop by the infusion unit so I could ring the bell. "The cancer in your body has stayed the same since the last scans. Unfortunately, we can't say there's 'no evidence of disease,' but I think we should take off the training wheels right now and see if everything still stays the same during your next scans. Does that sound okay to you?"

"Do you still think cancer will kill me?" I asked.

"Most… likely," my doctor said, "but there is hope. I really think if you can just hang on four more years… They might have a cure for the specific mutation of melanoma you're facing. Enjoy your trip, Elisa."

So, with Kara and Mike in tow, I approached the Zildjian gong on the other side of the second floor. My hand shook, holding the mallet. I shut my eyes and prayed for everyone in that infusion unit. I could hardly believe I stood there, staring hope in the face. "God, please give strength to everyone who hears this."

I turned to Mike. "I can hardly believe I'm here."

And then, I swung so hard that the people probably heard the "bell" across three states. I didn't do a simple hit, though. Instead, I played a fun rhythm many people know: "Shave and a Haircut." Some of the patients looked over and giggled, and everyone clapped. I could hardly contain my joy. I couldn't believe it had actually happened—and all within a moment's notice.

A nurse came over a few minutes later and brought out several blankets for me to choose from.

"What is this?" I asked.

"Different people make these for our unit, so we can give them to patients after they ring the bell. That way, you can always remember this moment."

287

"I promise I will never forget it," I said. "Are you sure you want to give me a blanket? You already gave me my biggest dream."

She nodded, and my heart soared as I studied the three blankets. They were all beautiful. Two appeared extremely fuzzy and warm. The third one, a quilt, seemed more practical and something my family would love too. "I'd like to have this one if that's okay." I pointed to the quilt.

"I just knew you'd pick that one," Kara said, laughing.

'I want it to *always* be on my bed. This is the best moment ever. I hope I'll never forget this feeling."

That night, I pulled out the letter I'd written to myself. It seemed so tired and worn, laying flat on my beautiful new quilt. Yet, the words written there held a value that's hard to put a price on.

First Night and a Lost Bag

I sat wondering how we'd ever repay the people who sent us to Italy. Despite whatever the future might bring, they gave our family — especially our kids — memories that no one can ever take from them. I messaged a few people I discovered gave us money to buy the plane tickets and explained how I got to ring the bell. "Are you sure you still want us to take this trip?" I'd asked. "I might be getting better. Someone else is probably way more deserving than I am."

"Enjoy this while you can," one of my friends wrote back. He's dying from cancer, yet he selflessly donated money to help make this possible. "Everyone should get to visit Italy at least once in their lifetime."

"But what *if* I get better?" I asked. "You all gave money as my Make-A-Wish."

"If you're getting better, that would make all of us so happy. That's what we want," he wrote back. "We want you to live a long, happy life, Elisa."

"You're feeling hot," Mike said, bringing me back to the moment. We'd been waiting at the baggage carousel so long that we missed our train.

"Mike, I think they lost my bag."

"We should probably stay the night in Milan," Mike whispered before glancing back at our four kids. "Do you think the kids will be sad if we change our plans?"

Ring the Bell

I blinked, unsure. "We'd be on the train most of the time anyway." I said this to placate myself because the whole situation seemed like my fault. I'd brought so much medication in my carry-on that the security officers in France did a full pat-down. She even felt *under* my bra; they're thorough in France. But... I'd left my emergency medicine in my main bag because I didn't want anyone confiscating it. You guessed it, though. That's the bag they lost. Without those steroids and antibiotics, I could be hospitalized in a foreign country. And this fever didn't look good.

"I'm sorry about this. I should've brought all the medicine on me. I don't know what I was thinking."

"It's okay," Mike said, putting his hand on my shoulder. "You need your clothes and everything too. It'll be okay."

We decided I'd roll over to the lost baggage area — thank God for my wheelchair — while Mike fed the kids and told them about my lost bag and our new itinerary.

The missing luggage line for Air France stretched for eternity, and I grew hotter by the second; apparently, flying over the ocean isn't the easiest when you're fighting cancer. I'd make a *terrible* astronaut.

Finally, I got closer to the front and listened as people yelled at the customer service representative. "I have my fanciest clothes and my best swimsuit in that bag. And you lost it?" a woman screamed.

I know it's wrong, but although I felt for the woman, I didn't understand why she yelled at the poor representative. And, selfishly, I got excited that I could understand what she said in Italian... (I know it's not angelic to be happy about linguistics when someone else is upset, but understanding some Italian *is* awesome.)

I always wanted to learn Italian, but I put it off before I got sick. I put off so many things from my bucket list. And then, when friends paid for us to visit Italy, I couldn't make excuses anymore. Our entire family of six started learning through the Pimsleur app, and it's unreal how watching movies in Italian with English subtitles helped too.

Anyway, the person in front of me cried to the representative because Air France lost their ski equipment, and they'd miss their entire Christmas holiday with their family. I couldn't imagine how devastating.

"Mom, are you okay?" Sky asked, and I nodded. Sometimes when everyone else is busy, Sky remembers to check on me.

The customer service rep called us then, so Sky wheeled me to the front desk. The depleted representative's eyes drooped. I studied his exhausted features, and instead of complaining about my bag, I used my Italian to ask how he was doing. This genuinely surprised him, and despite my fever and pain, I mustered the brightest grin because the tired man appeared to be having an *awful* day.

"Bene." Good. "You-a have a lost-a bag?" he asked. "I speak-a English. If that's-a easier for you."

"You're awesome," I nearly squealed. "English is great."

Ring the Bell

"You have-a your luggage number?"

I dug through my fanny pack.

"We can get it on the next flight from France. It will be here in a few hours. Does that-a work for you-a?"

"Perfetto." I glowed.

The machine in front of him fritzed. It's different from the electronics we have in America. He immediately opened it toward me, like the steampunk maw of a crocodile, pushed a few wires back in place, and spun a couple of gears. Then he shut it.

"Wow," Sky and I said in unison, staring at the machine and then at each other.

"You like-a?" He laughed so hard that it echoed around the room. "I-a do it again?"

Before we could leave, the man asked, "Ma'am? Why-a... Why are you two-a so happy? We lost-a your bag. Everyone else... " He motioned to people in the room. "Are... how-a you say... pazzo?"

"How can we be upset? We're in Italy. We're actually *in* Italy," and then I giggled, "and we get to meet people like you."

He blushed and waved at us before placing his hand on his heart. "You two-a were the best part of my week-a. Grazie."

So we caught the shuttle and got a room nearby before Mike brought Ruby and Sky out for a beer (since people can drink at 18 in Italy). Trey, Indy, and I immediately fell asleep, so grateful friends gave us this trip as a gift and just hoping my fever would abate.

Busking to Use a Bathroom

"I'm related to the Coglione family," Mike said to the bartender, and the man almost fell over, violently laughing.

"That means... testicles," he finally coughed out the words. Then his eyes grew wide as he poured another drink. "Oh. You must mean Colleoni. Coll-e-oni." The pronunciation sounded barely different to my American ears, but apparently, it's pretty drastic to a native Italian. "That sounds close to a well-known mafia family here in Italy. Maybe don't tell people you're related to them."

The next day, we prepared to visit Trento, where the testic—I mean—Colleoni family is from. But transporting a woman in a wheelchair and rousing four people (21 years old and younger) takes time, and we missed our train by two minutes.

Mike parked me against a wall in the Milan Central Station, and the kids piled their backpacks around my wheelchair like a pyre. "I'll be back. I think the next train to Trento doesn't leave until later tonight. We might have to skip it and go straight to Florence."

So, Mike left to get tickets sorted, and about 20 minutes later, Trey whispered, "Mom, I need to use the bathroom."

"Me too," Indiana said.

"So do I," said Sky.

Ruby appeared to be the only one who *didn't* want to visit a European bathroom.

Ring the Bell

"It costs money here," Sky said. "A euro per person to use the bathroom. And they have bidets."

Everyone looked horrified. Bidets could be fun, though... right? *Right?*

I dug through my pockets and cursed under my breath. Mike had taken all of the money with him by accident.

"Mama, what are we gonna do?" Indy asked. "He might be gone for a long time."

I remembered being a homeless street musician in Hawaii when I was 17 and 18. The memories gave me an idea. "This'll be great," I told the kids. "Can you guys put my violin case in front of me?" I'd brought my electric violin to Italy, hoping to play it on the streets of Rome, but the biggest train station in Milan seemed even better.

I played the first song that came to mind, SOMEWHERE OVER THE RAINBOW, and put my soul into it because although my electric violin isn't a silent one, it's still reasonably quiet. People gathered and started listening, and as the crowd grew, magic filled my fingers *and* my soul. The words to the song appeared in my head, making Yip Harburg's lyrics feel so true at that moment.

I couldn't believe we'd made it to Italy. Despite things going "wrong," the trip so far had a beauty all its own:

"Where trouble melts like lemon drops. High above the chimney tops. That's where you'll find me... Somewhere over the rainbow, bluebirds fly. And the dream that you dare to, why, oh, why can't I?"

Ring the Bell

At the song's end, my four kids stared at me with happiness displayed on their features. "You made money," Trey said, dumbfounded.

"We can use the bathroom." Sky grinned.

And when I looked in my case, I realized we'd made seven euros—even more than expected.

Sky took Trey and Indy to use the bathroom, and Ruby stayed by me. It seemed like missing our train had opened the door to grand adventures.

A man walked past, whistling, GREENSLEEVES; I stole the chance to jump in on the fiddle. He glanced back, shocked, and spoke in such passionate Italian.

"Mi dispiace," I said, apologizing. "Io Americana, e non capisco." I'm American, and I don't understand. "Puoi rallentare?" Can you slow down?

"Wait? You're American." He studied me. "But your smile... That smile is Italian."

I giggled because Italians are *the best*. "My mom's family is from San Giovanni in Calabria."

"That makes sense. You're a middle Italian.

"Middle Italian?" I paused. "Che cosa?" What?

"You're part Italian. My family is from Southern Italy too."

Right before Mike and the kids returned, another man approached me and Ruby. "Your music... is wow. Bellissima." He kissed his fingers and spread them into the air as if he'd just tasted the best meal in Milan. "But you are brave, signora. You can play over there, away from la polizia. But you chose to play *right* by them." He pointed to the sign not too far from our heads. "I like you." He laughed with such joy. "I do." He flicked a couple of euros into my case and walked away, mumbling. "Música vicino alla polizia." Music near the police. "Mamma Mia."

So, our second day in Italy was filled with excitement too. We got to eat fancy food in a well-known Italian train station, bought a belt in the world's fashion capital, played music for the police, and earned enough money to use the bathrooms. Plus, I hope my kids will never forget how we made an adventure out of thin air. Every moment can become magical if we dare to search for the good.

The next day, we headed to Florence—and I must admit that it's one of the best places in the world.

Florence is hard to describe because it's so beautiful. Streets spider-vein around, all practically leading to one central location: the Cathedral of Santa Maria del Fiore. People visit, watching street artists, eating gelato, and discussing the fun items they discovered at surrounding shops. But, as always, our adventures became somehow hilarious. And no matter how hard I tried to be fancy, we ended up having a hysterical real-life moment.

I waited outside the art building, unable to go in because of our music cases. We had the mandolin, violin, and ukulele with us, but the security guards had some safety concerns about the music cases and wouldn't let them in.

Ring the Bell

"You can leave them here," a guard said. "But they might get stolen."

I blinked, appalled. "I'll stay with them," I volunteered. I honestly felt okay with this because I loved watching people go in and come out after seeing Michelangelo's David. So I sat in my wheelchair and studied people who trudged in... glum, bored, eager, or just filthy rich. When they came out, it seemed they'd been touched by the hand of God himself, brought back to a gentler, humbler state of being. After many individuals were reborn, I could hardly wait to see Mike, Trey, and Indy's reactions.

Ruby and Sky had gone off into the city alone. Since Ruby is a tattoo artist, she decided to find the best tattoo shop in town to get a matching tattoo with Sky: wine glasses.

Mike stepped from the building first, dazed and amazed—as if he'd stood under a rocket ship and somehow survived the blast.

"That sculpture of David must be one hell of a thing," I said.

"He is big... As tall as our house. Elisa, it was astounding. I can't describe what I'm feeling. Imagining one man carving that by himself—and it's in such perfect condition after all this time... "

Then Trey came out. He pulled his ukulele from his backpack and started playing. He's an excellent guitarist, but since we told him he couldn't lug that around Italy, he conceded to bring his uke. "That girl just looked at you," I said. Trey is like a California surfer boy from the '60s, and apparently, the Italian girls loved it.

"Yeah, I know," he said. "I made eye contact."

I stifled a laugh and readjusted my position in my wheelchair. "Where's Indy?"

At that moment, poor Indy stumbled from the building. "Indy? Are you okay?"

"Mama... " She stared blankly ahead, looking but not seeing. "He was naked. Haven't they heard of Adam and Eve — even they knew to put clothes on? I was fine with the six-pack. But his… *thing* was so big. I couldn't… I couldn't pull my eyes away. And it was so gross. I hope that's not what boys really look like."

Mike started pushing me across the cobblestone so we could get gelato. "Was he seriously as tall as our house?"

"Yeah." Mike showed me a picture from their adventure. David's toes were about eye level, and he seemed completely skewed.

"Well... " I looked at David's schmeckle and thought Indy needed some validation. "They could've named this piece David *and* his Goliath. That's bigger than a door."

"Right?" Indy said. "I kept asking if we could leave. Dad said it was art." She paused. "Scary art."

So, we went to the grounds of the Cathedral of Santa Maria del Fiore and had a gelato, just like one of my favorite uncles, Uncle Roger, recommended.

After that, Mike, Trey, Indy, and I jammed in the piazza (or square). People took pictures and videos, probably feeling nostalgic since Mike and Trey had learned the TARANTELLA on the mandolin and ukulele, hoping for a moment like this. The two appeared happier than I'd seen them in years, and that's when Indy jumped in, playing rhythms on a wooden bench. Her band class really paid off, and I felt glad she'd quickly recovered from her foray into art.

We had such a fantastic time just waiting to meet up with Ruby and Sky. And right there in my wheelchair, I fiddled my heart out on the streets of Florence. Nothing else existed except the wind, the melodies, and the kind of history that unites nations. The music became a tapestry let loose from our fingers. It warmed my soul and the wintry air around, but I couldn't help feeling like each of us traded being the capstone in an Italian arch, all vital to the song in our own ways.

As the music wound tighter, becoming more multifaceted, I remembered the first time I played by ear after years of taking lessons in elementary school. Jewish melodies had always inspired me, and the anticipation of playing without written notes felt exhilarating. This mirrored the day I married Mike when he removed my veil. I couldn't wait to see my soulmate moments before we'd walk down that aisle to eternity. Initially, playing by ear felt like irrevocably falling into that kind of passion. Maybe it's because my violin *was* my first intense love, something I would never be free from. A wooden lover that had gotten into my veins and under my skin.

As the music built in force, I could've sobbed because although I remained in that confining wheelchair, my heart soared without disabilities. Something I'd felt compelled to do as a child remained my lifeline through some of life's hardest challenges. And when the song ended and I finally opened my eyes, people stared. Despite language barriers and everything finite beings deem worthy of dividing us, music had bound us together in some type of fermata.

An older woman dropped money into my case as Trey started strumming his ukulele, ready for more.

"Thank you," I said brightly.

"You're all American?" she asked.

"So are you?"

She nodded. "I'm from New York."

"We're from Idaho."

Her features warmed even more as she studied me. "By the way, that was truly beautiful."

"You play something too? Don't you?" I caught a knowing sparkle in her eyes.

"Why, yes. I do. I play the violin. I played professionally in a symphony for years."

Before turning and sauntering away, she added, "You guys are good. Trust me; I would know."

Ruby and Sky darted over to us moments later, showing us their new tattoos and raving about their experience. They spoke so quickly that I lost the New Yorker in the crowd. That's when I knew we'd all had an unforgettable day.

"He asked me to come back and do an apprenticeship here," Ruby said, euphoric.

"Who did?" I felt my eyes widen in wonder.

"The owner of the tattoo shop in town. He saw some of the tattoos I've done on myself."

"Isn't that awesome?" Sky said.

Ring the Bell

"Wow," I said, nearly speechless. "Ruby, you should totally do it."

I felt so much peace then. Whether I beat cancer or not, those memories from Florence would live on with Mike and the children.

After everyone fell asleep, I tried hopping on the internet and felt lucky we had a good connection. My cousin, Farrah, had messaged me to see how the trip was going. She had been my maid of honor; over the years, I've found myself increasingly grateful for her friendship. It's funny because we weren't very close growing up, but our grandma always told both of us that we needed to spend some time together.

"Grandma," I said one day, "we don't have anything in common."

"That's what you think." She laughed. "One of these days, I bet the two of you will be best friends." And after our grandma died, Farrah and I did become the best of friends. And I started calling her when I'd normally call my grandma.

Anyway, she'd asked how the trip was going and sent me some pictures she took from when I got engaged to Mike. I smiled over the photos. Farrah owns a company called A Mother's Eye Photography, and she's incredibly talented.

"Today, I saw something I never anticipated when I took these engagement pictures." I read her words and felt so happy to have this message from home. "As an artist, I am most comfortable when

Ring the Bell

I'm creatively expressing myself, but I also like to tell stories with my photos. They should be accurate and true to the person I'm photographing. I'm sure that comes from my work as a family history consultant. Looking back on our ancestors and their lives can help us learn many things about families and ourselves. With that experience, I viewed these photos and reflected on the challenges you've gone through in the last couple of years."

I turned the light down on my phone so I wouldn't wake Mike, and I thought about my fight with "terminal" cancer. So many times, I've felt like I'm tied to the train tracks, just watching those terrifying lights come closer as I'm completely helpless.

"I thought about how you were diagnosed with stage 4 melanoma and given two years to live," she continued. "You know these pictures were taken years before that diagnosis. Mike has faithfully rescued you repeatedly through his actions, love, and (I'm sure) a shared fear at times. I love seeing how these pictures represent the two of you. Notice him picking you up and removing you from the oncoming danger of certain death. If only to give you a little more time."

I looked at the pictures then, stunned as I made the connection to her words. There's a historic train near where Farrah lives in Southeastern Utah. It's been retired and lives on a small length of tracks that reaches just a little farther than the train's actual length. For our engagement pictures, we decided to have Mike tie me to a chair and then pick me up in front of the legendary train. I'm still unsure how she did it, but Farrah made this scene appear as if Mike rescued me, carrying me in his arms as he ran from an oncoming train. We'd used this picture on the front of our engagement announcements with a quote from Winnie the Pooh: "I knew when I met you an adventure was going to happen."

"These pictures perfectly capture the relationship between you and Mike," she added. "Mike has fought to rescue you from what looked like certain death—and you've kept *smiling* and putting full trust in Mike and God, even when you've suffered… tied to a chair—now sometimes a wheelchair. Mike is still picking you up and taking you to magical places that help you escape the danger of the oncoming train." I had to wipe my eyes at this point. Farrah is such a gifted writer, and this deeply touched me.

"I love both of you very much, and you both mean the world to me. I look to you and Mike, your example of how to live life and face trials, so I can be more heroic in facing mine. I'm so grateful you and your family are getting to experience Italy."

With tears still in my eyes, I quickly responded to one of my favorite people in the world. "You'll never believe this," I wrote back, "but the story I want to tell you involves a *train* and a train station. I needed money for the kids to use the bathroom, and I got to busk there… "

First Night in Rome

The train that night pulsed with anxious energy. Trey said it reminded him of the Polar Express. Attendants came through and gave each of us a little treat like Edmund's Turkish delight in THE LION, THE WITCH, AND THE WARDROBE, and I couldn't get over the magic swimming around us, so thick you could taste it.

We spent many hours traveling and sleeping on the train—and I loved it. After we came to our stop, Mike set up my wheelchair and helped me onto the platform. "Look," I whispered to Mike and pointed at the kids after I sat down. All of them had such wide eyes, filled to the brim with excitement, but the two who seemed especially elated were Sky, who enjoys history, and Indy, who adores the movie ROMAN HOLIDAY.

"Rome," Sky said, a mature solemnity in her 18-year-old voice. Her blue eyes sparkled as if she'd just vowed to live more intentionally.

Indy squeezed my shoulder three times for "I love you." She did this little hop-skip that I adore. "Mama, can you believe we're visiting the same city where Audrey Hepburn came?"

"It's amazing," I said, and Mike chuckled because Indy and I have watched ROMAN HOLIDAY together more times than I'm willing to admit.

Trey wanted to find our Airbnb apartment because the sooner we dropped our backpacks off,

the sooner we could eat authentic Italian pizza.
"And I need to use the bathroom," Ruby said.

So, it became a rush. We tried to save money by
having Mike and the four kids walk everywhere
while Mike pushed me in the wheelchair. But the
cobblestone was a bit aggressive, the family seemed
tired, and I got the kind of stone massage no one
hopes for. All of our worries dissipated when we
looked to the left. There, tucked amidst apartment
buildings, the chaos of a modern city, and more
people than there are in New York, we spotted the
Colosseum.

"It's... It's just right there," Sky said, immediately
taking pictures. "This is so cool."

Describing what that ancient building can do for
one's soul is hard. You start thinking about the
people who have been there — and those who have
died amid its walls. The Caesars, gladiators,
peoples, and kingdoms have risen and fallen with
time. And the travelers, like me and my family, who
will continue to visit because it's so enormous and
profound. It's hard seeing something that brutally
majestic and realizing people built it so long ago.
One might even say it *feels* infinite even though it's
finite, like we all are.

Someday it will be gone like the people who
made it. That's the thing about Rome. You're just
walking around, traversing a busy city, or eating
incredible food, when suddenly you stumble upon
an excavation site where they found more ruins.
Rome is a treasure trove of wonder, art, and
opportunities for reflection.

Ring the Bell

We finally made it to the front of our "apartment," but the door loomed, a massive drawbridge to a dungeon. "I really need to use the bathroom now," Ruby whispered.

"I'm trying to hurry. But I don't know how to open this thing." Mike wiggled the doorknob, which appeared tiny in contrast to the looming door. He kept fiddling with it for a moment longer, and to our surprise, a tiny door opened within the massive door. Inception.

"It's like a movie," Trey said, absentmindedly strumming his ukulele. I swear he even slept with that thing.

Anyway, so many incredible things happened in Rome. I loved hearing the bells from the church down the road. I reveled in the dilapidated apartment we rented, with so much character and charm. Some of the lights didn't work, the floorboards would come up when you walked, and there were big bars on the windows, but none of us will ever forget it—or its 10-plus locks on the front door. Indy even went around taking notes about the apartment "for her future self" so she can one day tell her children what it was like when she was a child.

I think I'll be trying to wrap my head around Rome forever. I'm glad we didn't go for a regular tourist experience. Mike brought us to places where people actually live, and we got to see what real life is like—or at least have a glimpse of it. Anyway, ancient architecture, art, beauty, and intrigue aside, the people we met were unforgettable... Isn't it interesting how it always comes back to people?

Ring the Bell

"Indiana," I said in the little Italian apartment as she helped me do the dishes from breakfast. "I brought these for you." I handed her a bag of coins with angels cut out of them.

"What are these?" she asked.

"They're angel coins." I paused because they meant more to me than she realized. When I first got diagnosed with cancer, a thoughtful friend mailed those to me. "If you really like someone during our trip here in Italy, give them a coin."

She nodded, tucked the bag into her pocket, and we prepared to leave for the day.

The morning and afternoon seemed filled with discoveries around every corner. The streets buzzed with people taking pictures of ruins and beautifully renovated buildings. It felt unforgettable, but still, my favorite memory happened that night.

The man in the tiny shop barely spoke English, and we tried our best in Italian. "Gelato?" he asked Indy and Trey.

"Si." Indy vibrated with happiness.

The man grinned, making the skin crinkle far across his cheeks like ripples in a stream. And I couldn't help but smile back. He embodied everything kind and good in the world. He'd probably seen so much in his years—haven't we all?—but he'd become gentle and wonderful instead of bitter and hard. "Size?" he asked in English.

Ring the Bell

"Molto grande," Indy said, and everyone laughed because "very big" (as she'd just said) wasn't on the menu.

"Oh." The man chuckled. "Molto grande?"

"Per favore?" Please. Indy's eyes widened as she pled.

"Okay... Okay... " He laughed so hard. "Quale?" He pointed to a few different flavors.

She tapped the glass in front of the tiramisu.

"Non per te." Not for you. "Piccola." Small. He pointed to Indy. "Piccola."

We looked at each other. Not understanding. "Piccola?" Indy pointed to herself. "Si." Then she turned to him. "Grande" She pointed to the ice cream, spread her arms wide, and gave a charming look.

He wouldn't give her tiramisu but four huge scoops of the other ice creams. Then he gave Trey a big bowl too. Trey is so shy and darling. Everyone thinks he's much older than he is because he's five-foot-ten and only 14 years old. "Grazie mille," Trey whispered and glanced up.

We went to the door where my wheelchair rested against the wall. Mike set it up on the cobblestone walkway outside the shop, and the man looked out the door with so much concern. I'd seen him watching how I stood in the store and knew he wondered what was wrong, but I couldn't fully tell him about my battle with cancer or how hard I'd fought to live. I couldn't even explain how my biggest bucket list item was going to Italy with my family and how generous people had made this possible. Isn't that how it goes? We all have a story, but we don't always share it.

He pointed to my wheelchair and placed his hand over his heart as if trying to express sorrow for what we might be going through.

"Arrivederci, piccola," Goodbye, small. He waved to Indy.

"Arrivederci, bello," Goodbye, handsome. Indy giggled when she said it, and the bellowing laughter from the man was worth more than almost anything.

The shop closed after we left, and we got to our apartment in record time. "Oh, no. I didn't get to give him a coin." The thought hit Indy too late.

"You can try tomorrow," I said.

"Our train leaves before the shop opens," Mike said.

"But I'm his piccola friend," Indy responded.

As we passed the gelato shop the next day, I noticed Indy sticking something at the bottom of the door.

"What are you up to?" I asked. "Slow down, guys. We don't want to lose Indy." Mike pushed me in the wheelchair, and the kids moved in line with us. That's how we went everywhere, from Milan to Florence, Rome, Naples, and Pompeii.

I got out of my wheelchair and struggled to pick up the paper that Indy had stuck in the door. "Sei amato. Piccola." Then she'd taped an angel coin to the paper. I thought about her words, "You are loved." And I hugged her hard. "He'll like this so much," I said to Indy. Then we continued toward the train station.

The Rare Beauty of Pompeii

Some clutched belongings while different people held each other — or simply themselves. I've thought about this often, especially at parties when some new-age philosopher asks, "If you were in a natural disaster and you could only save one thing, what would it be?"

No one heeded the earthquakes just years before, and 2,000 residents of Pompeii (up to 16,000 people in all, counting surrounding areas) perished after Mount Vesuvius erupted in 79 A.D.

It's odd to think some of these victims' final moments have been immortalized. I read about it in elementary school and never forgot. The whole place seemed curiously morbid and yet beautiful in its agelessness.

Somehow, while fighting cancer, that's been one thing I've pondered. I don't want to be forgotten. But we'll all be forgotten someday. We can't even see the "end" of our ever-increasing universe. The speed of light is even slow compared to how long it would take to reach what we foresee as the *end*. Yet, we worry about being remembered. By whom? Everyone we've known will have passed away within a century after we die.

And yet, people worry about the silliest things: If a waiter forgot their soda. If their haircut looks nice. Maybe people aren't impressed by their new car.

What *really* matters?

311

Ring the Bell

Still... Pompeii is so much more than a philosophical catalyst. And when Mike and I went through the once-majestic city, my soul ignited with passion, and I watched the same thing happen to Sky. I can't run or sprint or skip, but I wanted to rush everywhere, exploring each home, courtyard, orchard, temple, and the 20,000-seat amphitheater. But I can't. Luckily, quite a bit of the city is wheelchair-accessible, and Mike pushed me across the uneven walkways. I would get up occasionally when Sky skirted down a road and told me I should "come check it out."

She ran and discovered precisely in the way I would've if I were in better health. She jumped and hollered, talking with so much animation about the new things she'd just found. At one point, when she led me to an amphitheater—that Pink Floyd played in for a documentary in the 1970s—I watched her, and tears filled my eyes. I'm just so proud of the curious, content person she's become. She's only 18, but she's already starting to accept who she is and wants to be. I saw that in Pompeii as she reflected on the ancient past and what she wants for her future.

At one point, the sun began setting, and although we'd seen casts of the deceased in the museum at the top of the hill, we hadn't found any in the city, which stretched much farther than what's shown in history books.

"These streets," Sky said, "it's just unreal to think how many people have walked these same streets and how advanced they were back then."

Ring the Bell

I nodded. "You know I'm not Christian anymore, but thinking this is how the world looked when Jesus was alive is strange." A rabbi once told me that Jesus was the greatest Jew who ever lived. It's neat to speculate about what the world looked like during his lifetime.

Just then, as Sky helped me along the street, she paused. "Wait. I think we found one."

"A what?" I asked. "A cast?"

She nodded.

I pushed myself out of the wheelchair and walked across the rocky street. Everyone else had gone far ahead to where a vast colosseum rested. But Sky and I stayed behind, pondering every detail.

At that moment, fate rewarded our patience, and we stood voyeuristically before a cast, feeling so much emotion. The man had died in obvious pain; you could tell by how his body contorted around the large object he held. "Do you think it's a vase?" I asked.

"Or a baby," she said.

I felt terrible that the cast showed so much; we could tell he'd been a man—a tall, skinny man. Vesuvius had left little to the imagination, yet I couldn't pull my prying eyes from him.

After facing my diagnosis, seeing someone's traumatic death from almost 2,000 years ago sent shockwaves through my body. I wondered what his hopes and dreams had been. But even more than that, I wondered what he held in his arms. Was he happy to be remembered in such a way? And how will... how will I die when the time comes? Will I be

313

hooked up to machines or at home? Will I be remembered for longer than several decades, and will it even matter?

I've always heard that when someone is about to die, they know death is coming days before it happens. People say they'll often talk about death or reach out to the people they care about. I think that's a reassuring lie we tell ourselves to make it seem like we have control. But trust me, it's unnatural to know the time of our demise.

That's something modern medicine has partially stolen from me. Yet, it gave me the ambition to visit Italy and inspired me to live with intention.

I thought about all of this as we studied the man's cast in front of us, and Sky must've had similar thoughts because neither one of us wanted to leave.

Our family spent almost three hours amongst the "ruins" of Pompeii and only saw a portion of the city: homes, roads, gathering places, art from the time, bathhouses, kitchens, and even writings perfectly highlighted by moss. Yet, it will remain the most breathtaking place I've ever visited (even topping a Jamaican bioluminescent lagoon Mike and I swam in on our honeymoon). It's rare for such a tragedy to yield beauty, but that's what I've decided to hope for in my final years. I want to be like Pompeii. I want my sickness and trials to yield something good, even if I am only a speck in time.

Skipping Through Italy

We left Pompeii slowly because the sun had set, and at one point, we used our cell phones as flashlights. If anyone thought it was hard pushing me in the wheelchair during the day, this became almost impossible at night. We finally made it out a bit after they'd closed and apologized profusely in Italian for being the last people to leave.

The guard waved kindly. "Stai bene," she said (you're okay). Then the woman grinned as if understanding how life-changing Pompeii could be.

"We might miss the train," Mike said.

Almost immediately, he and the kids started running uphill toward the station. Mike pushed me so quickly, impressing me with his resolution, and I glanced back, wishing we could camp amidst the ruins and soak in the beauty of the star-filled night.

"It's gone." Mike huffed when we reached the top of the hill. "I just watched it leave." He seemed so deflated as he hunched over and placed his hands on his knees, breathing hard. "Another train will come, but we'll have to wait hours."

The kids didn't complain, but they did seem disappointed. "Is there anything else we can do?" Ruby asked. "Could we try for a cab... or something?"

I checked my phone, but I didn't have service, and no one else seemed to be around the station except our family.

Ring the Bell

"There is another train," Mike said after a minute, "I know how to get there... but it's over 10 miles away."

My eyes widened, and that's when Ruby took the opportunity to shine.

Ruby is so strong and hardworking. When she gets it into her mind to do something, that kid will move mountains to accomplish her goals. I still remember when she told us she wanted to become a tattoo artist. She was only 17, and I didn't expect her to devote her heart and soul to it for years, sometimes spending over 80 hours a week working at the shop and drawing samples for clients at home.

As Mike told us our options, I watched Ruby's mind whir. "We can do this," she told her siblings like a reincarnated Joan of Arc. "Do you want to sit here for hours? Or do you want to run through the city with me and catch that other train?"

I still don't know how she did it, but everyone jumped on board, thinking that running 10 miles was a grand idea. And after a moment, we rushed through the streets leading to Sorrento. This might sound straightforward, but the wheelchair started rocking as everyone shoved me along.

The kids got tired after several miles. *Shocker.* I couldn't believe they'd made it so far. "Elisa, how close are we?" Mike asked.

I used the calculator on my phone to figure out the distance with an average of under three miles an hour. "Well, if you stay at this pace, you might make it to the train station with six minutes to spare. We're only a few miles away."

Ring the Bell

"Kids," Mike hollered. "Skip. Let's all skip."

"Yes." Ruby nodded. "Skip."

And everyone did. With Ruby in the lead—the Pied Piper of Sorrento, I'm sure the locals thought we were half-mad: several frantic people skipping and sporadically pushing a redhead in a wheelchair.

"It's... so... beautiful," my words came out joltingly because that's what it feels like when someone skips and pushes you at the speed of light. But Sorrento *was* glorious—so much prettier and down-to-earth than I would've imagined. It's not too far from where my mother's family lived in Italy before they came to America, and it felt surreal seeing it at night with all of the nightlife and everyone laughing right after we'd pondered death at Pompeii: the perfect dichotomy.

Emotions overcame me as I gazed back at my skipping children and my husband, who has stood by me through much more than cancer... He's held my hair as I've thrown up in the toilet after treatments. He's rubbed my feet when I've suffered the kind of pain I only knew from childbirth—it's the devastation cancer wreaks when it's gone into your bones and eaten your nerves. He's stayed with me through bad choices, crying fits, and much more. But seeing his joy as he skipped and looked at every one of our kids—and then down at me—that joy moved me to tears.

Ruby continued, courageously leading everyone to a place so close to where our ancestors came from, and somehow, I felt that if they could see us, they would be proud.

Ring the Bell

We made it to the train with only a few minutes to spare, and all the kids acted as if they'd won the Olympics. A couple of passengers stared at us quizzically, and we could not stop laughing.

"This might be my new favorite memory," Trey said, "skipping through Italy to catch a train."

I hugged Trey and winked at Ruby.

"Mama, you're right." Indy took a bite of a complimentary cracker a train attendant had given her. "Sometimes bad things can turn good if we just look hard enough."

The Protagonist of Our Own Stories

Almost a decade ago, I gaped at the hundreds of papers on my desk and grabbed a strong cup of coffee. My kids had just gone to bed, and I finally got to read the query letters I'd set aside—300 in total.

"This is unreal," I whispered to myself. We'd just opened the press for nonfiction submissions, and the amount we'd received felt unmanageable. Yet, as I read through various pitches, something beautiful happened that night. I learned about one woman's journey to fame as she became a successful songwriter. I became awed by a man who'd traveled the world and seen God in everything. I cried for a mother who'd been abused but somehow found the bravery to escape. And with each query, I became intensely conscious of how astoundingly different life can be for each of us. One person detailed their story of resilience while another clung to pain, and on and on, the stories continued until the night had passed, and I'd made it through the pile of paperwork and several cups of coffee.

Although this happened so long ago, the power of the moment is timeless. No matter where I am, I'll ponder the fact that we're each the protagonist in our own plays. When I say hello to someone in the elevator or watch people at the airport, I wonder what their "adventure" is and what brand of "memoir" they're creating for God. Which moments are so powerful they'd be used as a medium to craft a book? These thoughts are so prevalent in my life that they even followed me to Italy.

Our family of six waited for the train in Naples. "It'll be hours," I said. "I'll wait by the luggage. Why don't you and the kids go get some food."

"We can't leave you," Mike said.

"I have my wheelchair," I said, patting it endearingly. "And I can read my book."

"And she has me too," Indy said, refusing to leave my side.

So, after Mike, Ruby, Sky, and Trey left, I told Indy about my experience with the query letters. I wonder what each of these people would want written about their lives." I motioned to various people who passed us at the train station.

Indy's eyes brightened with curiosity. "It's such an exciting thing to think about." Then she paused for a moment. "Mama, if this were a moment in a book, what would you want to happen?"

"Well, I'd have an amazing conversation with you—which we *are* having—and then I'd pull out my violin and get to jam with a stranger."

She laughed. "That's one of the reasons you wanted to visit Italy. Like how you played in Staten Island and the New York subway?"

I smiled. "Yep. This is on my bucket list too: Jam with a stranger in Italy. But it hasn't happened so far, and our trip is getting closer to being over."

Indy knelt and started taking out my violin. "We don't have anything else to do. Why not try?" She handed me my bow and seemed hopeful. That kid has such a spirit of adventure. It reminds me of when I was young, so I took her advice and started playing. Soon, a small crowd formed around us, and Indy pulled out her phone, happily snapping a few pictures.

I caught movement to my right and turned just in time to see a tall man with blonde hair. He wore a guitar slung over his back and put something in my case.

"Oh, no. I can't take that," I said because he'd tried to give us several euros. "Can you jam with me instead?"

"Jam?" he asked.

"Play." I made a strumming motion.

At this point, another man with a guitar stood by the first. His dark hair perfectly accentuated his eyes as he began to interpret. "Patrick, she wants you to play with her," he said.

I looked at both of them. "It would mean so much to me," I said. "I... I have terminal cancer, and it's on my bucket list to jam with a stranger in Italy. Would one of you mind playing a song with me? It would mean the world to me."

The blonde-haired man looked stunned by my confession, and as he wiped something from his eyes, he turned to his dark-haired friend. "I can't play. Will you?"

"Well... " He looked at me and my family, who had returned then. "Yes. I will." He held out his hand. "My name is Jin."

"I'll play a song I just wrote," Jin said in English so good that he hardly has an accent. Then he began playing, and the song completely overtook everyone around.

Music really is the universal language. It transitions me to another world where musicians' souls sit across from one another. This place is void of all earthly distractions. You can learn so much about fellow musicians in this space by the way they jam, transition into choruses, and share — or steal — each solo.

After the song ended, I told Jin that if he ever wanted to visit Idaho or Yellowstone, he should come and see us.

"I will," he said. "But just know that when I make a promise, I keep it."

A Real-Live Angel

The morning had been a whirlwind of excitement. I went to an Italian laundromat, got a free coffee from a man who owned a shop across the street, and made a couple of friends who were also washing their clothes. I don't know how, but at the end of the last spin cycle, a young man and I cried over cancer, hardships, and the beauty of fulfilled dreams.

"Go after whatever you want in this life," I said. "Don't wait until you're almost 40. Because you could end up like me, and it could almost be too late."

He nodded.

"You won't forget?" I asked.

"I'll never forget this," he replied.

Mike came in with the kids and didn't even seem surprised to see me and this man with tear-filled eyes.

"How was lunch?" I asked everyone as they helped put the clean clothes into their packs.

"So good," Trey said. "I just love Italy."

They'd all gone to lunch and a farmers' market while I washed our clothes—the caveat being that we'd visit a famous synagogue in Milan that afternoon.

But later that day, everything seemed against us. We couldn't get there on foot, a train couldn't take us, and none of the taxi drivers could fit six people and a wheelchair into their cars. I closed my eyes and prayed. "God, if I'm really supposed to see this synagogue, please send an angel to help us." It sounded silly, praying for an angel, but God can do anything if it's meant to be, right?

I gingerly stood from my wheelchair and went up to a taxi driver. He couldn't understand English or my Italian. So, I started speaking in Spanish. My mouth fell open when he responded—he'd understood every word.

"¿Seis personas?" he asked, and I nodded. Within moments, he'd made every effort to get us a cab. When I thanked him, he kept talking in Spanish. I wondered what my Spanish accent sounded like to that Italian man. How hilarious.

Anyway, I knew the driver was extraordinary when we got in the cab. I sat up front, and he explained he didn't speak English. Although I could understand him fairly well, I couldn't speak much. Despite that, I somehow explained that we wanted to visit the main synagogue in Milan—one of the most beautiful buildings in the world.

His eyes widened. "Potrebbe essere difficile." It could be hard. "Ci sono un sacco di polizia e sicurezza lì." A lot of police stay around the synagogue to offer security.

But we decided to try anyway, and luckily, when we got there, the policemen even let the taxi driver take a picture of us in front of the building.

Our whole trip to Italy seemed predestined, but when I stood in front of that synagogue, I felt the sheer power of God.

Sometimes when I play my violin, I get so lost in the music that I can almost feel God's presence around me. It's so peaceful and intoxicating. It doesn't have the constraints of religion or bureaucracy. It's just me and God, a simple being worshipping her creator. And that's what it felt like standing in front of that synagogue. Emotion filled my eyes as the taxi driver took our picture because I knew for some reason that I was supposed to be there.

After we returned to the cab, the driver gave us a fantastic deal to bring us to our hotel. Mike and I nodded, deciding to take him up on his offer — after all, he'd somehow gotten our picture in front of the synagogue.

On the 45-minute drive, Mike and I spoke with the driver in Italian. He worked with our family, helping us understand every word, and this interaction became a treasured memory. We told him about our lives, and he reciprocated by sharing stories about his beautiful, accomplished daughters who are truly making the world a better place. The conversation became such that my soul glowed just as brightly as it had in front of that synagogue.

Toward the end of the drive, I wanted to tell him I prayed for God to send an angel to help us, but I didn't know exactly how to say all of that in Italian. So instead, I introduced myself and then asked for his name.

"Angelo," he said — the Italian word for angel! — and chills ran up my spine. The whole day made sense. How hard it'd been getting to the synagogue... It seemed impossible to catch a train and find a big enough taxi.

Ring the Bell

Sometimes when "obstacles" fill our lives, it's simply an opportunity for God to point us in the right direction.

After hearing his name, Indy gave him one of the coins with an angel cut out of it. "An angel for an angel," she said. Then Mike told him about my ongoing battle with cancer and that friends and family had paid for us to go on this trip.

Angelo's eyes welled with tears. "I am so sorry," he said several times in Italian. "So sorry."

When he dropped us off at our hotel, I asked him to wait a moment. I'd brought a copy of my memoir, TWO MORE YEARS, to give to someone special on our journey, and I knew it was him. I handed him the book, finding it hard to speak because he'd been so kind and given us far more than a simple trip to a destination.

Later, I saw that he'd sent me a message on Facebook. He'd told one of his daughters about my memoir, and she'd already begun reading it and translating it to him in Italian. There are times in my life when I look back in complete wonder. I know I've had some difficult things happen, like experiencing the death of a child or fighting terminal cancer, but the good far outweighs the bad. I meet such exceptional people. And just like this taxi driver, I'm so fortunate to have angels around me.

We Are Whom We Judge

Trey is such a philosophical kid. I knew that even when he was a toddler. Other kids would be racing toy cars, hugging dolls, making choo-choo noises, or even fighting with each other, but Trey would sit quietly, observing everything like a wise old man. Because of this, I wondered what he'd think about Italy—especially the brutal history of the Colosseum.

"If you became a gladiator and had to fight someone truly evil, would you kill them if it was your only chance of survival?" I asked, and he thought hard. "Well, would you do it?" I reiterated.

"If I could make that decision so easily, how could I be trusted with anyone's life—good or bad?"

I leaned back, taken off guard, letting his words sink in. "But what if they actually were evil?" I asked.

My 14-year-old shook his head. "I don't know what circumstances made them who they are. It would never be my place to take someone's life. So, no. The answer is 'no'—I would *not* kill them because it's not just killing someone; it's erasing everything they could've done. It's removing what only that person could add to the world. What if they could change the course of... everything, and I just ruined that chance? Plus, who am I to say they're really bad anyway?"

This was one of our first conversations in Italy, but it stayed with me the whole trip as Trey, Mike, and I jammed everywhere we went. I fiddled while

Ring the Bell

Mike strummed chords on the mandolin, and Trey played lead on the ukulele. But each place we jammed, no matter how beautiful, ancient, or serene, I kept thinking about Trey's words.

I guess they hit home because I almost stopped getting treatments at different points during my journey with cancer. Thank God I didn't because I would've missed so many things, like jamming with Trey in Italy. It's just a reminder that life is worth it. When someone dies, they're erasing future opportunities... and everything they could've done but didn't.

My eyes widened because I've rarely seen a plane so massive—with 42 seats. "I'm all by myself," Trey said. "I'll be okay. But I'd wanted to sit by Mike."

I looked at his ticket: 42E. The rest of us sat in row 41. "Tell you what." I smiled. "I'd just hoped for some alone time." I feigned surprise. "And I'm sitting right by Mike. Would you mind trading?" He didn't need to sit alone for almost 10 hours.

So, we traded, and I got much more than I bargained for. The lady next to me complained about everything. "Why are we in the back?" she asked the man beside her. "Don't they know who I am?"

Was she famous or something? "I love the back," I said, trying to help her see the bright side. "We're not too far from the bathroom."

Ring the Bell

"That's part of the problem." She flipped her hair and set her designer purse on her lap. "I don't want to put my purse on the floor back here."

"You know," I said a bit softer, "I think these seats are normally for crew members if we hit a rocky patch of air. I feel bad we took their seats. At least we have somewhere to sit."

At this point, the woman resolved to hate me. "I want an upgrade." She said it so loud, hoping the blonde-haired stewardess could hear. "I said—I want an upgrade."

Ruby and Sky turned around not long after this. "Mom, you're the one fighting cancer." Ruby's eyes darted to the woman on my left.

"You should be up here by our family," Sky said. "One of us can go back there."

"I'm all right," I said. "It's… nice back here."

"So much for an upgrade." The woman next to me gawked like I had leprosy, then she put in earbuds and leaned away.

It wasn't long into the flight when Mike came over. "You should probably walk around," he said. "You don't want to get another blood clot."

I nodded. Mike is the sweetest man. He held my hand and helped me walk to the back area. "I wish my doctor could see me now." I laughed. "But she said if she couldn't stop me from skydiving… "

After a moment, Mike said something to a stewardess in the back. She was one of the most beautiful people I've ever seen. "How was your trip?" she asked.

I felt like telling her our story. "I'm fighting cancer," I said. "Friends and family paid so we could take this trip to Italy because it was the biggest thing on my bucket list. It was life-changing."

After telling her everything, I burst into tears. "I'm so sorry to cry," I said. "I'm just so happy we got to go. I wasn't supposed to live this long."

She wiped tears from her own eyes. "There's a seat open at the front of the plane. I want you to take it."

My mouth fell open. "Oh. That's okay. I want to be by my family. Just send me a friend request on Facebook. That's all I want," I said cheerfully because this woman seemed like the sweetest person on land or air.

"Okay. But then I'd like to give you *two* seats up there, so someone can sit by you. I insist."

I could hardly believe it because I've only seen things like this in movies. Plus, my dad always flies first class—even holding diamond and platinum status. He told me about the fancy seats, and I'd devoured every detail, thinking I'd never see them.

Indy came to sit by me first. She could walk behind the seats because there was so much room. "We have a footrest." She giggled. And we even got a gift: handmade purses in the seat pockets. They came with ChapStick and all sorts of fun beauty supplies.

"This is so exciting," Indy whispered.

Each person got an opportunity to rotate up, and at one point, when Danielle, the stewardess, had rechecked on us, I turned to Mike and cried. "They're so nice," I said. "People are so wonderful."

330

Ring the Bell

He took a sip of his free wine. I couldn't get over how fancy this was—complimentary *fancy* snacks. *Fancy* drinks. Curtains? Reclining seats. This. Was. Living.

"Did you hear the woman in the back? The lady who was complaining?" I asked him.

"I think everyone heard her," Mike said. "You should've seen her face when she realized you got upgraded."

A little while later, Danielle came back. "I sent you a friend request, and I've been reading some of your stories. They are so touching."

This woman, a real-live angel, had made my year. "We've arranged for you to go to the Delta Sky Lounge for your layover in Cincinnati; that way, you and your family can rest and get a nice meal."

"I can't believe you're doing all of this for us," I said. "You've made the end of our trip unforgettable. Thank you. Thank you so much."

The sweetest woman, Patty, met us at the gate and treated us like royalty. She led us around and ensured we made it flawlessly through customs. Then she brought us to the lounge and gave me a huge gift. "People like you and your family are why we love our jobs."

I wiped tears from my eyes. "We didn't do anything, though. It's all of you who have been so nice to us."

She asked if she could get a picture, and after she took it, all of us kept talking about how exciting the trip had been. Even when we returned home to Idaho, the kids talked about everything that had

331

happened. "It was amazing," Indy said, clutching her purse.

"I think so too. That entire trip, from start to finish, was just perfect. I wouldn't have changed a thing."

"I'm so glad we got to go to Italy," Trey said. "It still feels like a dream."

"You'll learn about Pompeii in school next year," Sky told Indy. "But you can tell kids you've *actually* been there."

My phone dinged. I'd just gotten a message from someone who helped fund the trip. Their mom died from cancer, and even though she wanted to visit Italy, she never got to go. "Your pictures warmed my heart," the message said. "My mom would've been so happy to know someone else who's fighting cancer got to take this trip."

I thought of our unforgettable adventure. Maybe my friend's mom was looking out for us every step of the way.

Praying This Whole Time

"I'm a pretty quiet person," the man said. "But I want to tell you a story. And I'm really nervous." This phone call shocked me because Daniel is the quietest person I know. He and his wife, Betty, are fun and down-to-earth. They're the kind of people you can call with any issue, and they'd be there without judgment—no questions asked. But Daniel was right; he didn't say much. I've only heard him say a few words at a time. And now, this gentle giant wanted to tell me a story?

I closed my laptop. I'd just been reading dozens of messages in response to an old post that started trending this weekend—it's about the day I realized I didn't believe in Jesus when an assistant pastor did an exorcism on me. Yesterday, one woman said my post is "dangerous" because it encourages people to doubt Christianity. "You will be accountable for all of those lost souls."

I shivered, thinking about her judgmental words. I don't want to be called dangerous because I encourage people to think for themselves. I shook my head and brought myself back to the moment. "I would love to hear your story," I told Daniel, more grateful for the distraction than he knew.

"When you first got sick," he said, "I started thinking about how much time I've wasted. I've never faced a really big problem, unlike what you've been going through with cancer." He paused, and I knew this must be hard for him. "And so, 250 miles from home, on the road to Scout Mountain, I decided to make a change." He cleared his throat. "Elisa, I started praying for you, and I never stopped."

"That's... " I didn't know what to say because this was a huge deal. Daniel doesn't normally share much about himself, but even I knew he wasn't religious. "Thank you," I finally said.

"That means so much to me. I can't believe you've been praying for me.

"I'm getting ahead of myself." He exhaled into the phone and gathered his thoughts. "When... your book came out, I bought it because I knew that would somehow help. And then I just suddenly felt like I should tell other people about it. I felt so bad for everything you were going through being constantly sick. And it became my mission; I could help by getting your story out there."

Tears filled my eyes. "Seriously?" I couldn't imagine this reserved man telling people about my story. It must've taken immense courage because he's so shy. The thought left me speechless.

"Yeah." He laughed. "And now, I've told so many people about it that I can't keep track anymore. And the weirdest things started happening when I decided to do this. People would approach me and ask if I knew of any good books. They would almost just come up out of nowhere."

"You made my whole year." I laughed. "This is so amazing.

"The strangest time was when a lady at work told me she ran out of books to read. We were in full bodysuits and I told her about your book.

Ring the Bell

People would come up like that, or I'd hear about people fighting cancer, and I'd tell them about you and how positive you are. One lady told all her friends about it because they read too." He chuckled about all of this, and I sat straighter, astonished.

"You and Betty are so wonderful. I can't believe how kind you have been through all this." Betty has sent me care packages or messages telling me she's thinking about us. Their son has come over and brightened Trey's days. And now this, from Daniel

"But I never wanted to tell you about it," he said. "I just wanted to do something in the background to help without you ever knowing. And then, I just felt like I needed to call you... like you needed to hear this for some reason."

I thought about some daunting emails I'd just been reading and suddenly wanted to thank Daniel for everything. "My book has made it to the bestseller list several times. I bet you were a big part of it. I've even had some people start following me from Wyoming, and I had no idea why."

"I'm not sure if I'm the reason, but I *have* been telling almost everyone I know in Wyoming. Your book did many things for me, but it was hard to read the parts about Christians saying they thought you were sick because of your sins.

"I want to think they tried to be helpful, but it was still hard.

"In the past, I went to church even though I never really followed. But I started to see some changes in myself this year. Elisa, I just got baptized." Excitement lit his voice, and even though I'd found my truth amongst the holy walls of a

335

synagogue, I wanted to celebrate with my friend. It doesn't matter that we believe different things; I'm so glad he's found God.

"That's awesome," I said.

"I've been praying for you this whole time, and somehow through all of this, I've gotten closer to God. His love isn't about judging people but being kind without asking for anything in return. And that's what I've tried to be. I never wanted to tell you about this, but maybe you needed the encouragement to know that our family loves you."

I breathed slowly to keep emotion out of my voice. "I'm so grateful for you, Betty, and your whole family." I pictured Betty spending time teaching me different art techniques over the years. Both Indy and I absolutely adore her. Then I envisioned tall, quiet Daniel, bravely pimping my book to strangers, and it just made me bloom with joy. "That was so gracious," brave, kind, *wonderful* — I didn't have the right word — "of you to tell people about my book."

"I really went outside of my comfort zone," he said. "Oh. And I've started writing songs. One is something I pray every night. Can I send that to you? It's just that reading about your experiences with God and your family out in nature reminds me of what I wrote."

I could hardly believe I talked to the same Daniel we'd spent so much time with before my diagnosis. He's a devout Christian now, practically my agent, and he's writing music.

"Yes. I would love to hear it."

336

Ring the Bell

We gave each other updates on our lives, work, and health. And with a grin, I told him how much the call meant to me. "Thank you so much for calling," I said. "That was pretty amazing timing."

"Yeah?"

"Yeah," I responded, thinking about the messages I'd just been reading from my doctor. I'd been experiencing more pain, and my oncologist worried the cancer had started growing again.

"I just wanted you to know that I found Jesus, and I've been praying for you."

"Thanks, Daniel. Prayers mean more than almost anything else. God bless you."

I hung up the phone and sat for a long time, wondering how miraculous life can sometimes feel. Daniel is right; the best way to show God's love isn't through judgment and cruel words; it's through compassion and kindness that doesn't ask for anything in return.

People Don't 'Lose'
Their Battles to Cancer

"This is the most beautiful funeral," I thought to myself. The vaulted ceilings loomed above us, and a disembodied voice floated so angelically that I closed my eyes, soaking in the sounds of Heaven.

The hymn ended far sooner than I'd hoped, and my gaze fell to reality: the casket only a few feet in front of me.

"We all die," a Filipino priest said, his accent adding a hint of urgency. "You will die... I will die." His eyes implored the crowd. "Emma lived to be a good age: 93. Such a long life. Not many people can say that."

I swallowed. Emma—my husband's grandma—hadn't just lived to the age of 93. She'd made it to 97. How could this man make a mistake like that at someone's funeral? But before I could think of anything else, words popped into my head: There are *no* mistakes.

No mistakes? Now there's a cliche I've never subscribed to because I make more mistakes than anyone I know, like going to tanning salons—and getting melanoma. I glanced at the coffin again. I'm only 39, *thirty freakin' nine*... but doctors have recently said that I'll be in a box like that in less than a decade. Six feet under.

"Look at this box," the priest said. "Someday, each of us will die. But whether you make it to

338

93... " Then he decided to invert the numbers for extra emphasis, "or 39... "

Chills ran up my arms. Could this guy read English, Tagalog, and minds? Of all the numbers for him to pick one–100, had he seriously mentioned mine? I reached over and grabbed my mom's hand. She sat beside me in the pew, just as stunned as I was.

"Yes, whether you're 93 or 39," the man repeated, "and you're facing death, that's okay. As long as you've lived a life of service and loved others, it's okay to die."

Tears filled my eyes. I've never—in my life— heard someone say that it's okay to die. And since this journey began, I want to triumph... to win. But my battle is rigged. And it's terrible thinking if I don't make it past 40 or even 50, I'll be some failure because I wasn't strong or valiant... If I'd just been more positive... Had more faith... Damn it. If I could just be *more*...

"My 31-year-old brother was just ordained in September but died two weeks ago after suddenly having a heart attack." He paused, looking at the crowd. So much emotion filled his face that I felt his pain and found it hard to breathe. A sudden pressure in my chest compounded each of his words. "Every one of us will die. So, how many people will come to your funeral when you leave this earth? How many people will sit in these pews, mourning the loss of your presence because you helped *them*?" His voice heightened. "How many?"

At the end of the funeral, I told the priest how much his message had impacted me and my entire family. "I have melanoma," I said. "There's no cure, and doctors say I'll die from it. Your words spoke to me, especially when you said, 'whether you're 93 or 39.' I... Well, I'm 39."

He seemed taken aback. "What's your name?" he asked.

"Elisa."

"I'll be praying for you."

At the repast following the funeral, Mike's Uncle David asked me what I thought about the sermon.

"It was a bit life-changing for me. I know that's a tremendous claim, but it's true. You know I'm fighting cancer."

He nodded, and his girlfriend came over to hear what I had to say.

"Everyone tells me not to say negative things. To never say it's terminal. To never admit that it could kill me." I sighed. "But doctors say it will. And I think it would be completely idiotic to live in denial. I need to treasure each moment, but there must be a balance between happiness and facing mortality. I have to enjoy the present wholeheartedly despite my circumstances."

"I worked with aids patients over 30 years ago. I remember them telling me this same thing. Their views changed my life, so I know exactly what you mean."

I nodded. "That's why the priest's words meant so much to me."

He nodded a bit sadly.

"He made dying okay. I want to live, but it's okay if I have to die young—if it's God's plan."

Ring the Bell

His girlfriend's eyes turned up to me, stunned.

So Mike and I left with the kids and drove back to Idaho. I had a niggling feeling that either God or Emma had helped prompt the priest to mention my age and that it's okay to die when it's our time because, unlike what many people believe, sometimes death is acceptable. Death is a part of life. It's not something to fear or be terrified of. After battling long and hard to make a difference, death is meant to be embraced when our job here is done. I know that's why I'm not so sad about Emma. She lived and loved well. She fought hard to make a difference during her time here. And even throughout her funeral, I think she tried comforting others too.

Rainbow Baby

I had a miscarriage after Zeke. It might sound terrible, but I wondered if the baby would've been born with birth defects again, and I just felt grateful God took the baby before I had to watch them suffer like Zeke had.

But when I got pregnant with Sky, I worried the further along I got. The doctors said that since I'd had one baby die, the chances went up of it happening again. I thought about this as I drove through a storm one day, white-knuckling the steering wheel in my pregnant paranoia. The weather seemed like my young life at times: beautifully tragic. If I could just get to the other side of that damn storm...

"Mama. Rain," Ruby hollered from the backseat. Ruby was so tiny then, and she loved the rain, seeing the world in a magical sheen I once loved. I looked in the rearview mirror, studying her curls. Ruby was my lifeline. When everything else seemed awful or too hard to bear, that perfect angel kept me going.

I patted my huge belly. "I wish I could have some sign that I'll never have a baby die again." I cried through the storm, and shortly after my words, I turned a bend.

"Rainbow." Ruby giggled. "Two, Mama." And she was right; we saw two huge rainbows just outside of the storm. I wiped away my tears, thinking that we would never have appreciated the rainbows' beauty if we hadn't traveled through the storm. I told Ruby that, and she listened with her big, green eyes making her appear even more like a perfect cherub.

I thought of God's promise to Noah in Genesis, how He sent a rainbow to tell that old man He'd never flood the earth again. Maybe this was my promise from God that I wouldn't have another baby with birth defects.

"What should we name your sister?" I asked Ruby.

She stared up at the double rainbow and grinned. "Sky." So, Ruby named her little sister, and the two have grown up to be best friends: my beautiful Ruby and Sky.

I thought about Sky, my rainbow baby, yesterday. That's actually what they call babies born after one who has died. Sky was quite sick yesterday, but she still came to talk with me and ensure I was okay because I'd been fighting a fever all day — and bad news from the doctor. She hugged me and asked if there was anything she could do. And after she'd taken some medicine and started to feel a bit better, she came and cheered me up.

True to her rainbow baby name, Sky knows how to bring joy after any storm. She told me about the exciting things she did over the weekend and how happy she was about her inner growth. As she talked, I couldn't help forgetting my fever and sickness because she made me smile. I'm so proud that she's only 18 and has already begun to figure life out because she knows what really matters: love. So many people spend their lives searching for the pot o' gold at the end of the rainbow; unfortunately, they forget the magic of seeing a rainbow in their fight for status, meaning, riches, fame, and achievements. It's sad, but the contentment that eludes them was there all along.

I'll head to get more scans at the end of this week, but whether I get good news or not, I'm just grateful to have so many wonderful people in my life.

My 40th birthday was the best anyone could ask for. I felt extremely loved and, for a moment, didn't think about cancer at all.

Dee Ready always explained that her 40s were some of her best years, but I didn't know if I'd make it that long. I just wanted to see what all the hype was about.

"Are you sad to be 40?" a friend asked in the middle of the day. "I had a total meltdown on that birthday. I just felt *so* old."

"I'm grateful to still be here." Turing 40 isn't something to grieve over. It's a gift, and I'm surprised people get that so skewed in their minds.

At one point, I smiled at my little family who'd gathered around for my big day. We decided to play games and even took turns playing Mario. This is always hilarious since we can struggle to work as a team. Trey sometimes intentionally throws us off cliffs — which doesn't even help him since we're on the *same* team. "Trey!" I heard Indy groan as Mike

and I got everyone a slice of cake. "Not the cliff...
again."

"What?" Trey chuckled. "You got an extra life.
You're fine."

My eyes met Mike's, and we held each other's
gaze. "Some days, I feel like you just got an extra life
too," Mike said. Then he set two plates down,
sneaked behind me, and wrapped his arms around
my waist.

"I'm so grateful for more time, Elisa. I don't
know what I'd do without you."

"Me too," I said. "I love you with everything in
me."

That night, after we'd finally passed a level and
everyone seemed full to the brim with cake and ice
cream, I grabbed my bucket list and climbed into
bed.

"What are you up to?" Mike asked.

"Just thinking about the memories and the last
few years. It's unreal that we've checked almost
everything off of my list." I fiddled in New York.
We'd gone skydiving, visited Italy, repurposed a
violin... In fact, life suddenly felt so good that it
scared me.

"Mike," I said, "you know how when you're
about to put a dog down, and you give them a steak
dinner the night before? I'm so happy right now
because today was so great. What if this is my steak
dinner from God?"

He laughed so hard and simply shook his head.

Ring the Bell

Just a year into this journey, when my liver started failing because of cancer treatments, my Aunt BoAnn and Uncle Frank came to see us from another state. They bought dinner, brought gifts for everyone in our family, and even watched the kids when Mike rushed me to the emergency room.

Each of our kids cherished their time with my aunt and uncle and took exceptional care of the gifts they received. But this especially made an impact on Trey. During that visit, he'd received several sand dollars and learned how to break them to release the "doves" inside.

But even as time passed, Trey didn't want to break them. "They're just so neat. I can't stand to destroy them."

So, I looked it up online. "But it's good luck," I said, then read the search results. "Once the sand dollar is broken open, the five jaw apparatuses are said to look like doves." I pointed to the "doves" from a cracked sand dollar in his room. "Broken sand dollars release goodwill and peace into the world."

He didn't quite agree with me. And although he loved the gift, he vowed to keep them safe. So, months and months passed, and despite Trey's best efforts, since sand dollars are quite fragile, some of them started to break on accident. I watched as a sand dollar at a time would disappear from his shelf, replaced by doves. And although I didn't ask Trey about any of this, I found it interesting until only one sand dollar remained unbroken.

I'd called in sick to work on Valentine's Day, suffering beyond words. "It seems there's no rest for

the weary," I whispered, and Trey must've heard
me because he looked at me thoughtfully before
going to school. That afternoon, when Trey and
Indy had finished their homework, he handed me
something wrapped in tissue along with a note.
"Read the note first?" he asked, and so, I read it
aloud.

"I am giving you a sand dollar," I read his
words, "but not just any sand dollar... the intact one.
Because out of all of us, you have stayed the
strongest the last few years. Not only that, but you
have inspired so many lives." My voice shook as I
continued reading his words. "You have earned the
one and only sand dollar." I smiled at my darling
son. "Use it wisely. From Trey."

I gave Trey the biggest hug. It's crazy that he's
almost six feet tall and has such a tender, loving
heart. I'm so grateful for him every single second of
every day. So, as I reread his words this Valentine's
Day, I realized once more the importance of telling
the people in our lives just how much they matter to
us. I hope my kids know how very special they are,
especially to me.

Life has changed so much for me. Every previous
trauma could be held at bay by what some would
call moxie, but as time progresses, I find it harder to
remain free-spirited. For example, as a kid, I got
locked in a tiny camper closet for hours. Being
babysat, I sneaked away from the house in search of
cherry taffy. But when the camper's closet door

sprung shut, I'd been trapped, sweating in that tiny space... sucking cherry flavor off my fingers in the darkness as my family frantically searched. And I'm lucky they found me. I'm unsure how much time passed because I'd cry and fall asleep, then call and fall asleep again. Despite this, I'd never been claustrophobic. Instead, I became a risk-taker who enjoyed cliff jumping and spelunking. I loved taunting death.

But now, doctors have found another brain tumor, and simple things send me into a frenzy. Boarding a plane feels beyond terrifying. Elevators are a death trap. And just visiting a hospital makes me relive numerous visits, like when I got strapped to a bed after having a surgery to remove the tumor that had overtaken my L3.

Once laughable thoughts race through my head: Maybe I've undergone radiation, infusions, and surgeries... for nothing. What then? What if this new brain tumor does kill me?

I never tell these thoughts to *anyone*, especially my children—who I hope are deluded into thinking I'm strong. But if you see me taking deep breaths, chances are I'm quaking inside.

I don't expect you to understand this. I never would have before cancer.

I finally decided to voice these thoughts to someone—anyone. The medical assistant folded her arms, and I immediately regretted my mistake. "You have to overcome your fears—because we're all terminal. We're all dying. Stop freaking out about everything. You have to *believe* you'll get well."

Ring the Bell

I looked at her sadly. I hate it when people say, "We're all terminal" or "We're all dying" because it minimizes what having terminal cancer is like. It's not always about dying; it's about the path cancer patients take to get there. Being sick at a young age is hard, enduring painful "cures." Like I once told my cousin, Farrah, it's hard being tied to the tracks and *seeing* the train coming.

As I looked at the young medical assistant, I realized, we both want a semblance of control. This woman must believe that if I'm optimistic enough, I'll win against cancer.

So, what about all the happy, positive cancer patients who've died before me? They certainly didn't die from lack of moxie. But this M.A. hasn't been around long enough to see that… yet.

"I'm doing the best I can," I whispered to her. "You know, I looked up the meaning of beauty yesterday."

"Um... okay?"

"Beauty... its Greek roots mean 'belonging to the right time or season.'"

She blinked. "What are you trying to say?"

"When something owns its current season— imagine a tree—turning green in the spring, blossoming and bearing fruit in the summer, turning new colors during autumn, and even being sprinkled with snow in the winter... it's beautiful. We all live through different seasons during this life. To truly own each one, well, that's a form of beauty. I'm not giving up and giving in. But if this is the winter of my life, I want to embrace it. I'll be vulnerable if it'll help other people know they aren't alone. I might get better, and I might not — *that* is the truth. And embracing this season, according to ancient Greeks, well, that is beautiful."

"I don't understand," she said.

And after she left, I blankly stared out the office window.

Patience and a Dash of Hope

I've told you that one of the biggest things cancer stole from me is the ability to play in a band.

I've cried several times since 2020, remembering what it felt like to perform for an audience, missing the warmth of the stage lights on my face and the cheers from a live crowd. And at times, the loss of that dream has felt like too much... too quickly.

"We want to bring you out," my dad said. "Bring your violin."

Since I got this terrible news about the new brain tumor, Trey and I decided to go see our family in Tucson, Arizona, and my parents seemed thrilled to see us.

I've heard they attend parties at a local RV park, and I could hardly wait to see it all in person. So, I donned a dress my parents had bought me earlier that day—a tight black and white number with bright flowers. "Do I look terrible?" I asked my mom because I could no longer stand straight anymore, and I hunched a bit more than normal.

"You look beautiful," she said as my dad packed my violin into the truck. I smiled at my mom. Oh, to be loved by my mother... it's a beautiful feeling.

Far Horizons, the RV park, is a lot different than I expected. People get up and dance. They really know how to have a great time. They're hilarious and fun, and I could see why my parents enjoy being retired in Tucson—it's an adventure.

Ring the Bell

"Why did they want me to bring my violin?" I turned to my brother. Trey had gone to hang out with his aunt and cousins, and I felt grateful Shane had stayed with me. Neither one of us knew anyone at the RV park except our parents, and that somehow leveled the playing field.

"I'm not sure why they wanted you to bring your violin," Shane said.

"Just wait for the band's next break, and you'll see," my dad said to both of us.

I felt stunned by the band's talent. Despite only having three members, they nailed song after song, even having the drummer sing lead *and* harmonies. Finally, they took a break, and my dad rushed up onto the stage. He chuckled and smirked; then he pointed to me.

"Are you okay?" Shane asked.

"I think so." I felt a rush of adrenaline.

"You're willing to just get up there and play?"

"Sure," I said.

He shook his head. "We're a lot alike, but you and Julie are a lot more extroverted than I am."

After that, my mom and I ended up going behind the stage. "They said you can play," my dad said. "She can play anything," he boasted to the lead guitarist, and I couldn't help blushing.

"You'll really let me play?" I asked.

"We just drop down a half-step. Are you up for it?"

"Of course I am." And I quickly retuned my fiddle.

Ring the Bell

The lead singer showed me their set list and then pointed to MARGARITAVILLE. "How about this one?"

I exuded joy because that's a song I always played with the old band, Rough Stock. "Sure," I said. "That... Well, that sounds great." I paused, then explained. "I have terminal cancer. I had to quit playing in my old band, which almost killed me more than the tumors in my spine. Anyway... " The drummer had come over and studied me seriously. "Thanks for letting me do this. It means a lot more than you might know." They nodded, not saying much, even if empathy shone from their eyes.

So, I played MARGARITAVILLE, hitting all the right notes and confidently playing the solo. I peered at the crowd, remembering how remarkable playing for a live audience felt. And even as my legs started to shake from the pressure of standing in one place for too long and my spine pulled awkwardly from the tumor at the base of my spine, I thought I couldn't be happier. The lead guitarist gaped at me as I played, and my parents and brother grinned.

After the song ended, tears filled my eyes as I stepped from the stage and felt blessed for a moment that transported me back in time. To a moment when I wasn't sick. When I could dance and fiddled my heart out among some of my favorite people on earth — the members of Rough Stock. And as I put my violin away, trying to steady my quaking heart, I felt so grateful for the memories. I might not be able to do the same things, but at least I can say I've really lived.

Ring the Bell

When we left, I threw some money into the band's tip jar, and the lead guitarist waved. "Thanks again to the guest fiddler, Elisa Magagna," he said into the microphone. So many people clapped and grinned at me, not even knowing how much their kindness lifted the previously sunken spirit of a 40-year-old who's still fighting to always find the good.

I sat in Arizona, mulling the contrasting meanings between hope, despair, and faith. The root meaning of hope is quite surprising; it means "to wait," something I've never been good at. When God blessed me with "chutzpah," He left patience out of the deal. But in my situation, that's all I can do: Wait. Unfortunately, without hope, when you feel like you can't be patient anymore, that's when you reach despair.

I've met other cancer patients who understand this even more than I do. They each traveled to the end of their road and knew when to retire their efforts. Their funerals were beautiful... But even during their final moments, they seemed different from me; first, they lost faith and hope. I've never even had faith to begin with.

This confession might sound terrible because I've traveled to different continents to get prayer. Leaders of numerous religions have laid hands on me and wished me well. People worldwide have read my story and begged God for healing—even if others deserved it more. And at the height of this debacle, when I almost died from sepsis while out of town, all I knew was that God will do what works for Him, just like when He took my oldest son from this world.

In the past, I've tried to believe, but it's simply not something you can force.

Belief is the confidence that your hopes will come to fruition.

I've been to visit my family in Arizona a few times since my diagnosis, and on each trip, I've had this strange feeling that I should visit a synagogue there.

Maybe this was because I love Jewish music, services, philosophical debates, and traditions. Even when people discouraged me from attending, I tenaciously went because, amongst those walls, like Rahab... I felt God. And even if He didn't heal me, I loved being by Him any way I could. If that was at the synagogue, so be it.

My parents pulled up to Bet Shalom in Tucson, and we felt surprised to meet two rabbis and a chef from Israel who stood on the sidewalk as if they'd been expecting us. We talked about my journey with cancer, and the kind cook said, "We didn't meet by chance."

Then, one of the rabbis, Avi Alpert, talked with me about Noah and rainbows, a sign that has dotted my journey with cancer since the beginning—my unlikely breadcrumbs to God.

"Can you pray for her?" my mother suddenly asked. "Please. Can you pray for my daughter?"

Avi began singing an evocative melody as he weaved Hebrew in a way I could only hope to understand. Then, as the melody grew in depth and power, something strange happened.

The Hebrew words enveloped me like incense, and something sprouted to life inside my soul. It wasn't merely hope or desire. I no longer felt that void of despair. Within myself, I sensed the beginning of faith in God's plan. I don't know if He will heal me. In fact, that isn't very likely. But what I do know is that this seed of faith brought patience with it. And patience is exactly what I need.

So, whether I'm getting closer to death or not, I'm learning to appreciate life in new ways, meeting strangers at synagogues, and seeing adventure within my own journey to finding God.

A Godwink from Grandpa

No one can avoid death; maybe it's best to come to peace with mortality now. We were all born, and we will all die. But sometimes, that's a hard reality to swallow when people are young.

My cousin Farrah's oldest son committed suicide, and we've all been devastated. Justice was a pretty incredible guy, so much like our grandfather. I guarantee at 26 years old; he had no idea what this would do to his family and friends. He was the third person I knew who committed suicide in a year. All of these people were healthy and young, while I battled even for an ounce of life.

Since Justice reminded me of our grandpa, maybe that's why I started thinking about the past…

As a single mom, I used to frequently bring the kids fishing. I'd heard about a lake we'd never visited before. People raved about a spot where the water descended quite deep and giant fish lurked. While the kids and I walked, I thought about how unpredictable life can be. A few years before, my grandpa had gone to fix an A/C unit and had fallen off the roof and hit his head on a curb. He ended up dying a few days later.

After arriving at our destination on the other side of the lake, these thoughts abated. We'd just begun fishing when a man walked toward us. I thought he wouldn't come too close because there's an unspoken rule amongst fishermen that you don't go right next to people. But he did!

He stayed quiet for a while, and soon, we introduced ourselves. Then his kids played with my kids, and after a bit of time passed, we talked about some pretty profound things: our hopes, dreams, and fears. At one point, Sol got extremely serious and said there *was* something he regretted and had even felt guilty about.

"What is it?" I asked.

"I rented a little house, but the A/C unit had something wrong with it, so I called the landlord." He sighed, struggling to get the words out. "The landlord was older, and I felt bad calling him in the first place. But… I called anyway. The landlord got up on the roof." Despair overtook Sol's face as he peered despondently into the trees. "He fell off of the roof, and he died."

At this point, I felt taken aback. "What… "I paused. "What was the landlord's name?"

"Clan."

It became hard for me to breathe. "Clan Stilson was my grandpa," I said. Then seeing the shock in Sol's eyes, I continued. "Sol, you have to let this go. It's incredible that I'm meeting you here while fishing today. My grandpa may have brought us together so you could have closure. He would never hold this against you. He died, but it was his time to go."

Sol and I both found such peace that day and have stayed friends over the years.

Ring the Bell

After Justice died, I thought about this memory and prayed for Farrah before going to sleep. Maybe that's why I had such a lifelike dream.

I walked around a massive apartment complex in Heaven. It loomed far into the sky, more luminous and iridescent than I could fathom. I didn't know why I was there, and finally, a few people said I should look for the maintenance man. "He can help you." As I searched, tenants explained that apartment sizes in Heaven were a direct result of people's lives on Earth. Some people owned entire floors, while others had tiny one-bedroom apartments.

But a lot of time seemed to pass, and I needed to find the maintenance man. "Where the heck was I? And why was I there?"

I eventually spotted him. He wore blue coveralls and faced away from me. It didn't take long to rush over and tap him on the shoulder, but when he turned around, I could hardly believe it. My grandfather faced me, just much younger and happier. He'd always been dressed in fancy clothes, even down to the shiny black dress shoes, so it seemed odd for him to be in blue coveralls. The shock slowly wore off, though, and I adjusted to seeing him with hair. (I never expected it to be blond.)

"My Elisa." He hugged me with such fondness. "I need to work on a few things. Do you want to come with me?"

"Of course I do," I said and could hardly wait.

"But why would you want to do this in the afterlife?" I asked as we walked.

Ring the Bell

"I enjoy helping others. It makes me happy, and it makes them happy too." He paused. "I own this building, Elisa." And he appeared genuinely content to check on tenants, fix pipes, and replace hinges.

As the day progressed, I remembered what it had been like being with my grandpa… the most fantastic guy. "Grandpa," I said at one point, "I want to stay with my family as long as possible. Am I gonna live a long life?"

"Elisa," he responded, "you're gonna live—" Then he stopped. "I can't—I shouldn't say that."

And then I woke up. I'd had dreams about my grandma, telling me not to be scared because she waited to show me around Heaven. It felt comforting to dream about my grandpa too.

A few days later, Farrah decided to meet me after treatments. I had never told her about that strange moment with Sol, and it seemed almost unshakable that I should share that memory with her and tell her about my recent dream.

That night, after eating ice cream, having a mini photoshoot, and trying to take our minds off hardships, I finally shared these stories about Grandpa with Farrah.

"I've dreamed about Grandpa too," she said. "He wore blue coveralls."

I gasped. "That's what he wore… in my dream too." Goosebumps ran across my arms.

"My mom said," she whispered, "that's what he always used to wear when he was really young." We both remained quiet for a moment, shocked.

Ring the Bell

"I don't know why, but I just had to tell you about Sol and this dream."

Farrah paused, holding back tears. "I wake up every morning at 6:30 a.m. It's my internal alarm clock, but this morning I felt different. When I woke up, I saw Justice and Grandpa laughing. Their arms were around each other, and they seemed to be working together. I wanted to believe — with everything in me — that Grandpa was actually *with* Justice, I feel like I have that confirmation now."

It seemed uncannily like the moment with Sol at the lake. And so, Farrah said she left that bench knowing Justice is with our grandpa, doing what they both loved: helping others.

Jin Contacted Us

Remember how I jammed with that stranger in Italy?

"I posted the video of us jamming in Naples," I wrote to him.

"Such an adventure," he responded. Then the following message popped up. "I came to Auschwitz. It's my last day here... and I just finished visiting the camps." I felt the devastation in his words. "The pain and sorrow overwhelmed me. And as soon as I opened Instagram to rest my mind, I found your post. It reminded me of the good in humanity and the power and love each of us can exude—as you and your family did when I met you. Thank you."

"I can't even imagine how I would feel seeing Auschwitz," I replied. Then I wanted him to know how grateful we were to meet him. "Our entire family is so impressed with you. You made our trip to Europe exceptional."

After that, he messaged me, Ruby, and Sky. "I'm making a trip to Nashville," he wrote. "I hope I can make it and see you and your family in March to get a tattoo. I'll try. Thank you—and God—that we were gifted such a moment in Italy. That moment still pushes me forward to this day."

I didn't know the logistics, but I didn't doubt his words for a second. He really wanted to get a tattoo from Ruby.

Ring the Bell

Do you ever wonder what the point of life is?

After being diagnosed, I thought, "If I can just make it until all my kids are adults." That seemed impossible, like sailing to the moon. Indy cried after initially hearing the news. That momentarily shattered my sensibilities, my dreams, and even my resolve. She was only 10, and seeing her crying— because of my mortality—nearly broke me.

Yet now she's 13, Trey is 14, Sky's 18, and Ruby is 21. As the months and years have progressed, my terminal illness has become part of my life. Some days I spend unable to keep anything down. I'll suffer from a fever, physical pains from tumors, or even sadness from lost abilities, but I do my best not to let this affect my family. I cry in the closet. I shield them from my pain. And I throw up as quietly as humanly possible, which in hindsight might look funny to God *if* He's watching.

But yesterday, as I felt incredibly ill, I huddled alone on the couch in the fetal position. Ruby is busy building a career, which makes me so proud. People have now come from across the world to have her tattoo them. She's booked out until November. Sky is getting ready for the summer semester of school. She's brilliant and usually busy studying her latest fascination in Ruby's room, which the two share even though Sky has her own room. Trey plays the guitar after school every second of every day. He's even teaching other kids how to play instruments now. And Indy either practices the drums or reads Manga to her cat, Nova. I'll hear her giggling in her "tent" (an odd assortment of haphazard blankets). "She removed her mask to answer the master," Indy read one day. "I may lose people in this life, but I must go on…" At that point, Nova meowed. "Oh, Nova. She has to be tough or she won't make it much longer."

I'm grateful my kids are content and happy. But Mike works afternoons and nights, and yesterday, I felt alone, wondering what the point is. I'm like Mary Poppins. It's not time to unfurl my umbrella and float away yet, but I have taken steps to prepare my kids. And I do need to take solace in the fact that I'm raising strong individuals who will be all right, even without me.

I pulled a fluffy blanket around myself, and that's when someone knocked on the door.

"Are you kidding?" I whispered, sliding a hand across my unruly hair and straightening my shirt.

"Elisa," Ralph said after stepping into our entryway.

"You... But you just had surgery," I stammered.

"I needed to get out of my house." He'd driven with an injured hand all the way to my home from Blackfoot—in a blizzard. He must love driving that Mustang.

Indy and Trey bounded from their rooms, excited to see Ralph. Indy hugged him right around his waist, and he grinned. "How old are you anyway?" Indy asked. "I forgot to ask on your birthday."

"Well," he said, sitting at our kitchen table, "how many keys are on a piano?"

Ring the Bell

"With the black and white ones?" She paused to think. "67?"

"You're a real charmer." He chuckled. "67? Ha. I wish. There are 88 keys."

"You're 88 years old?" Trey's eyes bulged. "That's... wow. I had no idea."

The kids returned to their rooms shortly after, and I just laughed.

Ralph and I talked about all sorts of things. I asked if he could repeat any five-year period of his life which one he'd choose. He picked 35–40 because he'd "finally figured things out about life." We played a game called Worst Case Scenario, and Ralph picked "taking a vow of silence" as his worst situation, even compared to wrestling a crocodile. Then, the conversation changed from beautiful memories of fishing, working, and raising kids to his worries about aging. "I know my days are numbered. I guess some of your feelings mirror mine," he said. "It's hard knowing your time is coming sooner rather than later."

I nodded.

"But I have to do things that give my days meaning. I might not know what the point of life is, but I know what I wanted the point of *today* to be."

Those words hit me, almost knocking me off my proverbial feet.

"What was that? The point of today?"

"To see all of you," he said. "Just to have a great conversation. To keep living even if it was difficult to get here. Some days aren't easy, and we must put in the effort."

365

Ring the Bell

I felt so touched. The kids and I had been someone's "point of the day." That felt wonderful.

Trey and Indy finally told Ralph goodbye. I hugged him before he could walk out the door. He's become like family to us, and I usually hug him awkwardly, wanting him to know that he matters. But this time, he hugged me and held my head against his chest. "You're getting so thin," his voice quivered. "We just want... " He inhaled shakily. "All of us want you to get better." He wiped his weathered eyes and held my wrist with his good hand. "Just take care of yourself, kid. And remember to give each day meaning as it comes."

He drove off, disappearing into gusts of snow as they billowed across the Idaho roads. And I still don't know why his words and that hug impacted me the way they did. I'll never understand how certain people have come into my life.

Our world is such a mystery. When we think we're lost, a friend might battle through a snowstorm just to show us the way.

Light from a Lighthouse

Ever since I got sick, I kept wanting to visit a spiritual healer named Dixie Nowell. She takes a holistic approach to healing, wielding oils, music, and books that detail information from ancient texts. Years ago, a dear friend paid for me to see her after my divorce, and I genuinely couldn't believe how much better I felt after seeing her.

"I'm fighting cancer now… Can I come to see you again?" I asked her. "I'd also like to bring one of my daughters, Sky."

"Yes. And come stay with me," Dixie quickly responded to my query.

I've had so many people altruistically offer me to spend the night at their homes close to the cancer center in Utah, but I rarely do it, not wanting to impose. Yet, for some reason, I agreed, feeling almost like we needed to stay with Dixie. This might sound hokey or ridiculous, but the night before we left for more cancer treatments and to see Dixie in Eden, Utah, I dreamed about a beautiful lighthouse with a blinding light shooting through the windows. It left me feeling pure and flawless despite illness, something I haven't felt since long before this whole ordeal began.

What Dixie gave me and Sky is hard to put into words. She spoke with both of us for hours and hours, and with each moment that passed, I somehow felt my load lighten. "You're changing so many lives," she said to me. "I read your posts."

Ring the Bell

"That—well, that means so much." Then I watched as my beautiful, vibrant 18-year-old transformed from carrying worries about losing her mom in the future to appearing hopeful that everything will go the way it's supposed to. There's nothing more important to a mother than seeing that her children are okay. And I think half of Dixie's gift is being a life coach; the other half is building others up to the brim with positivity and kindness.

We finally went into the healing room, and as Sky and I closed our eyes to pray, I felt so much joy beating in my heart. I don't know how much longer I truly have or how excruciating my cancerous death may be, but I am trying my hardest to remain present and hopeful. I'm enjoying every minute, taking opportunities to experience new things, and cherishing time with the people I love the most. The longer I sat, it almost seemed as if my dream about the lighthouse had been for this moment, that the sun shone through *my* soul, and God filled me with such light and love.

After the session ended, Sky practically glowed and hugged me. "Thank you for bringing me here, Mama. I'm glad I got to meet Dixie and experience this with you."

Dixie appeared very content hearing these words. "Let me show you to your room."

I gingerly walked down the stairs. "Here it is." Dixie radiated kindness.

I gaped at the wall, completely dumbfounded and momentarily unable to speak because in the corner—large and impressive—hung a striking picture of a lighthouse with light shining directly through the upper windows.

"Is everything okay?" Dixie asked, taking a step closer to me.

"Ye—yes. I'm just so... grateful for your generosity. And your friendship." I paused, willing her to know how much it all meant to me and Sky. "Thank you for letting us stay here, Dixie. Your kindness... means far more than you might know."

The next day, I received test results from earlier that week. They showed a new tumor.

"I hate to be the one to tell you, but this is very bad news," my oncologist said over the phone.

I sighed and wracked my thoughts for something positive to say since I've made it my personal vendetta to try shocking the hell out of my doctors. "At least that gives me a good excuse to buy a new dress," I blurted. "How can my husband get mad when I tell him I got a new dress and another tumor."

The line stayed quiet, and I didn't mean to, but I laughed.

"You're taking this news awfully well," she said, dumbfounded.

Yes. I'd done it again. Bwa-ha-ha. "I had an awesome experience this week," I admitted. "It put everything in perspective, and I'm grateful to be here at all. I can't believe I actually exist. It's hard to even fathom that I've lived longer than expected. I can't believe I got to have a family, experience love, and see the beauty of our world. Death is just part of the bargain." I sighed.

Ring the Bell

"You... Elisa... Sometimes you amaze me," my doctor said.

"Same to you. Thank you for helping extend my life," I replied. And after I hung up the phone, my thoughts returned to that unforgettable lighthouse, the one with the light shooting straight through the upper windows.

"Dear God," I silently prayed. "I hope you love me. If you do and you can find the time, can you please give me the strength to get through the next leg of this journey?" Then I sat down, and thinking about the future, I cried.

Reuniting with a Stranger from Across the World

Months after the jam session in Europe, several of us waited to pick Jin up near a bus stop. "I see him." Indy squealed, and then we all spotted Jin.

We talked so fast, excited to see him. And when we brought him to soak in hot pots, he peered around thoughtfully. "It's surreal to think that just a few months ago, we all met on the other side of the world."

"This journey with cancer has been hard on all of us," I whispered, pointing to the kids. "But you gave us something so wonderful to look forward to. Thank you for coming to see us."

Each member of our family needed to meet Jin for a reason. He may be young, but he's wise beyond his years and shows such generosity of spirit. During his visit, we all made memories that we'd never forget. He helped Trey with his guitar, got a tattoo from Ruby, played card games with Indy, hiked with Sky, and went out to some bars with Mike.

What I loved, though, was hearing his stories. Jin has traveled around the world, going anywhere from Greece to Iceland to Idaho to Japan. I'll never know what inspired him to come to see us, but I think it might've been providence.

After a few days, Jin prepared to leave, and we all wanted to give him a card. Since I enjoy etymology, I'm very intentional about what I write to people. That particular day, I felt almost compelled to write in Jin's farewell card, "You are *unforgettable*."

Jin looked up at me after reading the words and appeared quite overcome with emotion. "It's interesting you would write the word *unforgettable*," he said. "The root of that word means 'truth.' And as I've traveled across the world, that's what I've been looking for—and finding: my own truth."

This resonated with me even more than any music we'd played while he stayed with us in Idaho. I thought then about my journey with cancer and how hard I've tried to persevere and remain optimistic despite each setback. Even when I pulled out my old bucket list, I never expected it to lead to such memories for our entire family.

At the end of it all, after I'd checked off so many crazy things, I realized what makes life matter isn't life experiences. It's experiencing life with the people we love.

We each hugged Jin and stated the very best of wishes. And when he walked out our door, I felt like we'd met someone who had somehow changed our lives forever. Indeed, life can sometimes feel unbearably hard, but it's also beautiful and miraculous. Who knew a stranger we met at a train station in Italy would become such a dear family friend?

An Understanding

"I don't understand you," the woman said. "How can you talk about death so calmly?" She'd recently been diagnosed and reminded me of myself at the beginning of this journey. "Quit saying you're terminal. Words have power."

"We each have to do what's right for us," I said.

"You're so strong and full of life."

"Elisa, so are you, but I feel like part of you is giving up."

"I *am* starting to get tired," I said. "This has been a long journey." I thought about my recent scans. The cancer is progressing, and although doctors say there will probably be a cure for this kind of melanoma in a few years, we don't know if I'll make it that long.

"Aren't you scared to die?" she asked.

"No," I said. "Not anymore. I'll get to see people who have gone before me." And part of me could hardly wait for God's loving embrace. I could almost feel His kindness encompassing me as I said the words. It felt like the synagogue.

"Why did this happen to me? Why is this happening to any of us?"

"I honestly don't know," I said. But I have learned a lot."

"Elisa, I want to accept things like you have."

"I'm still working on it, but I'm getting closer every day."

"You're really not scared, are you?"

Ring the Bell

"No," I said. "God comes to us when it's time. He's a good God." David's words from Psalm 103:8 came to mind, and I couldn't help but smile. "You know, I prayed for God to put me through the refiner's fire the year I got sick. I started studying Shadrach, Meshach, and Abednego. A lot of people say it's a story of healing, how the three men went into the fire and came out okay. But I realized later that it has nothing to do with physical health. Although the people in that story physically escaped the fire, they grew in the ways that truly matter, and they left everything else behind."

Something must have hit her because she cried right there in my front room. "I can't do this," she said, and I put my arms around her.

"I've felt that way too—so many times. But I promise that somehow, it'll be okay. It has been for me."

"But doctors say this is what you're dying from," she said.

"And even that became okay once I found faith that God has a plan."

After she left, the kids asked if we could do something as a family, so Mike set up the badminton net in the backyard. I can't play badminton anymore, so I sat in my wheelchair, cheered, and smiled as I watched Mike and the kids play.

At one point, I breathed deeply, overcome by irony: I'm the happiest I've ever been and the sickest.

I'd reached a new season in my life. Instead of playing the game and enjoying the ability to make the birdie soar, I found more joy in simply watching my family. I worked for years to give my kids the best of everything, to raise them to be strong, kind individuals. And seeing that come to fruition is more than Mike and I ever hoped.

Since the day I got diagnosed, I wanted to ring that bell and have a second chance to just *live* for my kids. I'd been so scared to die. To no longer be an active participant in my family's lives. An impenetrable glass wall would loom between us. I'd desperately watch Mike, begging him to feel my presence at our kids' graduations and weddings. I'd watch *all* of them as time changed everything except my untimely death. And somehow, I'd remain obsolete... forever.

But as I sat, cheering my family on during their game of badminton, something odd happened. I finally understood that this journey through illness was never about ringing the bell and surviving this fire. I've had what mattered all along. The only thing more powerful than fear, sickness, regret, and loss. The only thing stronger than death... is love. Nothing can take that away. Not bitterness. Not sorrow. Not even time. Love will always tie me to Mike and the kids.

So, whether I die in my 40s or someone pulls through with a cure, I'm finally at peace. My purpose was never about playing the violin or writing books. My life wasn't about the jobs I had, the degrees I attained, the places I'd seen, or the goals I accomplished.

My life was *always* about making people feel loved. And somehow, as I sat in my wheelchair, reflecting on the time God gave me, I realized I'd done exactly what I needed to do. And… that was enough.

WE HOPE YOU
ENJOYED THIS MEMOIR.

**After reading RING THE BELL, please consider posting your heartfelt review through the retail site where you purchased your copy. Reviews are vital to helping authors succeed.
We appreciate your time and support.**

**Don't stop here. Keep reading for more, including a Book Club Guide and a Special Sneak Preview of:
THE RED FEATHER by EC Stilson**

Book Club Guide

1. Could you relate to this story on a personal level?

2. Did this memoir make you feel specific emotions? If so, why?

3. How do you try to find peace when you're struggling? Did the author relay helpful examples?

4. Do you have any regrets about your past? If so, how can you live without having any regrets in the future?

5. Is there anything you'd like to accomplish that you haven't already done? What, and do you have a plan to do so?

6. Did your opinion of this story change as you read? If so, in what way?

7. What's the one thing you will never forget about the author's experiences?

8. If you could talk to the author, what questions would you want to ask her?

9. What was your favorite and least favorite part about this memoir?

10. Have you read other memoirs by EC Stilson?

Acknowledgments

I want to thank the most incredible husband in the world, Mike Magagna. He's spent many hours reading this memoir and helping me implement the necessary changes. His patience and kindness have seemed almost never-ending since I got cancer. My children (Ruby, Sky, Trey, Indiana, and little Zeke) are the reason I continue to fight against all odds. I would do nearly anything just to try to make them proud. Braydon Jenkins is so awesome; he always remembers me on Mother's Day and is such a great guy.

My parents, Philip and Ruby Stilson, generously have RVers across the nation praying for me, and my mom has worked so hard editing this memoir. I'm so lucky to have Steve and Maureen Magagna as in-laws. They make my visits to Utah fun and are always there when I need them—even at a moment's notice. Grandma Alice Hartley has been such an incredible example of kindness, strength, and love. She's one of the people I really look up to in this world.

Dee Ready—whom I've adopted as family—is so dear to me and such an inspiration. My good friend, Ralph Hauser, for his encouragement and that unforgettable ride in his Mustang.

In addition to this, my siblings Julie (Gregg) Laub, Shane (Kazuna) Stilson, Theresa (Jason) Kunzler, and Angela Lupcho have shown such support throughout this journey. My aunts, uncles, cousins, nephews, and nieces are the best anyone could ask for. (I hope all of you know how much I love you.)

Without my friend, Ford Forkum, this book would not exist. He's been there for me through some very difficult days, and our philosophical conversations have given me so much peace.

I so appreciate Scott and Colleen Hancock for the many trips they've made to Pocatello when I needed love the very most—and for checking up on me every single day.

I'm grateful to Andrew and Terri Lasslo for the many prayers. I also want to thank Rabbi Avi Alpert, Jenna Thompson, Jeff and Joanna Lee Doster, Emilie Laudie, Amy Campbell, Johnathon "Pun" McReynolds, Lolita Mercer, Daniel and Betty French, Ben Ditmars, Pablo Rodriguez, Dixie Nowell, Bryon Gundersen, Casey Nuttall, Daniel San Souci, Denise Klingler Portmann, Douglas Sayer, Nicole Walters, Jennay Pound, Dustin Bartrop, Bob Stuart, Stephanie Clark, Carolyn Wold, Burgan Hobbs, Romi Clark, Sue Harvey, Pastor Alfred Murillo, Victoria Bromley, Roberta Turner, Ann Marie Anthony, Jerry Russrad, Danielle Mussman, Garrett Pete, Alex Shaw, Dan Nelson, Angelo Palattella, Ashlee K. Thomas, Barbara and Vern Kilbourn, Kim and Gloria Hansen, Natalie and Terry Bergevin, Jennifer and Jared Grover, Terry Morris, Trent Porter, Jim Schaub, Harry and Patsy Sherman, Lisa and Jim Workman (along with their amazing family), Shaun Buck, Rachelle Lerner, Sheri Neeley, Mark Gabriel, Kristine Murray, Laurie Allen, Emily Thornton, Kara Saunders, Candiss

Ring the Bell

West, Nicole Nauman, Katy Williams, Donna Bergman, David and Bayle Goodman, Rabbi Sara Goodman, Dan Meir, August McLaughlin, Robb Grindstaff, and Inger Wiltz—**your kindness is what makes people want to keep moving forward despite otherwise unbearable hardships.** My book club friends, especially Tasha Chambers, Mysha Ashbocker, and Ashlynn Oborn, have made me smile—even on the toughest days.

I'm also extremely fortunate that Katie Leoni perfected this cover—she did an exceptional job.

And last but not least, thank you to my friends on social media. Without your wonderful feedback, I may not have found the strength to finish this memoir. God bless all of you!

Special Sneak Preview

The Red Feather

The room ran so high with stringed instruments that it utilized a rolling ladder similar to those found in ancient libraries. A whimsical-looking woman slid down one of the closest ladders and grinned at me. "Well, finally. You're here!" Two guitars swayed near her, and I wondered if she'd ever accidentally knocked one to the marble floor.

381

Ring the Bell

"Do I know you?" I finally asked. She reminded me of a cross between Amelia Earhart and Bilbo Baggins.

"I'm Emma. The Master Luthier." She stuck out a stained, calloused hand. "I make all kinds of stringed instruments—anything anyone could ask for."

"That's quite a skill," I said, taking in the unimaginable details around me.

"We heard you have some questions." She tilted her head to Henry as if the mechanical bird had told her about my situation.

I shook her hand, and Henry swooped onto a nearby workbench, deciding to stay by me. I smiled at him warmly. Little Henry seemed far more than a bird, and I wondered if he was really something—someone—else.

"You're one of those humans who's always trying to earn God's love," Emma said, interrupting my thoughts. "What a silly concept! God's love exists just like time. Just like energy. Just like… God. Nothing you do can change how much God loves you. Why do you think that could be?"

"Because God knows the beginning and the end. Predestination?"

Emma's left eyebrow raised. "Now, there's a word that can get people in a mess. And it has. Have you studied it before?"

"I learned about it while getting my bachelor's degree. Then I heard people—of three different religions—arguing about it once."

"Well, no wonder you're confused with all the people preaching what they want to hear!" She spun with such animation I worried she'd accidentally hit one of the instruments with her hands. "The living have such a hard time understanding the simplest things. Let me show you, so you can fully understand God's love."

Emma's hair stuck out sporadically, and the huge apron tied around her waist dwarfed her. "Take your time and find the instrument that calls to you."

"I can pick any one?" I asked. "But there must be thousands of instruments in here. How can I possibly know which—"

"It won't be that hard. Trust me. You favor the guitar, right?" she asked.

I nodded. "Yes."

"Then pick a guitar," she said. "That narrows it down a little bit."

Guitars dotted numerous rows of instruments for as far as my eyes could see. Narrows it down? That didn't help me at all.

I walked toward the closest row of instruments, feeling quiet trepidation, and Henry cocked his head.

My fingers trace the surface of a burl-top guitar, and its energy rushed up my arm as if the instrument were alive. Woah. It felt like someone's soul...

—**End of Special Sneak Preview**—
For book release details, please visit the following website: ECWrites.net.

Meet the Author

EC Stilson has authored over ten novels; three of her memoirs have become No. 1 bestsellers on Amazon for women's memoir. She lives in the rustic mountains of Pocatello, Idaho, where she is grateful for every second she has with her husband and children.

Although she continues to fight stage 4 melanoma, Stilson enjoys blogging, making daily TikTok videos, speaking at events, and encouraging families at grief support groups.

If you enjoyed
RING THE BELL
Check out the Prequel: TWO MORE YEARS

"This memoir [TWO MORE YEARS] is a precious life lesson for me as it made me realize that a mother's strength is unimaginable and that my legacy shouldn't be about the trouble I caused but about the good I could do."
–Emma Megan, Readers' Favorite Books Reviews
(5 STARS) ☆☆☆☆☆

Books by EC Stilson

NOVELS AND MEMOIRS
TWO MORE YEARS
A STRANGER'S KINDNESS
BEST OF ECWRITES
ONE WING IN THE FIRE
HOMELESS IN HAWAII
THE GOLDEN SKY
THE SWORD OF SENACK
RING THE BELL
THE RED FEATHER

NOVELLAS
HOW TO AVOID HAVING SEX
GET LUCKY
THREADED DREAMS

CHILDREN'S BOOKS
HOW TO LOSE A TOOTH
THE SMALLEST PEACH

SHORT STORIES
(EC Stilson's stories appear in the following anthologies.)
CHRISTMAS LITES I
CHRISTMAS LITES II

Ring the Bell

FRACTURED FAIRYTALES
FRIGHTENING FABLES
MY FUNNY MAJOR MEDICAL
OPEN DOORS I
OPEN DOORS II
(EC Stilson's stories appear in the following magazines.)
BINGHAM MAGAZINE
RUBY FOR WOMEN
SAVVY DAD

For photos and videos from
TWO MORE YEARS and RING THE BELL,
please visit the author's website:
TwoMoreYears.net

Made in the USA
Columbia, SC
21 April 2024

647b426f-f693-4df8-8587-afd28cb236d0R03